HELP!
*For Parents of
Children from
Birth to Five*

HELP!

For Parents of Children from Birth to Five

Jean Illsley Clarke
and Gail Davenport, Marilyn Grevstad,
Sue Hansen, Nat Houtz, Samara Kemp,
Maggie Lawrence, Darlene Montz,
Gail Nordeman, Mary Paananen, Ellen Peterson,
Judith L. Popp, Judith-Anne Salts, and
Melanie Weiss

 HarperSanFrancisco
A Division of HarperCollinsPublishers

Originally published in four volumes: *Help! For Parents of Infants from Birth to 6 Months*, copyright © 1986 by Jean Illsley Clarke, Samara Kemp, Gail Nordeman, and Ellen Peterson; *Help! For Parents of Children 6 to 18 Months*, copyright © 1986 by Jean Illsley Clarke, Darlene Montz, Judith L. Popp, and Judith-Anne Salts; *Help! For Parents of Children 18 Months to 3 Years*, copyright © 1986 by Jean Illsley Clarke, Gail Davenport, Nat Houtz, and Maggie Lawrence; and *Help! For Parents of Children 3 to 6 Years*, copyright © 1986 by Jean Illsley Clarke, Marilyn Grevstad, Sue Hansen, Mary Paananen, and Melanie Weiss.

The developmental affirmations for children are adapted from Pamela Levin's therapeutic affirmations in *Becoming the Way We Are* (Deerfield Beach, FL: Health Communications, Inc., 1988) and are used with the permission of the author.

FIRST REVISED EDITION

Library of Congress Cataloging-in-Publication Data
    Help! for parents of children from birth to five/ [edited by] Jean Illsley Clarke [et al.].
— 1st rev. ed.
        p. cm.
    Combined rev. ed. of: Help! for parents of infants from birth to six months. c1986; Help! for parents of children from ages six to eighteen months. c1986; Help! for parents of children from ages eighteen months to three years. c1986; and Help! for parents of children ages three to six years. c1986.
    Includes bibliographical references and index.
    ISBN 0-06-250159-3
    1. Child rearing—United States. 2. Child care—United States. I. Clarke, Jean Illsley.
HQ769.H485 1993
649'.122—dc20   92-56404
                                                                                  CIP

93 94 95 96 97 ❖ RRD-H 10 9 8 7 6 5 4 3 2 1
This edition is printed on acid-free paper that meets the American National Standards Institute Z39.48 Standard.

To all our children,
who insist that we grow in ways we never imagined.

Contents

Appreciations   *xi*

Foreword   *xiv*

What Is This Book About?   *xv*

How to Use This Book   *xviii*

Parents Get Another Chance—Recycling   *xix*

I. Help!
For Parents of Infants from Birth to Six Months

Ages and Stages   1

Affirmations for Growth—Being   4

Parents of Infants Get Another Chance—Recycling   6

Common Pitfalls   9

Keeping Babies Safe   11

    1. Crying   13

    2. Breast- and Bottle-Feeding   22

    3. Sleeping   30

    4. Bonding and Growth   36

    5. Changes in Marriage   46

    6. New Parents Have Needs, Too   54

    7. Grandparents   67

    8. Working Parents   73

    9. Who Helps with the Baby?   77

    10. Out and About   84

    11. Second-Baby Blues   91

Moving On from Infants to Toddlers   95

II. Help!

For Parents of Toddlers Six to Eighteen Months

Ages and Stages		97
Affirmations for Growth—Exploring and Doing		100
Parents of Toddlers Get Another Chance—Recycling		102
Common Pitfalls		104
Keeping Toddlers Safe		106
12.	The Nature of the Toddler	108
13.	Now I Lay Me Down to Sleep	116
14.	Nursing, Feeding, and Weaning	122
15.	Siblings and Such	131
16.	Coping with the Explorer	138
17.	Keeping Them Safe	149
18.	Who Raises the Kids?	157
19.	Parents Have Needs and Problems, Too	167
20.	Working Parents	180
Moving On from Toddlers to the Terrific Twos		187

III. Help!

For Parents of Children Eighteen Months Through Two Years

Ages and Stages		189
Affirmations for Growth—Thinking		192
Parents of Two-Year-Olds Get Another Chance—Recycling		194
Common Pitfalls		196
Keeping Two-Year-Olds Safe		198
21.	The Nature of the Two-Year-Old	199
22.	Tantrums and Other Power Struggles	204
23.	Toward Cooperation	214
24.	Good Night, Sleep Tight	220

25. Toilet Training 225
26. Nursing, Eating, and Weaning 230
27. Brothers, Sisters, and Playmates 238
28. Coping 243
29. Keeping Them Safe 251
30. Parents Are in Charge 257
31. Hassles with Other Adults 264
32. Parents Have Needs and Problems, Too 270
Moving On to the Preschool Years 278

IV. Help!
For Parents of Children Three, Four, and Five Years of Age

Ages and Stages 279
Affirmations for Growth—Power and Identity 283
Parents of Three-, Four-, and Five-Year-Olds
    Get Another Chance—Recycling 285
Common Pitfalls 287
Keeping Preschoolers Safe 290
33. The Identity of the Preschooler 292
34. Behavior Problems 302
35. Brothers, Sisters, and Other Kids 316
36. Not Again! Toddlerhood Revisited 322
37. Responsibility 327
38. Coping with Special Stresses 333
39. Picky Eaters 339
40. Things to Do 344
41. Bodies and Sex 349
42. Hassles with Other Adults 353
43. Parents Have Needs, Too 363
Preparing Your Child for Grade School 371
How It Feels to Be a Parent of a Preschooler 375
Moving On to the School-Age Years 376

Appendixes

Developmental Affirmations for All Ages 380

Signs of Abuse and Neglect 384

How to Start a Backyard Center 386

How to Set up a Child-Care Co-op 390

Time-Out 392

How to Lead a Suggestion Circle 394

Where to Go for Additional Support 398

Resources 401

Index 415

Other Learning Materials Available 423

About the Editors 425

Appreciations

We have many thanks to give. Our appreciation goes to:

All the parent educators and Self-Esteem: A Family Affair facilitators who contributed to this book.

The hundreds of people who asked for or gave suggestions for circles including:

The Nurture Company, Parent-Infant Education classes, and the Acalanes Adult Center

The "Mothers' Retreat" participants at Westerbeke Ranch

The members of the Healdsburg group

The group of young parents and their babies at Modesto Junior College

The Self-Esteem: A Family Affair support groups, especially Steve and Mary Dunn, Shari Miller, Ed and Karyl Sakir, Yvette Podlogar, Diane Karsh, Eileen Burt, Meg Murray, Don DuPont, Rose Chait, Jason Davis, Annette Holmberg, Jane Kincaid, Nanette Mills, Kathy and Bart Simmons, Mike and Donna Spoon, Joan Hobbs, Karen Hobbs, Cal and Beth Darrow, and Eileen and Mark Pleticha

The Parent Education Cooperative programs in Washington State

The Yakima, Washington, schools' Backyard Center parent support groups, the Early Childhood Program staff, the members of La Leche League, the Yakima Valley College Cooperative Preschool parents, the Educational Service District 105 parents, and the members of the Yakima community

The Yakima School District, a national leader in providing programs that support parents as the first and most vital teachers of their children

The Family Life program at Edmonds Community College

The parents at North City Cooperative Preschool

The people at Hilltop Day Care and the Saint Patrick's Day group

Parent Education Associates, for bringing Self-Esteem: A Family Affair classes to the state of Washington. Through them, ten of the editors had the opportunity to meet and write.

For their thoughtful support and special insights, we thank Annye Rothenberg, Alice Van Der Laan, Gwen Bradley, Nedra Callard, Helen Peterson, Rosemary Rief, Barbara Durr, Gloria Myre, Mary Lou Rozdilsky, Becky Bottino, Cindy Fortier, Liz Bentley, Becky Monson, and Sandra Jolly.

We especially thank:

- Am and Barbara Englund, for inviting us to edit at the Mountain View Motel

- Tom Grady, for sharing his wonderful skills as an editor and a daddy

- Pediatrician Christine Ternand for connecting abuse with lack of knowledge about child development and for editing the book for medical accuracy

- Deane Gradous for conceiving the idea of publishing the Suggestion Circle books

- Becky Monson, Athalie Terry, and Barbara Beystrom for their support, encouragement, and dedicated typing.

Finally, hugs and kisses go to our families, who taught us that it is OK to try something new.

The Editors

Foreword

Reading through this book is an emotional experience for me. It reminds me that parenting is a series of courageous and simple acts. In those moments when we give our best, with humor and caring, to our children, we learn over and over how to love them, as both our needs and skills and their needs and skills change.

Here are the voices—nameless yet familiar—of parents from around the United States and Canada, who met in their communities to share support and offer thoughtful suggestions on how to solve the problems of family living. The editors, in gathering and arranging the suggestions in this book, convey a message of strength. Ideas from each parent are made more valuable because they are grouped with related suggestions. The editors have also offered their own expertise, gained from working with parents and with children at each stage of their early lives. The book is a celebration of possibilities. Reading it will remind you of the ways in which you are already a good parent and will invite you to continue to give your best.

Mary Lou Rozdilsky
Author of *What Now? A Handbook for New Parents*

What Is This Book About?

This is a book written for parents by parents.

It is for the days when you don't know what to do or for those when what you're doing isn't working. It is *not* a theoretical book about the times when things are going smoothly. It *is* a book of specific, practical suggestions on how to handle problems for which parents have sought solutions in parenting classes around the country.

These parents have participated in groups led by a facilitator who is trained in the techniques used in Self-Esteem: A Family Affair classes. One of these techniques, called the Suggestion Circle, is used to collect options for parents with problems or questions. Here's how it works. In class, members sit in a circle and listen to a parent describe a problem. Each member of the circle then offers his or her best suggestion for dealing with it. In this way, the person with the problem benefits from the collective wisdom and experience of the whole group and goes home with a list of suggestions or options.

The Suggestion Circle process is different from brainstorming, which encourages people to offer every idea that comes to mind. It is also different from listening to the teacher or the expert provide the "correct" answer. In a Suggestion Circle, *every* answer comes from an "authority"—a parent, daycare provider, uncle, aunt, or grandparent. And every answer is "correct," since it worked for the person who discovered it—sometimes after many years of experience. The resulting list provides a variety of suggestions and encourages flexibility in the listener or reader. It may even suggest a new way of perceiving the problem.

For this book, we chose 346 questions and their related responses because they deal with problems that we hear about repeatedly in classes or that seem particularly difficult for parents. Leaders collected the suggestions and asked the parents if we could share them with you. Each list of suggestions, then, is followed by the name of the facilitator who first sent the problem to us and the location of his or her class or group. Since similar problems come up in different parts of the country, we have combined suggestions from more than one group.

You will notice that often the answers contradict one another. This needn't bother you. Parents, children, and homes differ, and what works for one may not work for another or at another time.

You will find the questions grouped in clusters according to subject matter. We have eliminated any ideas that advocated violence, both because child abuse is illegal and because we do not believe that violence helps children. We have also eliminated suggestions that implied that parents or children are helpless or that a problem was not serious. We assume that if parents ask for help, the problems are important and serious to them.

This book is divided into four parts, based on the age and related developmental stage of the children described. At the beginning of each part, we have outlined the characteristic tasks of this stage of development and described how parents may abuse children if they misunderstand these tasks. We have also given short explanations of the affirmations, recycling, common pitfalls, and safety issues that apply to each developmental stage. All of these topics are important parts of the Self-Esteem: A Family Affair class, and they are referred to throughout the book.

So here they are, 346 collections of the best ideas on parenting, from parents who have been there, to you who are there now.

The Editors

How to Use
This Book

You can use this book to help you think. When you want ideas about how to solve a problem, look in the table of contents for a title that seems to include your problem. For example, for the problem of a two-year-old having tantrums, look under "Tantrums and Other Power Struggles" in Part Three, "Help! For Parents of Children Eighteen Months Through Two Years." Or look in the index for words that describe your problem (like *tantrum, yelling, biting,* or *anger*) and then turn to the questions that sound most like yours.

Reading about what other parents have done will remind you that there are many ways to solve problems and that you can discover and try out new ways that work for you and your child. If you read a list over several times, you will probably find ideas that you missed the first time. Some of the suggestions may not fit your situation or your parenting style. Many of the lists contain contradictions, since there are lots of ways to raise children. Think about which suggestions sound useful for your particular problem.

Whenever you think of a suggestion that is not listed, write it in your book for future reference. Our purpose is not to give "one right answer" but to support and stimulate your thinking by offering the wisdom of hundreds of the real child-rearing experts—parents themselves.

Remember that these suggestions are *not* listed in order of importance. They were offered by a circle of people. If we had printed them in circles, this would have been a very big book indeed! We have printed them in lists in order to make this book convenient to use, not to imply that the top suggestion is best.

Use the short sections at the beginning and end of each part as you need them. The section called "Parents Get Another Chance—Recycling" reminds us that our own growth never stops and that we, too, are working on developmental tasks.

At the beginning of each part, you will find a description of normal behavior under "Ages and Stages" and "Common Pitfalls." You can use this information to think about whether your expectations of your child are reasonable.

The "Affirmations for Growth" sections are about healthy messages or beliefs that children at each age need to decide are true for them. You can ponder these affirming messages and all the ways, verbal and nonverbal, in which you offer these ideas regularly to your children.

At the end of each part, there are additional tips about living with children at that stage. When you need more help, you can look at "Where to Go for Additional Support," or you can follow the directions in "How to Lead a Suggestion Circle."

So read and think. Honor yourself for the many things you do well with your children. Celebrate your growth and the growth of your children. Change when you need to. Remember that your parents did the best they could and that you are doing the best you can. If you want to learn some new ways of parenting, it is never too late to start.

Note: Throughout this book, we have alternated masculine and feminine pronouns; in one question or subsection, the child will be a "she," in the next a "he." For "he" or "she," please read "all children."

Jean Illsley Clarke

Parents Get Another Chance—
Recycling

Parenting young children can be rewarding and exciting. It is also a demanding and sometimes exhausting and confusing task. The process, however, benefits not only the children but also the parents. At each stage of a child's growth, the parents get a chance to experience their world anew through the eyes and antics of their child and to recycle their own need to grow in new and exciting ways.

Recycling is the name given to the rhythmic, cyclical growth process that individuals go through, often without noticing it, in which they learn to accomplish important developmental tasks in ever more competent and sophisticated ways. The theory is described in Pamela Levin's *Becoming the Way We Are*. Recycling does not mean that we adults regress to a childlike state but rather that our life experiences demand that we continually develop more skillful ways of completing life-supporting tasks. Besides having a natural rhythm of our own, we parents often recycle or upgrade the tasks of the stages our children are in. I have talked with hundreds of parents about this idea. Many of them have reported, often with some surprise, that they are working on some of the same tasks as their children. This is a normal, healthy, and hopeful aspect of living with growing children. In the "Parents Get Another Chance—Recycling" section at the beginning of each part in this book, you will find specific ideas about tasks that parents can recycle when their child is that age.

Jean Illsley Clarke

I

Help!
For Parents of Infants from
Birth to Six Months

Ages and Stages

No baby in the world is just like yours. Nature's pattern for development is universal, but each baby has his own style and timing. Here are some examples:

- No two days are alike: sleeping and eating times may vary widely.

- Babies have likes and dislikes from day one.

- Some babies want to be held and carried almost all the time; others don't.

- Some babies like vigorous handling; some like to be handled gently.

- Some babies lie quietly and observe their world; others wave and kick like cyclists.

- Some babies poop every time they eat; some poop every couple of days.

- Boys and girls are different from the start in many more ways than just their genitalia.

- Some babies reject everyone's care but Mom's for now.

- Few babies can simply be put to bed. Most must suck, cry, or be rocked first.

- Babies' sucking urge is so strong that it is usually not satisfied during feedings alone.

- Most babies cry for two or more hours out of every twenty-four.

- Babies are often fussiest during evening hours.

- Colic is intense crying for extended times throughout the day. Babies usually outgrow it by four months.

- Some babies are easy, and some are just plain hard to live with at first.

- Babies are learning all the time. They imitate and differentiate and categorize.

- Babies begin their use of language with lots of different sounds. They imitate human sounds, rather than the clock or refrigerator. They concentrate on the sounds of their parents' speech: Swedish babies focus on Swedish sounds.

- Babies like to look at faces, especially eyes. They can see clearly about ten inches away at birth—just the distance for focusing on your face when cradled in your arms.

- Babies become extremely distressed when parents break a normal, happy exchange and stare blankly at them without speaking.

- Babies have a variety of smiles, including a special one for Mom and Dad. Others smile after solving a problem, for strangers, and in relief after realizing that something frightening is not really threatening.

- Babies learn very fast, perhaps taking in and assimilating more information in the first six months of their lives than in any other similar stretch of time.

- Babies need to keep you close, so they come packaged with several traits that make it rewarding for you to stay near them. Parents need not fear that open, unabashed displays of affection will "spoil" an infant.

- Babies' skin invites caressing, and their cheeks are made for kissing.

- They fit perfectly in your arms.

- Babies like an easy transition from the womb; they respond to hearing Mom's heartbeat, feeling warmth, being swaddled, and being walked.

- They don't have adult motives like revenge or "teaching you a lesson."

- They are forgiving.

- They display relief when you are dependable.

- They are wonderfully cute and fascinating.

Reading your baby's clues and responding to them effectively will help you make a good beginning together. Keep your baby close, learn with him, protect him, and celebrate love.

Ellen Peterson

Affirmations for Growth—Being

Affirmations are all the things that parents do and say that let children know that they are lovable and capable. The support, care, protection, and love that parents give help children accomplish the developmental tasks of their current life stage.

An important emotional and social task of infants is to learn to trust, to decide to be. They need to experience and to feel sure that it is all right for them to live, to be who they are, to have needs, and to find ways to get those needs met. Babies reach out with eyes, voices, and wiggles to the people in their world, and their most important people are you, the parents. When they trust (bond with) their parents, they can learn to trust their world. Babies need to hear these messages:

Affirmations for Being

- I'm glad you are alive.
- You belong here.
- What you need is important to me.
- I'm glad you are you.
- You can grow at your own pace.
- You can feel all of your feelings.
- I love you, and I care for you willingly.

You give these positive messages by the way you respond to, hold, look at, talk to, and care for your baby. Saying the affirmations or singing them several times a day reminds you to express them through your care, and babies often respond to your voice with serious alertness or calmness.

Of course, you have to believe the affirmations in order for them to be effective. Otherwise, you offer conflicting messages that confuse children. Infants who believe that their adults mean these life-giving messages are encouraged to grow and to undertake the important task of learning to trust their environment and themselves.

You can read more about what affirmations mean and don't mean and how to use them in families in Clarke's *Self-Esteem: A Family Affair* and Clarke and Dawson's *Growing Up Again: Parenting Ourselves, Parenting Our Children.* (See "Resources.")

Jean Illsley Clarke

Being
—Birth to six months and ever after—

I'm glad you are alive.

You belong here.

What you need is important to me.

I'm glad you are you.

You can grow at your own pace.

You can feel all of your feelings.

I love you and I care for you willingly.

Copy these ovals and color them red.
Post them for daily reading.

Parents of Infants Get Another Chance—Recycling

Not only are parents of infants taking care of their babies but they, like their children, also have developmental tasks to accomplish.

Recycling Tasks of Being

Parents who are taking care of a new baby have the opportunity to rethink and feel their own being and dependency needs.

They may experience a wish to withdraw from the demands of the outside world. Moms and dads at home may long for someone to take care of them. Dads or moms at work may find themselves daydreaming about the baby and wondering what is going on at home. Or they may simply experience a heightened emotional state: "I don't know why I've been feeling so touchy lately," they may say, or "I feel good about the whole world today!"

Many moms report that they are acutely alert to the needs of their babies, while their thinking about other things feels "mushy." Many also note that they are less interested in getting back to work outside the home than they had thought they would be.

Parents who didn't get the Being affirmations, listed in the previous section, the first time around can take them now as they offer them to their children.

You can say them to yourself like this:

- I'm glad I'm alive. I belong in this world.
- I'm glad I'm a woman/man.
- I can grow at my own pace. I don't have to be a perfect parent, only willing to learn.
- I can have all of my feelings.
- I am lovable.
- My needs are important.

Parents during this stage need to receive care and nurturing from other adults and should arrange to get all the support that they can. Because of the infant's newness and needs, the needs of the parents are often overlooked both by the parents themselves and by anyone else who could serve as their caretaker.

Parents need to be nurtured. Their needs are

- To be held (getting lots of hugs)
- To be fed (having meals prepared)
- To get rest (getting lots of sleep to support lots of baby and family changes)
- To have a clean environment (including bedroom, bathroom, laundry, kitchen)
- To hear positive messages ("I'm so glad to see you and talk with you!" "What a wonderful mother/father you are!")
- To be shown concern ("Tell me about your day." "How was your night last night?")
- To get support for their parenting skills (*not:* "They never did it that way in my day.")
- To have a source of accurate parenting information
- To have time alone together to renew themselves and their relationship. This is essential and not a luxury.

Recognizing these needs and getting them met are vitally important to the parents and also to the welfare of the next generation: their baby. As partners in this endeavor, parents can get some of these needs met by each other; however, having outside support people to help is also important. One doctor we know writes prescriptions for help that moms and dads can present to their closest support persons.

Remember: A truly fulfilled parent is indeed the best parent available!

Jean Illsley Clarke and Samara Kemp

Common Pitfalls

As children go about their developmental tasks, they sometimes do things that can be misinterpreted by parents, who then may be overly severe or hurtful in their attempts to stop or control these behaviors or who may worry about spoiling an infant. When parents keep their children from doing what is developmentally correct and normal, children are hurt physically or emotionally.

The following behaviors or characteristics of children at this age are frequently misunderstood:

- *Extended periods of crying.* An infant cries to let you know she has a need. A baby should be learning to trust those who are important to her. She needs *unconditional love* and *caretaking.* Her needs may seem exhausting or even overwhelming to a caring adult. (The caring adults must realize that adults require adequate support in order to meet the infant's needs, because tired adults may act and speak abusively despite their best intentions.)

- *Being wakeful at night.* Infants frequently take three to six weeks to establish a normal light/dark sleep cycle. (The womb was always dark.) They are not deliberately trying to keep the adult exhausted by being active at night. They may need guidance to help synchronize their sleeping and waking periods to match those of the rest of the family.

- *Grabbing and biting.* Babies have strong reflexes for sucking and grasping, and they may inadvertently cause parents physical pain by pulling hair, grabbing skin, or biting. Parents may misinterpret these reflexes as willful attempts to hurt, and they may respond harshly or hurt the child back. Parents need to remember that only nurturing touch should be used with the baby.

- *Being real, not ideal.* The difference between the ideal baby (or the "Gerber baby") and the baby the parents bring home is often difficult for parents to accept. They may mistakenly try to fit their baby into the "Gerber image" instead of accepting the child as she is. At this age, the child should be learning and simply being herself. Well-meaning parents may inappropriately try to get their child to "do things" (such as raise her head, smile, look at flash cards, and so on) before the time when she would do them naturally. Parents should celebrate the new life and be with the child, not push the infant to perform.

- *Being male or female.* Since the child needs to experience unconditional acceptance, the sex of the child must be accepted and affirmed. If you wished for a child of the other sex, grieve that loss as much as you need to and then accept this child as fast as you can. Enjoy boys for being boys and girls for being girls, and encourage other adults to do the same.

Christine Ternand, M.D.

Keeping Babies Safe

We keep babies safe and physically protected when we

- Refuse to leave a child alone in a house or car
- Always use car seats when traveling with a child in a car
- Use safe toys, cribs, and other infant equipment
- Carefully supervise a baby on a changing table, in an infant seat, and in a shopping cart
- Set firm limits on a baby-sitter's activities, and remind the sitter that the infant comes first
- Allow other young children to be around the baby only with constant supervision.

We ensure physical and emotional security when we meet our infants' needs with respect and caring. Infants learn to trust when we provide the following:

- Adequate food but not overfeeding. If you are bottle-feeding a child, the child should be held and given eye contact during feedings; he should not be left with a propped bottle. The baby should be in charge of when and how much to eat unless a physician guides otherwise. (It's OK to "waste" an ounce here or there.)

- Touch, including frequent skin-to-skin, not just skin-to-clothing, contact. Touch that hurts, such as pinching a baby's cheeks, is not appropriate. Touch that surprises, such as tickling or "raspberries," sometimes delights babies and sometimes overwhelms them. Let the baby be in charge.

- Warm clothing. Dressing the child as warmly or as lightly as you dress yourself is a convenient rule of thumb unless the infant gives clear signals that her thermostat is different from yours.

- Prompt attention to distress. Children should never cry for more than fifteen minutes without an adult reassuring them.

- Dry diapers. Some children are more tolerant than others of wet or dirty diapers. This may depend on what type of diaper is used. It is important that all children have this area of their bodies cleaned in *matter-of-fact and nonsexual ways* so that they learn about the acceptability of their genitalia. Touching a child in a sexually stimulating way is always wrong.

If you suspect abuse of any kind, find a way to protect your child. Get help if you need it. Report the abuser to the child protection service in your area. See "Where to Go for Additional Support"; "Common Pitfalls"; and "Signs of Abuse and Neglect."

Christine Ternand, M.D.

Chapter 1

Crying

1. My baby cries and fusses. What do I do?

- Start infant massage every day for about half an hour.
- Bundle her, hold her close, and take a walk outside.
- Warm a blanket for her with a hot water bottle.
- Hold her over your shoulder and keep moving.
- Tape-record her own cry and play it back. Try it!
- Put her in a Snugli or back carrier.
- Take a shower or bath with her.
- Rock and sing to her. It helps both mother and child to relax.
- Go for a car or stroller ride.
- I do relaxation techniques for myself, like yoga, massage, and meditation, imagining her quiet, comfortable, and happy.
- Cut out stimulation like the television, lights, or toys.
- Help her find her fist to suck.
- Take off her clothes, then let her lie on her back and kick.
- Touch her with calm, confident hands.
- Rhythmic movement helps—swinging, rocking, dancing, walking.

- Wrap her in a blanket and lay her on the dryer. The heat, warmth, and sound may be soothing. Stay close to hold her there safely.

- Try an infant swing.

  (See also questions 2, 5, 25, 72, and "Ages and Stages.")

  Thanks to Ellen Peterson,
  Suggestion Circle from Concord, California

2. My colicky two-month-old cries for more than an hour at a time and cannot be comforted. Why does he cry like this, and what do I do?

- He cries because he is in pain. He is distressed.

- It could be gas. Lift his knees and push them gently against his chest.

- He could have what is called an "immature" digestive or nervous system. Hang in there with him until he grows out of it.

- If you are nursing, keep track of your diet and see if certain foods you eat cause your baby to cry six to twenty-four hours later.

- Ask your physician. Listen to her assessment.

- The baby may be wound up and tired.

- Put him in bed for ten to fifteen minutes, and then try comforting him again.

- Do everything gentle and nurturing you can think of. Understand that you may never know why he cries.

- Stay with him, rocking, singing, or just holding him so he knows he is not alone in his misery.

- Get help from someone else.

- Don't look at it as your failure.
- Offer extra feedings if he wants them.
- Don't let yourself get beyond control. Take breaks when you need to.

(See also questions 1, 7, and "Parents of Infants Get Another Chance—Recycling.")

Thanks to Ellen Peterson,
Suggestion Circle from Lafayette, California

3. My baby is fussing. How do I know if she's teething, and what do I do?

- When babies are teething, they chew on their lips or bite things.
- Give her a cold, wet washcloth to chew on. If it comforts her, she may be teething.
- She may arch her back a lot if she's teething.
- Feel her gums to see if they are taut like a blister. They will look white before the tooth breaks through.
- Wrap an ice cube in a washcloth and let her chew on it.
- Offer safe things to gnaw on, like toys and measuring spoons.
- Try the special teething rings that are filled with fluid and can be frozen.
- See if her gums feel tighter and harder.
- Let her chew on crushed ice tied in cheesecloth.

Thanks to Darlene Montz,
Suggestion Circle from Yakima, Washington

4. My three-month-old screams for over an hour whenever he's left with anyone but me. I seem to be the only one who can comfort him.

- Whenever the sitter is holding or feeding him, make sure that the same music is playing and that she is wearing the same robe or cologne you wear when you feed him.

- Arrange to work in your home and have the care provider there so the baby can see you.

- Give it time. He'll outgrow it.

- Let him be in lots of people's arms.

- A mother and child have a special relationship at three months. It is not a good time to introduce a new person. Accept the situation for now, and try again in a month or two.

- Tell the baby, "You are OK," while he is with someone else. Say, "You are fed and are in good hands."

- Tell the baby that it is OK to cry.

- Enjoy the reward of being the one who can soothe him.

- Help him use a "blankie" or "lovey" that he can hold when you are gone.

- Try another care provider with a new style.

- Stay home more and have people come to you for now.

  (See also question 2.)

Thanks to Ellen Peterson,
Suggestion Circle from Lafayette, California

5. My baby is fine all day but has a crying spell for three or four hours in the evening. What can I do?

- Know that babies generally have a fussy period each day and that evening is a typical time.

- Some tiny babies like to be swaddled—that is, wrapped snugly in a blanket.

- Take turns with your partner caring for the baby during the fussy time.

- See if taking a bath with the baby helps.

- Dance around to music. It may help her to burp!

- Lie down on your bed. Put a warm water bottle or a heating pad on a low setting on your belly; then settle your baby on top, tummy down.

- Give yourself a nice evening away each week. It's OK to get a sitter for a crying baby.

- Play classical music while you stroke her softly.

- Talk to her; use your voice to soothe her.

- Take her for a ride in the car in an approved car seat.

- Put her in a swing and swing her while you sing to her.

- Plan your schedule to have time to devote to the baby during fussy periods.

  (See also questions 1, 2, 7, and 52.)

  Thanks to Ellen Peterson,
  Suggestion Circle from Alamo, California

6. Are you spoiling a baby if you pick him up every time he cries?

- No, he needs to be held.

- Babies are not mean. If you tend to them now, they'll trust you and cry less later.

- "Spoiling" is an idea forty years out of date.

- Let him entertain himself in gradually increasing amounts of time.

- It is unnatural for a baby to be away from his mother when he wants to be close.

- No, yet you need to get other things done, too.

- Doctors say you can't spoil an infant.

- Crying isn't "good" for babies, even though many of our parents were taught it was.

- This is his only way to call for you. He can't talk yet.

- Avoid always picking him up in anticipation of his needs. Sometimes, when he cries, pick him up immediately so he will learn that you care. Other times, let him come to a full cry and then respond immediately, so he will learn he can call out to get his needs met.

(See also questions 7, 8, 33, and "Ages and Stages.")

Thanks to Ellen Peterson,
Suggestion Circle from Lafayette, California

7. How long should we let our baby cry?

- Respond right away.

- Not long.

- Trust your instincts and feelings each time.

- Not more than fifteen minutes before you comfort her. She may cry long after that but do hold, talk to, or attend to her.

- Check for pins, wet diapers, and so on; then trust your feelings.

- Watch to see if your baby cries at predictable times. Arrange your schedule so you can respond quickly and give time to the baby then.

- Let her cry until the song or the music box has finished playing.

- I think five minutes is enough.

- Some babies need to cry ten minutes or more before sleep. It won't hurt your baby to try this.

- Learn to recognize your baby's different cries and what each one means. Use this knowledge as a guide in each situation.

- Respond after the baby comes to a full cry.

  (See also questions 6 and 8.)

  Thanks to Ellen Peterson,
  Suggestion Circle from Berkeley, California

8. When do we start discipline? I feel like my six-month-old has us wrapped around his finger. Whenever I leave the room, he fusses and cries. What should I do?

- Discipline begins early. When your infant hurts you—by pulling your hair, grasping, or biting your breast—teach him that it is not OK by gently removing whatever he's hurting.

- Take him with you.

- Call to him. Let him know you're there when you leave the room.

- A baby is not mature enough to know you will return when you leave a room. Get him interested in a toy or music box before you go.

- Remember that the word *discipline* means "to teach." Think about what you want to teach him. Discipline is not punishment.

- A baby fussing for a short while when you leave the room is OK. Congratulate yourself that your baby has bonded well with you and is "checking in." You have things you need to do; do them.

- Make sure he is in a safe place before you leave any room.

- Are you sacrificing yourself for him at every turn? Babies will adjust to family needs and patterns. You're the adult. Take charge.

(See also questions 1, 6, 7, 71, "Ages and Stages," and "Common Pitfalls.")

Thanks to Ellen Peterson,
Suggestion Circle from Lafayette, California

9. When my child cries, I want to shake her. My physician says this can cause brain damage. What can I do with my anger that won't hurt anyone?

- Get relief immediately for yourself. Put your baby down and stomp on the floor in another room, or shake a pillow instead.

- Let someone else take over for a while.

- Call Parents Anonymous in your area.

- Set your baby down in a crib or safe place, and call a neighbor or friend for help.

- Yell (someplace away from the baby).

- Do some deep breathing and center yourself.

- Cry.

- Count to ten.

- Turn energy into action: shoot baskets, clean the house, go for a walk, pull weeds.

- Get support from your friends.
- Get more rest.
- Get some counseling to find out the root causes of your impatience.

(See also question 44, "Common Pitfalls," and "Parents of Infants Get Another Chance—Recycling.")

Thanks to Ellen Peterson,
Suggestion Circle from Lafayette, California

Chapter 2

Breast- and Bottle-Feeding

10. How can my newborn be hungry? I just fed him less than two and a half hours ago. Should I feed him again?

- He's really tiny. So is his tummy.
- A newborn's tummy is the size of his fist. It needs to be filled often.
- Yup.
- I'd do it.
- Offer to feed him.
- Go ahead. He will extend the times soon. Remember, in the womb he had a constant food supply.
- Trust your intuition about yourself and your baby.
- Sure.
- Throw away your watch.
- He's just getting himself arranged. Offer a pacifier or finger for sucking first. If it's not just a sucking need, offer food.
- Are you sure the child is hungry when he cries? Go through your checklist of what a newborn would cry for.

  (See also questions 13 and 14.)

Thanks to Gail Davenport,
Suggestion Circle from Alderwood Manor, Washington

11. Where can I get help with breast-feeding problems?

- Call a hospital's postpartum floor.

- Your YWCA or YMCA may offer infant-care classes.

- Try childbirth education classes.

- Talk to other breast-feeding parents.

- Contact La Leche League or other lactation consultants.

- Call your doctor or nurse practitioner. Any time you take drugs, get your doctor's OK because some drugs concentrate in the milk. Drugs that are helpful to adults may be harmful to babies.

- Talk to friends who have successfully breast-fed.

- Read books on nutrition and breast-feeding. (See "Resources.")

- Ask midwives.

Thanks to Samara Kemp,
Suggestion Circle from Ceres, California

12. What do you do with a baby who is bottle-feeding and doesn't want to stay in your arms?

- Sounds like she's finished. I take my baby's cues. I just say, "No more? OK."

- Be aware of the moods of your child, and feed her when she is calm.

- Have someone else feed the baby at times. See if she settles in better, and note how that person holds her.

- See if feeding in a quiet, darkened room that is free of most distractions helps.

- Don't prop the bottle! Lay her down next to you and hold the bottle.
- Make sure your arms are safe and protective and are not suffocating or squeezing the child.
- Let your baby feed in the way she prefers.
- Let go of doing it a certain way. Be flexible.
- Nestle with her in the corner of the couch, chair, bed, whatever.
- Let her lie down and take the bottle. Keep touching, patting, or caressing her.
- Lie down next to the child. Talk to and touch her. Be responsive; sing; maintain intimacy while feeding her in whatever ways you find comfortable.
- Give her lots of cuddling, hugs, and holding at other times.

Thanks to Samara Kemp,
Suggestion Circle from Turlock, California

13. How long should I breast-feed if it's frustrating for the whole family?

- Have each person take responsibility for his own frustration. Talk about it together. Then decide.
- It depends on your patience level.
- How important is it to you to nurse? Resolve this first.
- Stop now if you don't really want to continue nursing.
- For three months. That way, you will have time to get your milk established and work out the kinks. Then decide what you want to do about it.
- Not long.

- Determine what's frustrating, the nursing or the demands on your time to do other things, and then decide what you want to change.

- You may need the support of your husband to accomplish the task of nursing. You should each voice your views on nursing to find out if you have some negative attitudes that affect your ability to nurse the baby. Then decide.

(See "Ages and Stages" and "Affirmations for Growth—Being.")

Thanks to Samara Kemp,
Suggestion Circle from Lafayette, California

14. How do I know if my baby is getting enough milk?

- Check with your doctor.
- If he sleeps well and gains weight, he is getting enough.
- If he spits the nipple out, he has had enough for now.
- From time to time, babies require more milk to grow. Feed your baby whenever he wants to eat.
- If the baby is growing and seems contented, he is getting enough.
- When he's done, burp him and offer the breast or bottle again. If he refuses, he's had enough.
- If the baby is losing weight or not gaining weight, he isn't getting enough.
- If the baby cries a lot, ask your doctor to see if he is having an allergic reaction to the milk.
- Plenty of wet diapers? Ask your doctor how often your baby should be urinating.

- Throw away your watch and feed him whenever he wishes.

(See also question 10.)

Thanks to Gail Nordeman,
Suggestion Circle from Healdsburg, California

15. My baby throws up after feeding. What should I do?

- Call your doctor or nurse and describe exactly what happens. Note especially how much is thrown up, how long after the feeding it happens, and how strongly the vomit is ejected. Follow the instructions.
- In addition to calling your doctor, call a La Leche League counselor with the same information.
- Burp her several times during a feeding, as well as after.
- See if it helps to feed her before she cries hard and swallows a lot of air.
- Lay her over your knees or high on your shoulder to "press" air up.
- Avoid juggling, swinging, or playing with her right after feedings.
- Some babies gulp in a lot of air as they feed; help them get the air up any way that works.
- Try burping her by rubbing her back while holding her in the "clam" position—sitting, doubled over so her head is close to her toes.
- If she's bottle-fed, consider trying another formula, but check first with your doctor.

- Watch your baby's weight-gain chart. If she's gaining according to her "norms," don't worry.

(See also question 10.)

Thanks to Ellen Peterson,
Suggestion Circle from Walnut Creek, California

16. I want to express my own milk rather than use a formula, but I am getting little milk. What should I do?

- Say to yourself as you pump or express, "My baby will benefit from this milk."

- Picture the baby in your mind when you express or pump.

- Massage yourself first to encourage the let-down reflex.

- First take a warm shower or apply a warm washcloth to your breasts to encourage milk flow.

- Have someone show you how on your breast or hers. I couldn't learn from descriptions in a book.

- Expressing breast milk is a learned skill that takes practice. Save whatever amount you get in the freezer and add to it until you get several ounces.

- Get a good pump, not just a bulb type. Rent an electric one.

- Call a La Leche League counselor in your area.

- For manual expression, press gently, firmly, and in a radial motion around the breast and the brown area around the nipple.

- Borrow pumps from friends. Some breasts work best with one pump, some with another, and some don't work with any pumps.

- Take your time until you get the hang of it.

  (See also question 11.)

Thanks to Sandy Sittko,
Suggestion Circle from Saint Louis, Missouri

17. When should I start feeding the baby "solid food"?

- Four to six months of age or after is the current recommendation of the American Academy of Pediatrics.

- When your doctor recommends it.

- When your baby lets you know—because he's not gaining weight—that he isn't getting enough calories. Even then, more milk may be the best answer.

- After six months, make your own baby food.

- Don't start because of pressure from grandparents or friends.

- Remember, even the experts disagree on this subject.

- When your baby sticks his fist in your food and sucks it off for himself.

- Read as much as you can on the subject, both pro and con, before you decide.

- When you can't stand to eat in front of your baby and not share!

- Keep your own nutritional levels high, and breast-feed your baby as long as possible.

Thanks to Gail Nordeman,
Suggestion Circle from Healdsburg, California

18. How do you move a breast-fed baby to a bottle?

- Replace one breast-feeding a day, starting with the late-morning feeding. After several days, replace the afternoon feeding, and continue until all feedings are replaced with the bottle.

- Try different sterilized nipples. Old ones are good. Borrow them from friends.

- Make sure you hold your baby in the regular close position as you feed her with the bottle.

- Offer the bottle when the baby is sleepy.

- Offer the bottle when you are walking around and carrying her.

- Warm the milk to body temperature.

- Get your doctor's recommendation on what formula to use.

- Put expressed breast milk in the bottle.

- Take your time.

- Have someone else feed the baby. She can smell your milk if you offer the bottle, and she may refuse to take it from a bottle.

- Give her the bottle after you've nursed her, when she is not so frantic. Slip the nipple in her mouth.

(See also question 16.)

Thanks to Ellen Peterson,
Suggestion Circle from Lafayette, California

Chapter 3

Sleeping

19. When will my baby sleep through the night?

- When the baby is ready. Tell her, "You don't have to hurry. You can take your time and sleep on your own schedule."

- When you stop feeling anxious about it.

- Maybe never. Babies wake for different reasons throughout infancy and childhood.

- Depends on the baby's development and the parents' stress level.

- When you take the baby to bed with you.

- When you least expect it—the night when you wake up out of habit and lie there listening to the silence!

- Some people think it depends on the baby's weight.

- When the baby is no longer hungry during the night. You may have to delay responding to see if she can go back to sleep on her own.

- My baby slept through the night after I took the wool and feathers out of her room. She was allergic to them.

(See also questions 22, 23, and 24.)

Thanks to Ellen Peterson,
Suggestion Circle from Sonoma, California

20. Our baby was sleeping through the night but now is waking up two or three times a night. I feel tense and a little crazy! What can I do?

- Check to see that he is OK. Then go back to bed and breathe deeply.

- Keep a journal of why and when he wakes.

- Pick him up, snuggle him, then put him down and pat his back.

- Let your mate hold the baby when you are tense, because babies pick up the tension and will cry more, thus creating more tension for everyone.

- Set a time limit for letting him cry. For example, wind up a toy, and when it stops playing, pick up the baby.

- Analyze what's changed in his life.

- Plan ahead of time and agree as a couple on what you will do in the middle of the night.

- Take the baby to bed with you. Say, "I love you. Your needs are OK. I'm here for you."

- Go ahead and feed him if he is hungry.

- Accept that he needs to wake up right now. Get some sleep during the daytime.

- Get in touch with your own feelings, and see a counselor about feeling crazy.

- See yourself getting more rest: naps, earlier bedtime, week-end sleep-ins. Then do it.

(See also questions 7 and 23.)

Thanks to Ellen Peterson,
Suggestion Circle from Orinda, California

21. Our three-month-old is sleeping in our room. When and how should I move her out? The baby's room is too far away from ours for us to hear her when she cries at night.

- In some cultures, whole families sleep in the same room. Think and feel about what will be right for you.

- Dr. Spock says six months is a good age to move her. (See "Resources.")

- Leave the baby in your room as long as you want to, and find someplace else to make love.

- Buy an intercom so you can hear your baby in her room. You can plug it into any room and use it during naps, too!

- When our baby was four days old, we moved her out. When she needs me, she really yells. I don't wake with the little noises, and she doesn't wake with ours.

- Consider rearranging sleeping rooms so the baby can be nearer your room or you can be nearer to her.

- Move her out gradually—just outside the door first, then down the hall, then farther away, and so on.

Thanks to Ellen Peterson,
Suggestion Circle from Sonoma, California

22. My baby has day and night mixed up. What can I do?

- Make sure the baby's needs for contact are met during the day so he doesn't stay up at night.

- Check the lighting and shading. Have lots of light during the day and no light at night. Do the same for noise—eliminate sudden noises at night.

- See that the baby isn't overstimulated during the day, causing him to stay awake at night.

- Gradually bring your baby's schedule forward by waking him up during his daytime nap so he'll go to sleep earlier in the evening. Take about two weeks to do it, and be consistent with what you do every day. Brazelton explains how in *Infants and Mothers*. (See "Resources.")

- Give the baby his bath in the late evening; then feed him and put him to bed.

- Read *Crying Babies, Sleepless Nights*, by Sandy Jones. (See "Resources.")

- Experiment with letting him cry himself to sleep for ten minutes. Some babies seem to get *more* stimulated when picked up.

- Offer light feeding and light stimulation—holding, talking—before bedtime.

- Many babies need at least three weeks to adjust after those long, dark months in the womb.

- Curl up in bed with him when he does sleep. Get some sleep yourself.

(See also questions 19, 20, and 23.)

Thanks to Gail Nordeman,
Suggestion Circle from Healdsburg, California

23. My baby's naps are so irregular, I can't make any plans. How can I get her on a schedule?

- The baby *is* on her schedule. Listen to the rhythm of the baby and adjust *your* schedule.

- Keep a record for seven days of when she sleeps and eats. To discover her pattern, divide a paper into half-hour segments and jot down what she is doing.

- Remember that in the early months a baby's schedule changes every few days. In *Your Baby and Child*, Penelope Leach describes this period as "unsettled." (See "Resources.") As the baby matures, her schedule will become more predictable.

- Bathe and feed her right before you want her to sleep for a longer period. Do this at the same time every day.

- Don't try to schedule her right now. Treat yourself to a baby-sitter a couple of afternoons a week, and use that time to get things done.

- Gradually change her schedule by taking the baby into an environment that is stimulating during the time you want her awake.

- Don't. This is an opportunity to quiet your life and take a break from the hectic pace of the world.

- Go ahead and make plans. Adjust them later if you need to. Think positively!

(See also questions 19, 22, 52, "Ages and Stages," and "Parents of Infants Get Another Chance—Recycling.")

Thanks to Jean Clarke,
Suggestion Circle from Minneapolis, Minnesota

24. How can I get enough rest and sleep?

- Remember, you will get more sleep as the baby gets older. In the meantime, sleep when the baby sleeps.

- Rearrange your priorities and be more insistent with your partner about your needs. Ask for help.

- Program yourself. Unplug the phone, put a note on the door, and nap when the baby sleeps.

- Practice good eating habits. Exercise, too!
- Let the house go, and rest. Get a cleaning helper.
- Have Dad father the baby while you rest.
- Lie down for ten minutes out of every hour.
- Your baby and you need quantity and quality time. Don't shortchange yourselves: you can't live this time over again. Enjoy the baby, and let others cook for you and pamper you.
- Don't pick up the baby every time he whimpers. Let the child come to a full cry first.
- Accept offers and ask for help from friends and relatives.
- Nurse your baby in bed. Relax and enjoy this age.
- Don't be a Supermom. Be real and recognize your own needs, too.

(See also questions 50, 53, 76, and "Parents of Infants Get Another Chance—Recycling.")

Thanks to Samara Kemp,
Suggestion Circle from Modesto, California

Chapter 4

Bonding and Growth

25. What is this bonding everyone talks about?

- Bonding is an attachment to the baby that continues throughout life.

- Bonding is a relationship based on an exchange through sensory experiences—namely, holding, feeding, and loving—between parent and child.

- Bonding is a psychological connection between the parents and the baby.

- It is the protective feelings of the parents and the infant's preference for her parents.

- Bonding is what babies need to grow and trust. Babies need parents who are willing to bond.

- It is nature's way of ensuring our survival.

- Bonding is an inherent desire to care for and connect with your baby.

- It is the invisible glue that keeps you close.

- It is the need for close physical and emotional contact with the baby, the desire to touch, look at, and respond to the baby's cry.

- It is reflecting your baby's smile so you and the baby feel connected.

- Read the highly inspirational chapter, "Wholeness," in Polly Berends's *Whole Child/Whole Parent*, for a beautiful perspective on connectedness. (See "Resources.")

(See also questions 26, 68, "Ages and Stages," and "Affirmations for Growth—Being.")

Thanks to Ellen Peterson,
Suggestion Circle from Lafayette, California

26. When should bonding happen?

- Bonding is a process that begins the moment your baby is born and continues from birth to five years.

- I think it happens before birth because even in utero, the baby shows his own style as he and Mom learn to live together.

- When you hear your baby cry, you begin bonding.

- The process begins from birth. Hold and touch your baby from the beginning. If you don't feel it right away, don't worry. The feeling will come.

- It happens when you see the baby and look into the baby's eyes.

- From day one.

- It starts *whenever*—for me, in utero.

- Right after birth unless a cesarean has been performed under general anesthesia. In that case, it begins as soon as Mom feels she is ready.

- It's lifelong! There is no one magic moment.

- Before birth.

- At birth.

- With some, it happens during pregnancy. With others, it doesn't happen until the baby smiles and responds or when the parent relaxes.

(See also question 27.)

Thanks to Samara Kemp,
Suggestion Circle from Sacramento, California

27. How can you tell that bonding is happening?

- When your baby is responsive to you and affected by your actions.

- When your baby smiles when she sees you. When your baby cries and you feel protective toward her.

- When you notice how much time you spend thinking about your baby.

- Bonding is a process, so it doesn't happen instantly. When you become more involved with your child day after day and you feel an overwhelming desire to care for and be with your baby, you are bonding.

- Klaus and Kennell describe it in *Bonding: The Beginnings of Parent-Infant Attachment.* (See "Resources.")

- When you feel that surge of love.

- When your baby shows she doesn't like you to be far away.

- T. Berry Brazelton says that the stages of bonding take four months to complete. (See "Resources.")

- Burton White says it takes three years to create a strong bond. (See "Resources.")

- When you are giving and believing the affirmations for growth, you are bonding. (See "Affirmations for Growth— Being.")

(See also question 26 and "Parents of Infants Get Another Chance—Recycling.")

Thanks to Ellen Peterson,
Suggestion Circle from Lafayette, California

28. Should we take our three-month-old infant on our four-day anniversary trip or leave him with Grandma? What would you do?

- Take him. I wouldn't want to leave my baby with anyone else.
- When you need to get away, go out to dinner instead, and plan a trip away from him when he is older.
- Your needs are important and so are the baby's.
- Go two days with him and two days without him.
- Take him. We had fun having our baby along on a similar trip.
- Listen to your inner feelings and then make your decision.
- Take him. Four days is very long, and parents and babies belong together.
- Only leave him with someone he is used to seeing every day and who already has a strong relationship established with him.
- Take a caretaker along with you so you can get out and still have daily contact with your baby.

(See also question 72 and "Ages and Stages.")

Thanks to Ellen Peterson,
Suggestion Circle from Lafayette, California

29. I've heard so much about infant stimulation. What is it? What do I do?

- It is supporting her need to know and grow *at her own pace, in her own way.*

- Offer something for all her senses—music, mirrors, massage with oils, laughter, lullabies, and your skin.

- Try an unbreakable mirror in the crib.

- Smile.

- Offer safe things to touch and taste.

- Talk to her a lot. Call her by name.

- Listen to her sounds and repeat them back to her.

- Before you decide to use a stimulation program, watch to see what kind of stimulation she responds to. Also, how much does she like?

- The trend today is to overstimulate. Enjoy your child instead.

- Hold her and give lots of loving touch. Learn about infant massage in books or a class.

- Use a ready-made infant stimulation program only if you have trouble holding, touching, and interacting with your baby.

- Read *Infant Toddler: Introducing Your Child to the Joy of Learning,* by Earladeen Badger. (See "Resources.")

- If you bombard her with sensory experiences, she may get frustrated because you are pushing her.

(See also "Ages and Stages" and "Common Pitfalls.")

Thanks to Gail Nordeman,
Suggestion Circle from Healdsburg, California

30. My five-month-old isn't turning over yet, and his cousin, who's the same age, is. How can I stimulate him to turn over?

- Don't worry about it. Let them grow at their own speed. Enjoy what they do.

- Know that your baby is the star in your heart.

- Babies do things at different rates. Timing is different for each one. Let him play on a blanket on the floor, where he'll have room to stretch and strengthen his muscles.

- Babies do things in different ways. Some wait a long time and then surprise you by doing a new task very well the first time.

- Sounds like unhealthy parental competition. Let him be on his own time clock.

- Don't. Let your baby roll over when he wants to.

- Refer to a good book on child development.

- Read Bob Greene's *Good Morning, Merry Sunshine* for one father's feelings and experiences during his child's first year. (See "Resources.")

- Read *Infants and Mothers*, by T. Berry Brazelton. It reports on the development of three different babies. (See "Resources.")

- This could be a sign of family competition. Don't act it out through your babies.

(See also question 31 and "Ages and Stages.")

Thanks to Ellen Peterson,
Suggestion Circle from Lafayette, California

31. My baby isn't at all like I expected her to be! Help!

- Hold your baby and look at her. Touch her often when you're not physically caring for her. It takes time to get to know one another.

- Let her grow on you.

- Close your eyes and just listen to her for a while.

- Your child may experience you as different, too. Take your time.

- You have already spent nine months together; draw on that.

- Don't feel guilty. Accept your feelings and take time to see your baby in other ways.

- Discover what it is about this baby that you *do* like, and write these things down.

- Everybody has a fantasy of what his or her baby will be like. You will adjust your expectations as you accept what she is.

- Examine your feelings without judgment. Let go of your imaginings.

- In *Between Generations,* Ellen Galinsky reports that accepting "this baby" is a common task for new parents. (See "Resources.")

- The more you love your baby, the better she will seem to you. Loving takes time.

- You can't control everything. Instead, enjoy your baby and thank her for being who she is.

(See also questions 25, 26, and "Affirmations for Growth— Being.")

Thanks to Gail Nordeman,
Suggestion Circle from Healdsburg, California

32. I am concerned that my baby's father doesn't hold our baby close and only engages in "rough" play. I want to encourage them to develop a close, nurturing relationship. What can I do?

- Tell Dad how you feel. Find out how he feels about the baby and what kind of relationship he wants with him. Ask him how you can help.

- Ask him to give a bottle to the baby.

- Agree on a time they will spend alone together.

- Have Dad take over in the evenings.

- Play is an OK way to be close.

- He may feel insecure. Ask him if he wants you to show him how to snuggle and cuddle the baby.

- Build up his confidence by commenting in a positive way when he nurtures you or the baby.

- If you are concerned about your baby's safety, intervene. If not, enjoy their playing.

- Get lots of different kinds of books—some about playing, stimulation, development, and so on. Learn together what is "normal." (See "Resources.")

- Recent research shows that males and females play differently with babies and that babies as young as one week old respond differently to a man or to a woman entering the room. Enjoy the difference.

(See also question 55, "Affirmations for Growth—Being," "Ages and Stages," "Common Pitfalls," and "Keeping Babies Safe.")

Thanks to Ellen Peterson,
Suggestion Circle from Sonoma, California

33. Is my baby getting enough love or too much? How do I know?

- Babies are very sensitive to feelings, and they get their first impressions of the world through them. Take good care of yourself so you can show lots of love to your baby.

- No, babies can't get too much love.

- In *Babyhood*, Penelope Leach says you can't spoil a child under six months old. (See "Resources.")

- If your baby is healthy and smiles at you, she is getting enough.

- There cannot be too much love, but there could be smothering. If you want to read about this, see Clarke's *Self-Esteem: A Family Affair*. Smother-love is called marshmallowing in that book. (See "Resources.")

- If she is developing well physically and learning to trust, she is getting enough love.

- A baby who is not responding may not be getting enough attention.

- One way to ensure enough love is to say the affirmations for growth and act on them every day.

- Take time to feel the love you share with your baby. Hear it and smell it.

(See also question 6, "Ages and Stages," "Affirmations for Growth—Being," and "Parents of Infants Get Another Chance—Recycling.")

Thanks to Samara Kemp,
Suggestion Circle from Lafayette, California

34. My infant is five months old. How long should I let him use a pacifier?

- Watch the baby and see when he decides he doesn't need it anymore.

- Let him use it until he has his first few teeth.

- Let him use it until he wants to stop.

- It is easier later to remove the pacifier than the thumb. So continue as long as he wants it.

- Gradually limit the times and places when it is OK for him to suck on the pacifier. Let him have it when he goes to sleep if he fusses for it then.

- Let him throw it away himself.

- Many children lose interest as their sucking need declines. Introduce another sleep-time lovey, like a quilt or stuffed animal, while gradually limiting the use of the pacifier.

- Poke a hole in the pacifier when the baby is about two or two and a half years old. Continue to let him suck it. He will soon lose interest because it will be less satisfying.

Thanks to Ellen Peterson,
Suggestion Circle from Pleasant Hill, California

Chapter 5

Changes in Marriage

35. How will my marriage change now that we have a baby?

- Tremendously. This is the most dramatic change your relationship will see: going from two people to three.

- Every marriage is different and unpredictable. Use this occasion to create what you want.

- The baby may trigger competition in the family. Make private time with each person, including yourself.

- Some couples become closer and much more intimate. Some couples have difficulty and move apart.

- You will need each other in different ways. If you listen to your needs, you both will grow.

- Your sexual feelings may be altered by the presence of a child in the house.

- You will probably become more mature and responsible.

- The demand for you to operate as a team will increase tremendously.

- You will have new expectations of each other in new roles.

- Babies take tremendous time and energy.

- You and your spouse may be recycling this stage, and you may need to be cared for yourself.

(See also questions 36, 37, 38, and "Parents of Infants Get Another Chance—Recycling.")

Thanks to Gail Nordeman,
Suggestion Circle from Healdsburg, California

36. My husband is jealous of the attention I give to our baby. What can I do?

- Ask him what he needs to do about his jealousy. Then tell him to do it.

- Tell him about your concern.

- Encourage him to bottle-feed the baby to get some of that good intimacy with the baby for himself.

- Separate what part of this problem is yours and what is his.

- Remember, moms and dads need loving, too.

- Give him Clarke's tape, *The Important Infants,* to listen to. (See "Resources.")

- Set up special times together. Go for walks together with Dad carrying the baby in a pack.

- Spend some time each day pleasuring each other.

- Ask about his day, and when he responds, really listen.

- You and he decide which chores you both can put aside for the next year so you can spend more time together now.

- Leave the baby with a sitter, and go see a movie or go out for dinner. Hold hands.

- Encourage him to hold the baby a lot.

- Take a shower with him.

- Talk, yell, rant, and rave until he hears that you want him to stop this jealous stuff and help raise the child.

(See also question 37.)

Thanks to Ellen Peterson,
Suggestion Circle from Lafayette, California

37. How do you keep parenting from overwhelming your relationship with your spouse?

- Make time for the two of you.

- Use sitters regularly.

- Take the baby for a walk together and talk about each other, not the baby.

- Buy season tickets for something—the theater, sporting events, and so on—then use them.

- Choose your outings for the two of you—dinner together, for instance, instead of a party with other people.

- Make a conscious effort to talk about news, books, and so on—one piece a day from the radio, a magazine, or neighbors.

- Stay up together after the baby is asleep.

- Each make a list of things you want to do with the other. Then practice the art of the possible.

- Both of you take care of your health, rest, and nutrition needs so you have energy for each other.

- Get sexy!

(See also question 36.)

Thanks to Ellen Peterson,
Suggestion Circle from Lafayette, California

38. Is there sex after babies? Help!

- Yes, cuddle a lot.

- Make sure you go out as a couple, without the baby, perhaps once a week.
- It's OK to say no to sex until you feel like it.
- Take the baby to a sitter's home so you two can be home together.
- Rent a hotel room for an afternoon.
- If you suspect a physical problem, check with your doctor.
- Rent an X-rated movie.
- Talk to other parents, especially ones with older kids.
- Listen to romantic music.
- Remain open to options of different times for making love. Make a date for 2:00 P.M. or 11:00 A.M.
- Give each other a massage with a lovely, fragrant massage oil.
- Have candlelight dinners.
- Share your intimacy desires.
- Play while being sexual.
- Explore other loving expressions.

Thanks to Ellen Peterson,
Suggestion Circle from Sonoma, California

39. Sex hurts! What to do?

- Get some vaginal jelly for lubrication.
- Call your doctor.
- Ask for lots of TLC from your husband.
- Spend more time on foreplay.
- Don't avoid sex. Experiment to find out what does feel good.

- Say no to intercourse. Do other sexy things.
- Go slowly.
- Maybe stitches are the problem. Fingers can gently stretch the vagina.
- If your fears are preventing pleasure, get counseling.
- Pay attention to the love being expressed by your mate.

  (See also question 38.)

Thanks to Ellen Peterson,
Suggestion Circle from Lafayette, California

40. At what point is counseling in order for the marriage relationship?

- When there is no longer an understanding of each other or the ability to work through conflict.
- When one or both are not getting their needs met in the marriage.
- When you've lost contact with each other.
- When you long for something better for yourselves.
- As soon as you ask if it's necessary. Counseling can be with therapists, friends, pastors, or parents, for example.
- When help is needed to solve problems.
- When you're not listening to each other.
- When one-on-one communication breaks down, impartial help can be valuable because the parents, as well as the baby, are "newborn" at this job and can use guidance in their growth.
- When one or both partners see that it is time.
- Whenever distress is evident and there is a willingness to improve the relationship.

- When someone is drinking too much or misusing other drugs.

- Whenever there is physical abuse.

Thanks to Samara Kemp,
Suggestion Circle from Turlock, California

41. My husband wants his wife home, doing the cooking and raising the kids, as in a traditional Italian family. I want to be out "in the world" and returning to school or work. What should I do to prevent a problem here?

- Read about how other mothers solve this problem in Kaye Lowman's *Of Cradles and Careers: A Guide to Reshaping Your Job to Include a Baby in Your Life*. (See "Resources.")

- Remind him that a good mother takes care of herself as well as of her baby and her husband.

- Consider part-time work or part-time school.

- Surprise him by playing the "traditional Italian mama" occasionally.

- Help him understand that you and his mother are separate people. It's a different time and you have different needs.

- Consider staying home full time while your child is young. You can return to work later, when your child is old enough for nursery or elementary school.

- Tell him your need to be out is not a reflection on his ability to provide.

- A recent survey showed that "at-home moms" had higher stress levels than working moms.

(See also questions 40, 52, and "Parents of Infants Get Another Chance—Recycling.")

Thanks to Ellen Peterson,
Suggestion Circle from Sonoma, California

42. Now that the baby is here, my husband says he'll share the housework, but he doesn't do enough. What can I do?

- Do chores together.
- Listen to upbeat music to lighten and quicken the chores you share.
- Say, "This *needs* to be done. Do you want to do dinner or bathe the baby?"
- See if some of the chores can wait six months.
- Make a scene about this if that's what it takes to get his attention.
- Do less yourself.
- Make lists of chores on weekends, and decide who does which tasks. Divide the jobs by the days in the week; for example, one might prepare dinner every other day. Divide baby care by the times of the day.
- Be willing to teach him how to do housework and care for the baby.
- *Assume* he's going to share.
- Tell him to get off his duff and help!
- Enjoy the clean, finished work that you've done together.

(See also questions 53 and 76.)

Thanks to Ellen Peterson,
Suggestion Circle from Lafayette, California

43. My spouse and I disagree about how to care for our baby, how long to let him cry, how to soothe him, how often to use a sitter, and so on. What can we do?

- If you know more about it than your spouse does, teach your spouse.

- Negotiate on the sitter issue.

- Don't let your baby cry for more than fifteen minutes, and find lots of ways to soothe him.

- It's OK to discover that your way isn't the only way! Sometimes my spouse's questions help me see another way.

- If both your ways are safe, each do it your own way.

- Think. Solve problems; don't compete.

- If a safety issue is involved, ask your doctor for advice, or call the police.

- Pick one topic, then each read something about it, talk to a parent of an older child you admire, compare notes, and decide on a way that pleases both of you.

- Keep your mouth shut while your spouse is learning something you already know.

- Agree to disagree.

- Take a parenting class together.

(See also questions 1, 5, 7, 40, 56, "Common Pitfalls," "Keeping Babies Safe," and "Where to Go for Additional Support.")

Thanks to Samara Kemp,
Suggestion Circle from Lafayette, California

Chapter 6

New Parents Have Needs, Too

44. Sometimes I lose patience, and I don't think I should.

- It's OK to lose patience—get help. Ask for what you need.

- If you can, schedule a sitter daily and take a break.

- Lots of moms fall into the "Supermom trap" and think they're not supposed to be human. Make a realistic list of what good mothers do or say. See Clarke's *Self-Esteem: A Family Affair* for an example. (See "Resources.")

- Build in ways to get a break.

- Take a nap when your baby sleeps.

- At stressful times, ask someone else to take over.

- Catch your feelings early, and get help right away.

- It is natural to lose patience; it's what you do about it that matters.

- Keep one place in the house as your special spot and go there. Turn on soothing music for five to ten minutes to regain your composure.

- Forgive yourself. Accept yourself as human.

(See also questions 7, 9, 24, 25, "Affirmations for Growth—Being," "Common Pitfalls," and "Parents of Infants Get Another Chance—Recycling.")

Thanks to Ellen Peterson,
Suggestion Circle from Lafayette, California

45. How do I make new friends with other parents?

- Know that you all have something wonderful in common and can share that.

- Ask the mail carrier if there are any other babies in the neighborhood.

- Search for church- or city-sponsored "new moms" groups. Go.

- Listen for news of baby-sitting co-ops.

- Join exercise classes or take courses at a nearby school to meet people.

- Visit parenting classes and nursery schools; join in parent-participation activities.

- Try the park on sunny mornings or the neighborhood pool on summer afternoons.

- Check community services and get involved.

- Baby stores and neighbors may serve as resources.

- Offer to baby-sit.

- Invite parents you meet to join you for a snack, a movie, or a walk with the babies in strollers.

- Help someone else out.

- Photo studios are often full of new parents and their babies. Start a conversation there with another parent.

(See also questions 49 and 57.)

Thanks to Samara Kemp,
Suggestion Circle from Modesto, California

46. How can I maintain friendships with people who don't have children?

- Invite a childless friend to your house.

- Make time for yourself. Get a sitter so you'll have time for the friendship.

- Set a limit in your mind on how much time you will talk "babies," and then focus on your friends and what they are interested in. Develop additional interests.

- Ask friends to bring food over, and you'll provide the drinks.

- Tell friends that their friendship is important, and ask them how you can work this out.

- Plan and schedule time together.

- If you are invited to do something with the baby, do it.

- Be willing to let go of some friendships and build new ones.

- Exercise together. Jog, work out, sauna, walk.

- Phone friends while folding diapers.

- Be open about your feelings and your needs.

- Ask for and get hugs!

- Get together for breakfast.

    (See also question 57.)

Thanks to Ellen Peterson,
Suggestion Circle from Sonoma, California

47. Why are new mothers so forgetful, and how can I cope with my forgetfulness?

- Hormonal changes in the body affect the brain and allow emotions to run rampant. People often forget to do things that are not high priority.

- Nothing is as important as the baby. Other things slide past.

- Fatigue affects memory. Get more rest.

- Ask people to remind you of important things.

- Lots of moms recycle this newborn stage and find that their thinking is baby-focused. Read Clarke's *Self-Esteem: A Family Affair* to find out more. (See "Resources.")

- Keep lists.

- Keep a calendar by the phone and write everything down.

- Use yellow stick-on notes on the refrigerator and your mirror.

- Slow down.

- List your priorities each day, and read the list several times during the day.

- I found Alan Lakein's *How to Get Control of Your Time and Your Life* helpful in suggesting organizational skills. (See "Resources.")

- Visualize a warm, bright candle clearing away the fog in your head.

    (See "Parents of Infants Get Another Chance—Recycling.")

    Thanks to Ellen Peterson,
    Suggestion Circle from Lafayette, California

48. How do I get back in shape?

- Check with your doctor first.

- Find a mother-baby exercise class.

- Watch an exercise program on TV. Gradually work up to full participation.

- Get an exercise record or tape. Invite another new mother to join you in doing the routine.

- Go for a walk every day for about half an hour. Walk briskly and don't stop to window-shop along the way.

- Take a yoga class.

- Keep track of your diet. Make sure you eat plenty of the nutritious foods, and keep junk foods and alcoholic drinks to a minimum. (Don't drink any alcohol if you are nursing.)

- Plant a garden.

- Walk instead of driving to do short errands.

- Get Jane Fonda's book, *Workout for Pregnancy, Birth, and Recovery*, and do the workout. (See "Resources.")

- Organize a jogging co-op with other new mothers; rotate child care and runs.

  (See also question 50.)

Thanks to Mary Paananen,
Suggestion Circle from Seattle, Washington

49. I'm the only one home on my block, and I feel so isolated. How do I deal with this loneliness?

- Call someone on the phone; listen to a friend for at least five minutes a day.

- Turn on the stereo and dance with your baby; sing.

- Attend an ongoing class with moms and babies, or form one that focuses on the needs of moms.

- Prearrange time for just you and your mate to be together.

- Look for an exercise class. Visit with others for a few minutes afterward.

- Seek postpartum help.

- Ask friends or relatives for what you need.

- Volunteer your talents to help others—for example, call an elderly person daily, work on a campaign, and so on.

- Invite a mother you know to bring her child and meet you for a walk.
- Talk to people wherever you are.
- Treat yourself to a massage.
- Join a baby-sitting co-op.
- Ask people over.

  (See also questions 45 and 53.)

  Thanks to Ellen Peterson,
  Suggestion Circle from Walnut Creek, California

50. I feel I never have time for myself. What can I do about it?

- Tell your spouse you *need* it. Find some really good sitters or friends you can count on, even on the spur of the moment for emergencies. Trade baby-sitting services with them.
- *Take* time for yourself (it will not be given).
- When your baby is napping, do something you love to do.
- Take a class—exercise is great because you feel better. Have lunch with friends.
- Take five minutes of every hour for yourself.
- Leave the baby with a reliable person at least once a week and get out of the house. A child-care co-op is good for this.
- Cancel everything you can.
- *Take* time for yourself; you deserve and need it. Taking care of yourself is a way to invest in the quality of the person who takes care of your baby.

- Do small things to love yourself—like drinking milk in a lovely stemmed glass or taking a bath with music and candlelight.

- Learn to use the moment. Do some deep breathing. Straighten your spine and feel a balance of body and mind with calm emotion. Read Gay Hendricks and Russel Wills's *The Centering Book*. (See "Resources.")

(See also questions 24 and 51.)

Thanks to Samara Kemp,
Suggestion Circle from Sacramento, California

51. I loved the attention I received when I was pregnant. Now it's just the baby that people notice and fuss over. What about me?

- Fuss over yourself.

- Tell your close friends how you feel, and then ask them to talk about you part of the time.

- Join a parent-infant class to talk about how important your new role as a mother is.

- Do something pleasing for yourself—send yourself a balloon bouquet, have a massage, buy new shoes, get a manicure or haircut, prepare a favorite childhood lunch treat.

- Write affirmations for yourself about your beautiful inner self.

- Post Mother's Day, Valentine, or birthday cards on your mirror. Read and believe them each day.

- Get your makeup done; buy new cologne.

- Get away; go out for an evening.

- Remember to say "thank you" and accept compliments for your baby, and then feel good about them yourself!

- Read parenting books to remind yourself that you are vitally important now.

- Read Leo Buscaglia's *Living, Loving, and Learning*. (See "Resources.")

Thanks to Ellen Peterson,
Suggestion Circle from Lafayette, California

52. I have a two-month-old. I feel frustrated about not getting anything done. I have worked outside the home and am used to measuring the results of what I've done at the end of each day.

- Say to yourself, "I'm doing what I'm supposed to be doing, and this is the most important thing I've ever done."

- Remember how fast infancy passes by. Some important careers show results over the long term, not every day.

- You have kept another human being alive for one whole day. That is an accomplishment!

- Make that laundry pile disappear! Display those finished thank-you notes! Get praise!

- Divide projects into short segments. Cheer when you finish each part.

- Make a star chart. List all the jobs involved in keeping a two-month-old alive, and give yourself a star for each one you accomplish.

- Remember that your career will always be there but that your baby won't.

- Brag.

- Listen to Clarke's tape, *The Important Infants*, and don't be so hard on yourself. (See "Resources.")

- Visit your old workplace. Mine seemed nearly meaningless to me after I had been home with my baby.

  (See also question 23.)

Thanks to Ellen Peterson,
Suggestion Circle from Oakland, California

53. I am asking the people in my family to care for me for the first time, but they're not used to giving me nurturing, especially my husband. What can I do?

- Ask your husband to say the affirmations to you once a day. (See "Affirmations for Growth—Being.") Then tell him what you need.

- Think about a specific thing you want. Ask for it. For example, say, "Will you bring out the old quilt and tuck it all around me?"

- Start with small requests they can succeed at. Thank them.

- Visualize them caring for you.

- Give and get massages.

- Ask to be held and cuddled. Explain that new moms need loving, too. (Read "Parents of Infants Get Another Chance—Recycling.")

- Get lots of hugs from your spouse and family, and give them hugs every day.

- Be organized and divide household duties among family members. Stick to the plan. Don't do their jobs for them.

- Look for others who can nurture you: good friends, professionals, services for the home, sitters, and so on.

- Look for nurturing in everything they do. When you find it, thank them.

(See also questions 42 and 76 and "Parents of Infants Get Another Chance—Recycling.")

Thanks to Ellen Peterson,
Suggestion Circle from Sonoma, California

54. I feel vulnerable about my baby. Everybody is telling me what to do, and I don't know how to stand up for myself.

- Talk to other mothers. Evaluate their experiences and decide for yourself.

- It's OK to tell people you want to think before you do what they tell you.

- Trust yourself and say affirmations to yourself.

- Ask yourself, "In this moment now, what feels right for me?"

- Think of your baby in order to reinforce your courage.

- Practice looking in the mirror and telling them off!

- Write your beliefs down. Read them aloud.

- Become like a mama bear and protect your cub!

Thanks to Ellen Peterson,
Suggestion Circle from Sonoma, California

55. What does "fathering" mean to you?

- Nurturing—same as "mothering."

- Concept should be "parenting"—either parent can care for a baby.

- Bonding with his child.

- It means "mothering minus breast-feeding": folding laundry, getting a snack for Mom while she nurses, and so on.

- Honoring, respecting, and encouraging children.

- Getting to *really* know the baby, not just doing tasks.

- Seeing your infant react to your attention.

- Sharing in the life of the child.

- It's not just raising a child but also learning about the idea of "family." The whole family needs to function.

- Being aware of the consequences of your actions.

- Having part of your mind and attention on someone else all the time.

(See also questions 25, 26, and 27.)

Thanks to Ellen Peterson,
Suggestion Circle from Lafayette, California

56. My wife wants me to help with our one-month-old son, but she criticizes me when I do. As a result, I don't want to help very much, and I feel guilty. What should I do?

- Decide what you feel is best, then go ahead and do it.

- Take a parenting class together.

- Ask her to teach you about infant care.

- Forgive her; she may be unsure of herself in her new role.

- Look inside yourself. See your own ways of loving your son. Start there.

- You *are* helping with the baby, you are *fathering.* Do it.

- What may seem like criticism may be helpful. Listen for what you can use.

- Hand her a sheet of paper and tell her to list things for you to do, *with standards.*

- Pain produces change; act on it.
- Tell your wife that you feel criticized, and ask for two constructive suggestions for every criticism.
- Give her recognition for doing a competent job and being a loving parent. Ask for the same from her.
- Say, "Ouch, that hurts. New dads are tender, you know."
- Ask for positive, loving messages about your abilities. Read Martin Greenberg's *The Birth of a Father* or David Laskin's *Parents' Book for New Fathers*. (See "Resources.")

(See also questions 32, 42, 43, 55, and "Affirmations for Growth—Being.")

Thanks to Deane Gradous,
Suggestion Circle from Minneapolis, Minnesota

57. How can I keep my brain alive with nobody to talk to all day but the baby?

- Study child development, and make a record of your baby's daily development.
- Take a course at your local Y, civic center, community college, or on television.
- Read some of the books you've always wanted to read.
- Listen to cassette tapes of intelligent people talking.
- Take your baby to the park, and talk to other mothers.
- Meditate.
- Get a baby carrier, and take the baby with you to stimulating events.
- Start a book club.
- Invite a group of mothers and fathers over to talk.
- Buy foreign-language tapes and listen to them.

- Watch "Donahue." Take a position. Share it.
- Take your baby to the library—read the front pages of two top newspapers.
- Play with a computer.
- Write poetry.
- Knit a complicated sweater or sew yourself a suit.

(See also questions 45 and 49.)

Thanks to Gail Nordeman,
Suggestion Circle from Healdsburg, California

58. I get so tired of all this; sometimes I want to walk out the door and quit.

- Don't.
- Go out on the back step and scream. Then go back in the house and think about how to get some help.
- Phone a friend or ask a neighbor over for a cup of coffee and a visit.
- Quit for an afternoon by having someone in to care for the baby while you get out for a break.
- Care for your spiritual life.
- Babies are big commitments. Adjusting to family life involves lots of growing up. Hooray for you for doing it!
- It's common today to say, "Take this job and shove it." With babies, you may want to, but don't do it.

(See also questions 52 and 53.)

Thanks to Deane Gradous,
Suggestion Circle from Minnetonka, Minnesota

Chapter 7

Grandparents

59. How do I tell my mother that I want to spend less time with her?

- By being very honest and doing it gently and kindly.

- You could tell her what you *do* need—positive things, like more time alone with your husband or baby.

- Tell her. Don't scold and don't hint. Be assertive about *your* needs, and tell her that you *do* care for her.

- Create a special time with her regularly, and then explain that otherwise your schedule is busy and demanding.

- Gently but firmly!

- Think about and decide how you *would* like to spend time with her.

- You are getting to know yourself, your baby, and your husband—just like a honeymoon—so you all need time to get adjusted. Ask your mother if she would please respect your new family needs.

- Put up a sign that says, "Mother and baby are resting."

- I used to ask her to take the baby for the morning or the day. That way, she'd have her grandchild, and I'd have time to myself.

- Clearly, repeatedly, and lovingly.

Thanks to Samara Kemp,
Suggestion Circle from Modesto, California

60. How can I respond when my mother says, "You should do it this way," and my way is different?

- Do what you think is right, and explain why you do it differently.

- Say, "Thanks, Mom. We're going to try it our way."

- Say, "We are doing what we feel is right for our situation."

- Say, "That's a good suggestion. I'll give it a try," if it's something you are willing to consider.

- Say, "Thanks, Mom, for your suggestion. We've been working on this and what we have tried should work. We'll give your idea consideration."

- Acknowledge that you heard what she said. Try it if it sounds like it should work. Ignore it if not.

- Smile and thank her for her interest.

- Nicely tell her how you feel or what your doctor suggests.

- Say, "Thank you for your viewpoint. I appreciate your input. I feel comfortable doing this my own way."

- Ask for more specific information or an example of how she did it. Listen, and then do what you think best.

- Say, "Oh, that's one good way, Mom. And you know what? I've learned that this is a good way, too!"

Thanks to Samara Kemp,
Suggestion Circle from Ceres, California

61. My mother-in-law cares for our five-month-old when I work. She is wonderful and my son loves her, but she is raising him in her old ways. I want her to raise him my way. What can I do?

- Discuss this problem with your spouse, and share your thoughts with your mother-in-law.

- Find a job you can take your baby to.

- Talk to your spouse. Maybe you need a new sitter.

- Attend a parenting class together; define some mutual goals and set some guidelines.

- Talk to her. Tell her what you would like changed and why, and ask if she is willing to make those changes.

- Compliment her when she does what you like.

- Remember her background. Teach by doing.

- Is it possible for you not to work and to raise your son yourself?

- Find a book that you agree with, insist that she read it, and discuss it with her.

- Wait a minute! She's not raising him. You are! She's the caregiver, not the parent. Your ways will have the stronger influence.

- Explore the possibility that the old and new ways can mix and that your son will benefit from both!

- Shorten the time your son spends with Grandma, perhaps by adjusting your work schedule.

(See also question 70.)

Thanks to Sara Monser,
Suggestion Circle from Lafayette, California

62. My in-laws are coming to stay for three days. I am hesitant to ask for help, and they seem reticent to offer it. What should I do?

- Ask your spouse to ask them to share the load.

- Be really honest and say, "This is our fussy time, and I can use all the help you can give me."

- Go ahead and ask them directly. Remember that people want to help.

- Don't act "tough" and capable if they offer to help.

- Tell them that you can care for the baby, but you *really* need help with dinner.

- Ask Mom to care for the baby while you take a bath and give yourself a manicure.

- Tell Dad that you expect him to get to know his grandchild, and then hand him the baby.

- See to it that you get time for yourself during their visit.

- Ask. Your in-laws may be waiting for the invitation.

- Figure out something that requires two people to do—for example, one bathes the baby while the other takes the pictures.

- Take time to teach them about your house: how things work, where things go, and so on.

(See also question 53.)

Thanks to Meg Murray,
Suggestion Circle from Lafayette, California

63. The grandparents buy gifts for our baby that are inappropriate. How can we get what we need for our baby?

- Tell them what your baby needs and ask them please to be helpful.

- Have a list ready with sizes, brands, and models in mind so you are ready when they talk about gifts.

- Give specific feedback, like "I really appreciated that sleeper. It's so practical."

- Say, "Sarah needs some overalls. If you happen to see some, will you pick them up for me?"

- Offer to shop with them.

- Can you exchange the gifts for things the baby needs?

- Say, "No need to bring a gift every time you wish to see your grandchild."

Thanks to Ellen Peterson,
Suggestion Circle from Lafayette, California

64. I want to use a pacifier, but the grandparents say, "Get that thing out of his mouth!" What should I do?

- He is your baby; do what you want to do.

- Listen to your doctor's recommendations on pacifiers.

- Use the pacifier when they aren't there.

- Let the grandparents see you try other comforts also.

- Read as much as you can about pacifiers. Get an article that supports your thinking, and give it to the grandparents.

- You're the parent. You're in charge. The baby needs you to fulfill his needs. Do what you think best.

- Tell the grandparents that the baby's need to suck is important, and it is better to use the pacifier than to overfeed him.

- Say, "I will, when he doesn't need it anymore."

(See also question 34.)

Thanks to Judi Salts,
Suggestion Circle from Yakima, Washington

65. The grandparents are coming, and I feel that I have to cook special meals and entertain them. But I'm too busy!

- One night while they are there, take them out to a special restaurant. All the rest of the time, follow your regular schedule.

- Treat yourself to a cleaning service during their visit.

- Have yourself a wild but harmless fit over this, then sit down with your spouse and decide how to solve the problem.

- Have "tea" every afternoon with them. Otherwise, maintain your normal schedule.

- Cook double meals the week before, and put half of them in the freezer to use when the grandparents arrive.

- Eat in the dining room and use your best china; otherwise, keep everything the same as usual.

- Grandparents are also parents; ask for help.

- Decide what you can do before they come; ask your partner for help.

- Let them treat you to dinner.

- Ask Grandmother to prepare a much-loved dinner from your childhood (or your spouse's).

- Buy frozen fancy foods.

- Send them out to sightsee or do errands for you.

- Have "rest time" for two hours a day. Go to your room, shut the door, and lie down. Take the baby if that works best.

(See also questions 50, 53, and 62.)

Thanks to Gail Nordeman,
Suggestion Circle from Healdsburg, California

Chapter 8

Working Parents

66. How can my spouse and I balance work and family?

- Ensure family playtime.

- Communicate your needs, wants, and hopes to each other. Let go of unrealistic expectations. Decide what is most important.

- Sit down and talk about it. Find out what is right for both of you. Everyone is different.

- Both of you pitch in with the work and care of the family.

- Discuss and juggle priorities, keeping them clear. Limit outside obligations. Right now, the baby comes first.

- Hire others to do tasks that neither of you enjoys or needs to do. Use that saved time for family fun or intimacy.

- Continue talking about it. Family is work. It is the most important responsibility you have.

- Consider finding less demanding work.

- Make a special time for family and a special time for each other that fits your work schedule and your other demands.

- Guilt is a squiggle that says something is not working. Let your guilts be your guides.

- Read *The Working Parents' Survival Guide,* by Sally Wendkos Olds, or *2001 Hints for Working Mothers,* by Gloria Gilbert Mayer. (See "Resources.")

(See also questions 35, 37, and 70.)

(See also questions 35, 37, and 70.)

Thanks to Samara Kemp,
Suggestion Circle from Modesto, California

67. How can I continue breast-feeding and go back to work?

- Nurse in the morning and at night only. If you start several weeks ahead of the time when you plan to go back to work, you can generally taper down your milk supply so you won't be terribly engorged during your first week on the job.

- You can express your milk at work. I did it. It is time-consuming and definitely only for the highly motivated. You also need an understanding boss.

- Nurse before and after work, and express milk and freeze it for midday feedings.

- Start learning how to express milk (manually or with a breast pump) early, and try to get your baby accustomed to a bottle.

- Find a sitter near work so you can nurse at lunch.

- Schedule breaks and lunch so the baby can be brought to you.

- Investigate job-sharing, flex-time, and part-time work options.

- Get a job that allows you to take the baby with you to work. This may mean being self-employed and working at home.

- Read *Of Cradles and Careers,* by Kaye Lowman, for more ideas. (See "Resources.")

(See also questions 11, 16, and 18.)

Thanks to Samara Kemp,
Suggestion Circle from Modesto, California

68. I am returning to work soon, and I will be leaving our baby with a wonderful caretaker. Will our baby love her more than he loves us?

- Remind yourself that babies love their mothers and fathers deeply. Love for a care provider need not decrease love for parents.

- Talk about the baby's progress with your sitter each day so that you feel connected with what your baby is doing.

- Plan time alone with your baby each day, perhaps fifteen minutes to an hour, without other duties or distractions.

- No. The parent-child bond is stronger than you imagine.

- Babies need to make attachments. He can be bonded to you and also be attached to his sitter.

- Focus on your relationship with your child and not on your child's relationship with the sitter.

- Enjoy fully every event you do share with your infant.

- No.

- If you are clear in your own mind that you are the parent—the most important person in that child's life—he'll know it, too.

(See also questions 25 and 27.)

Thanks to Ellen Peterson,
Suggestion Circle from Lafayette, California

69. Should I stay home with our baby or go back to work? How can I decide?

- Discuss this with your spouse and come to a decision together.

- Make a decision based on realities. Consider money, time, resources, your needs, and the baby's needs. Then decide.

- Trust your feelings to guide you.

- Write down the reasons to stay home, the reasons to go back to work, and weigh the options.

- Talk to parents who stayed home; talk to parents who went back to work.

- Look for ways you can do both. *Of Cradles and Careers*, by Kaye Lowman, is a good resource. (See "Resources.")

- Stay home now; work later. This is your only chance to be at home with this baby.

- Babies need happy, fulfilled parents. Look to your own well-being as well as your baby's.

- Take your time to decide.

- Stay home, at least for the first three years.

- Think of your child. Consider the quality of the child care available, and decide whether you want that person to guide your baby at this particular age.

(See also questions 66, 70, and 72.)

Thanks to Ellen Peterson,
Suggestion Circle from Lafayette, California

Chapter 9

Who Helps with the Baby?

70. How do I find quality child care?

- Consider using relatives if it's possible for them to help.

- See if you can find a friend who has had experience caring for a baby.

- Trust your gut when you interview people.

- Ask people with kids the same age for recommendations.

- Call the state licensing agency for names of candidates, and then check the people out thoroughly.

- Call a local church and ask who the good baby-sitters are in the congregation.

- See if the local YMCA, YWCA, or recreation departments run baby-sitting courses. If they do, get lists of graduates.

- Call the local sponsor of the child-care food program. Find the sponsor through the state licenser.

- Start early. Give sitter and baby a trial run before your first day back at work.

- Visit several places several times.

- Write questions. Make a checklist.

- Drop in unexpectedly on potential caregivers.

- Join a parenting class. Ask there.

- Put an ad in your local paper. Be specific about hours, days, and references.

(See also "Where to Go for Additional Support.")

Thanks to Jean Clarke,
Suggestion Circle from Minneapolis, Minnesota

71. I feel better if I say good-bye to my baby when I leave the house, but she cries unless I sneak away. What should I do?

- Say good-bye. Say it lovingly and then leave.

- Give the baby a kiss instead.

- Don't be afraid of hearing your child cry when you leave.

- Call home about half an hour later if you are uncomfortable.

- Don't stay home just because she's crying. It's less traumatic if you go when you say you are going.

- If you leave with confidence, your baby will probably stop crying as soon as you go.

- Picture sitter and child happy together in your mind's eye.

- Don't sneak away. That's harder on your baby.

(See also question 72.)

Thanks to Ellen Peterson,
Suggestion Circle from Walnut Creek, California

72. What is a good age to leave an infant with a sitter?

- Have the sitter be someone you can trust—a grandmother, a good friend, another mother from a parenting class—and start before nine months.

- One week of age if all is right. Be careful of falling into the trap of saying, "It never feels right."

- Burton White, in *The First Three Years of Life*, says do it regularly *after* six months. (See "Resources.")

- Any age as long as the sitter is adept and trustworthy enough to care for the child.

- When our infant was three weeks old, we left him for a few hours about once a week.

- Go with your feelings. The "right age" is when you feel ready.

- Look at the importance of the outing, then decide.

- Listen to your heart.

- Leave an infant with a care provider only for short periods. Save the long trips until the child is older.

Thanks to Ellen Peterson,
Suggestion Circle from Walnut Creek, California

73. I am going to a concert tonight and am leaving our infant son with a sitter. He will not take a bottle. What can I do?

- Leave an eyedropper or an infant spoon for feeding formula or breast milk.

- Try a bottle warmed to the same temperature as human milk.

- Try formula, not your milk.

- Feed him just before you leave and as soon as you come home.

- Have the sitter hold him as though she were breast-feeding him.

- Pump your breasts and use your own milk.

- Use an old soft nipple on the bottle.

- Have the sitter offer a bottle at the first sign that he is hungry.
- Call the sitter during intermission. Return home if necessary.
- Call your doctor. Ask if any infant food can be offered. If yes, get some for your sitter to give him.
- Try offering water.

  (See also questions 16, 17, and 18.)

Thanks to Ellen Peterson,
Suggestion Circle from Sonoma, California

74. What do I do about my five-month-old who screams at night when I'm gone, even after she's had an eight-ounce bottle of expressed milk?

- Your responsibility is to hire a sitter who knows about her screaming and can handle it. Give the sitter a few suggestions, and don't worry after you are gone.
- Limit your evenings out for a couple of months, and see if your daughter grows out of this.
- She may need more sucking or holding time. Try a pacifier.
- Leave more breast milk or formula if hunger is the problem. Have the caretaker give her lots of cuddling.
- Tell your caregiver to try different solutions, like a massage or walking the baby to classical music. Tape your voice singing a familiar lullaby, and leave the tape for your sitter to play.
- Know that this behavior doesn't last very long.

- Get a reliable, consistent caretaker whom the baby can get to know. Then go out anyway for short periods of time.

(See also questions 1, 2, 4, 7, 70, and 72.)

Thanks to Samara Kemp,
Suggestion Circle from Turlock, California

75. I feel intimidated by my pediatrician and obstetrician. I don't feel like I get enough time to ask them the questions I want to ask. How can I change this?

- Say, "I would appreciate more time here." Offer to pay more if necessary.

- Write down your concerns and review your list when you talk with the doctor.

- Ask for an allotted amount of time. Know that you deserve the doctor's time.

- Think clearly about what you want. Your questions are important.

- The doctor is only another person. If you are not successful after several attempts to get all your questions answered, find a new doctor.

- Make "I" statements: "I feel," "I need," and so on.

- Grab the doctor's hand and don't let go until you get your questions answered.

- Doctors are your employees. Remember why you've employed their services.

- Ask them to sit down, not stand, when they're talking to you.

Thanks to Nancy O'Hara,
Suggestion Circle from Minneapolis, Minnesota

76. My husband changes our baby's diapers, but that is about all. I hoped he would see things to be done and do them without being asked.

- Confront the situation. Show him a list of jobs to be done. Ask him to mark what he will do.

- Ask for help on something specific.

- Maybe he doesn't do things because he doesn't know how. Teach him.

- Give him a choice: quiet the baby or get dinner.

- If you feel mad, let him know it!

- Recognize differences in timetables and priorities, especially when he first gets home.

- Some studies show that men and women think differently and that men do not "see" what needs to be done. Put the vacuum in the middle of the floor, ask him to use it, and tell him where.

- Remember, he can't read your mind.

- Talk honestly and nicely to him about the problem.

- For crying out loud, corner him and *tell* him what you need.

- Men may be caught in roles or imprisoned by images. Ask him what his dad did and what he thinks "good" dads do.

- Discuss a way for him to have a relaxing break after work—don't expect him to shift gears immediately.

- Make a list of things to be done. Discuss it. Post it. Ask him to do some of the things.

(See also questions 42, 53, 56, and 82.)

Thanks to Ellen Peterson,
Suggestion Circle from Lafayette, California

77. As a person caring for a drug-withdrawal baby and her constant needs, how do I care for her and myself?

- Realize drug-withdrawal babies are different from normal babies—that is, they are more irritable, sensitive (physically, mentally, and emotionally), and less capable while they are withdrawing and recovering from drugs. What worked for you with other children may not work with these babies.

- Watch for the baby's clues (having the jitters, sneezing excessively, yawning, averting eyes, refusing to eat, and splaying of fingers or toes) to gauge the amount of stimulation the baby can tolerate.

- Use swaddling (wrap the baby firmly in a blanket), a pacifier, or vertical rocking while decreasing the external stimulation (noise, touching, strong odors, bright lights).

- Be flexible—adapt to the baby's schedule.

- Try making only one change at a time with the baby.

- Be sure you take a nap at least once a day.

- Make sure you spend one-on-one time with your partner or spouse daily.

- Find a support system and use it regularly.

- Be alone for short periods daily and for long periods (such as two to three days) monthly.

- Line up reliable respite care, or use a crisis nursery.

- Use the services of your county public health nurse.

- Remember that what you are doing is extremely important.

Thanks to Samara Kemp,
Suggestion Circle from Modesto, California

Chapter 10

Out and About

78. My infant is ten weeks old. How do I manage grocery shopping with him along?

- Put your baby in a Snugli, and then buckle him into his car seat. When you get to the store, all you have to do is put the Snugli on because the baby is already in it.

- Bring the car seat into the store and put it in the shopping cart.

- If your baby starts fussing in the store, leave the cart in the store, take him out to the car, and feed or comfort him there. When he's settled, go back into the store and resume shopping.

- Shop with a friend or your spouse. One holds the baby while the other shops.

- Leave the baby at home with a trusted caregiver.

- Ask your mate to do the grocery shopping.

- Make sure the baby is well fed before you go to the store.

- Dangle a toy from an infant seat in the cart.

Thanks to Ellen Peterson,
Suggestion Circle from Lafayette, California

79. We're going on a long car trip with our baby. What can we do to make it pleasant—or even tolerable?

- In many states it is a law to keep a baby in a car seat at all times for safety.

- Plan to take twice as long as usual on the road, so you can stop and take her out to feed her and let her move about and play.

- Take her out of the car seat at rest stops and rub her back. Rub the adults' shoulders, arms, and backs, too!

- Sit in the backseat with your baby some of the time.

- Listen to soothing music.

- Drive at night.

- If you're changing elevations, pull over and feed her when you feel ear pressure, so she will swallow and clear her ears.

- Put a sunbonnet on her to protect her from the glaring sun.

- Take some new and different toys along.

- Hang a towel over the side window for protection from the sun.

- Feed the baby before you go.

- Tie toys onto the car seat, and hang pictures from the seat in front of the baby or on hooks above her.

- Sing.

Thanks to Ellen Peterson,
Suggestion Circle from Danville, California

80. I'm taking my baby on an airplane. Help!

- Let the airline know you are traveling with an infant when you make reservations.

- Arrive early, early, early.

- Ask for a bulkhead seat when you make your reservations; there you will get more room and more privacy.

- See if an airline bassinet is available.

- Take an umbrella stroller along.

- Help your baby swallow during takeoff and landing by feeding him. This helps avoid pain from ear pressure.

- Fly at night.

- Ask someone to take you to the airport and help you get onto the plane.

- Ask a flight attendant to hold your meal until your hands are free to eat.

- Accept help when it is offered.

- Take new toys and a change of clothes along in the diaper bag, in addition to all the usual baby items.

- Arrange for a car seat to be available at the other end of the trip, or take yours along.

(See also question 79.)

Thanks to Ellen Peterson,
Suggestion Circle from Lafayette, California

81. Although I like to show my baby off, when I've been out for a day, I'm exhausted, and I pay for it the next day with a fussy baby. What should I do?

- Try to get a good night's sleep before you go out.

- Get a sitter and leave your baby at home some of the time.

- Bring a partner when you go out. It is easier to do anything when you have help.

- Shorten your list of errands. Go for an hour at a time.

- Get home by noon.

- Listen to your body during your day out. Stop *before* you are exhausted.

- Time your trip around the baby's best times.

- Plan an easy day for the day following your day out.

- Plan several small social outings over two weeks instead of one big day out.

- Watch the clock. Make your visiting time shorter.

- Avoid rush hour.

  (See also questions 1, 24, and 53.)

  Thanks to Samara Kemp,
  Suggestion Circle from Lafayette, California

82. It hardly seems worth it to go out. When my husband is taking care of the baby, he only watches her; he doesn't do anything about the house. I come home to a mess. How can I get him to share the house and baby chores?

- Go away for a day. Make a schedule of things to be done and give it to him. Ask him to see that the baby is cared for.

- If your husband won't help, get a baby-sitter who does help one day a week.

- Trade jobs with your husband. Tell him, "I'll mow the lawn, and you take care of the baby."

- When the father cares for the baby, keep your hands off, notice what he does well, and compliment him on it.

- Ask your husband what he notices about the baby and expect him to be excited about her growth.

- Get him Klaus and Kennell's book, *Bonding: The Beginnings of Parent-Infant Attachment*, and ask him to read it because dads are so important. (See "Resources.")

- Sunday is "my" day. I sleep in and my spouse does everything but nurse the baby, especially in the morning.

- Compliment him on everything he does well with the baby and whenever he picks up or cleans something around the house.

(See also questions 42, 53, and 56.)

Thanks to Ellen Peterson,
Suggestion Circle from Sonoma, California

83. At family gatherings, our three-month-old is passed around a lot. Children especially want to hold her, but she is only content when she's in my arms. What can I do?

- Put her on the floor for everyone to enjoy.

- Set her on your lap; let others come to you to touch or play with the baby.

- To the children who want to hold the baby, say, "Yes, you may hold her. I will call you when the baby's ready."

- Tell them, "It is hard for me to quiet the baby after she gets wound up, so I'll hold her and have you touch her here."

- Say, "No, thank you, she isn't ready for that yet."

- Put her in a Snugli, so it's hard to take her out.

- Strap her into an infant seat and ask that she not be taken out.

- Say, "She's too young."
- Wait until the baby is happy, and then allow her to be held for only a short time.
- Only let children hold her if they aren't sick, have washed their hands, and sit cross-legged on the floor with her.

(See also question 87 and "Ages and Stages.")

Thanks to Ellen Peterson,
Suggestion Circle from Lafayette, California

84. I am going to a conference Saturday. My husband feels unsure about feeding and caring for our infant all day, especially since I'm nursing the baby. What can I do?

- Write down what the baby usually does during the day. Give Dad the schedule as a guideline.
- Remember that the baby won't starve himself.
- Babies often take bottles better when Mother is not around.
- Let your husband know that you trust him to care for the baby and that he doesn't have to do everything exactly the way you do it.
- Let them have a couple of hours of practice ahead of time with you out of the house.
- Call home and encourage him.
- Express milk ahead of time so that your husband can give it to your baby.
- Let him know that the baby cries when you are taking care of him, too.
- Don't call home. Trust your husband to cope and to get to know his baby.

- Let your husband practice bottle-feeding the baby using breast milk and perhaps trying several different nipples.

- Ask him if he has any questions for you before you go.

  (See also questions 1, 16, 32, 55, and 76.)

  Thanks to Ellen Peterson,
  Suggestion Circle from Lafayette, California

Chapter 11

Second-Baby Blues

85. We are expecting our second baby, and I'm worried that I don't have enough love for two. What can I do?

- Light a candle. Light another from it. Light one for each of you. See that the light is not diminished by each addition. Rather, it is increased.

- After the baby comes, set aside time for your first child and your spouse.

- I have two children and had the same fear. Now I bask in the love my two sons have for each other.

- Remember that there is always enough love. Do not confuse time with love.

- Remember to show your love through touching.

- Children don't need to compete for our love and attention. We can teach them to compete or not to compete.

- Set aside time to love yourself so that your needs are met.

- Eliminate outside pressures so your love has room to flow.

- Be confident that love begets more love.

- Affirm yourself that you are capable and can love many people at the same time.

- Rely on your personal experiences: count the people you've added to your heart, and know there's always room for more.

(See also question 53.)

Thanks to Samara Kemp,
Suggestion Circle from Lafayette, California

86. After our first child was born, my husband was helping a lot. He doesn't seem as interested in this new baby and stays at work late. What can I do?

- Tell him you need his help even more than you did with your first baby. Make sure he hears you.

- Ask him if he will spend twenty minutes with each of the children three or four times a week so both you and he can have twenty minutes alone with each child frequently.

- Let him know that you appreciate his wanting to be a good provider. Remind him that his children need love and attention as well as money.

- Ask him to help with the older child.

- Confront him. Ask for very specific contracts: "I will be home on Tuesday by 6:00 P.M. to care for both children for two hours."

- Don't let him get by with this stuff.

- Sounds like a serious problem between the two of you. Talk it out and decide together how you can both get more of what you need.

- Perhaps he is at a place in his career or with his company where he has little left over to give to his family. This is a dilemma that he can solve with encouragement from you.

(See also questions 25, 40, 42, 53, 55, 76, and 82.)

Thanks to Jean Clarke,
Suggestion Circle from Wayzata, Minnesota

87. How can I protect my infant from our older children?

- Teach the older children where it is OK to touch and where it's not OK.

- Set clear limits for the older children and follow through.

- Give the older children another way to show their feelings (especially their negative ones) for the infant. (Hit the pillow, *not* the baby; touch gently; and so on.)

- Help the older children feel loved by spending fifteen minutes a day alone with each.

- Put the baby in a safe place and keep an eye on the other kids.

- Teach the older children how to be with the baby. For instance, say, "Hold out your finger and the baby will grab hold," or "Touch or pat the baby very gently." Let them practice with you.

- Tell them about how you (or someone) protected them as babies and how you taught others to touch them in the right way.

- Read or tell them stories about when they were little and vulnerable. Show them their own baby pictures.

- Keep the infant with you in a Snugli.

- Get Karen Hendrickson's *Baby and I Can Play*. Read it with the older children and talk about it. (See "Resources.")

(See also question 83.)

Thanks to Jean Clarke,
Suggestion Circle from Minneapolis, Minnesota

88. What can I do so I'm not "torn apart" by two children who both want Mommy?

- Involve the older child in helping with the little one.

- Read to the older one while you nurse the baby.

- Get your spouse or another adult to take one child for a while so you can spend time with the other one; then switch, so you get individual time with each.

- Make sure you are not encouraging the children to compete for your attention by comparing them.

- Think about whether you are subtly encouraging the children in this behavior because you want to feel wanted. If so, find another way to feel worthwhile.

- Coping with this is part of learning to live with two kids rather than one. Know that you can't be perfect but can learn to do a good job.

- Say to yourself, "I have enough love, strength, and so on to give. I am enough."

(See also questions 85 and 87.)

Thanks to Jean Clarke,
Suggestion Circle from Plymouth, Minnesota

Moving On from Infants to Toddlers

You will look back on the first six months with your baby with a sigh. You'll think of the exhaustion and hard work involved, yet you'll also cherish the special excitement of getting to know a new soul and starting to build your new family system that includes this baby.

Infants who were given responsive care during the first six months have developed a strong healthy base from which to move out and enjoy the world. They can be confident and curious as they wiggle out of our arms and into everything. If you have accepted your baby for all that she is, have enjoyed holding her, and have not rushed her to grow up fast, she will move out in her own time.

New challenges face parents with each new developmental stage. You deserve help and support with the important job of becoming capable and loving parents who make good decisions for your babies and yourselves. As your child moves into the exploratory stage and becomes a toddler, remember that you don't have to be perfect to be a good parent, only willing to learn and to love. In the next section of this book, you can read about parenting your growing baby.

Ellen Peterson

2

Help!
For Parents of Toddlers Six
to Eighteen Months

Ages and Stages

It is during the six- to twelve-month stage when "babies" turn into walking or near-walking one-year-olds. They learn amazing skills and grow tremendously.

The toddler's primary adult caregiver may be the mother, the father, or another person. We will use the word *mother* to indicate any of those.

Here's what we know about six- to twelve-month-olds:

- They depend on adults to provide a safe and stimulating environment.

- They don't like to share their mother's time or attention with anyone.

- They want to be physically close to their mothers and may panic when she's out of sight.

- They can sit up and crawl.

- Some will walk. Many will not.

- They use their mouths a lot to check out things.

- They can grasp a cup or bottle with both hands and can manage finger foods.

- They can imitate simple actions like clapping hands and playing peekaboo.

- They begin to imitate new sounds.

- They like books that are sturdy and slobberproof with simple pictures.

- They may sleep from nine to eighteen hours a day.

- At around nine months, they may resist being put to bed.

- They are quite competent and can figure out solutions to many of their problems.

Let's go on to the twelve- to eighteen-month-old stage to see how these skills are refined and what new developments unfold.

Here's what we know about twelve- to eighteen-month-olds:

- They are constantly on the move.

- They can express whole thoughts with one word. ("Car" means "I want to go for a ride.")

- They can understand far more than they can express.

- They learn by doing.

- They cannot anticipate consequences or decide what's right or wrong.

- They may begin to resist naps.

- They like to play *alongside* other children.

- They like to stack blocks, pull things, fill and empty containers.

- They are *not* ready to be toilet trained.

- They often intensely dislike having their hair washed.

Exploration is the key word in describing this time in children's development. They are actually "soaking up" knowledge from everything they hear, touch, smell, and taste. So even if there are days when you imagine that your child is "hyperactive," he is probably just a normal, curious, searching, and enthusiastic explorer!

Darlene Montz, Judith L. Popp, and Judith-Anne Salts

Affirmations for Growth— Exploring and Doing

Here are some special affirming messages that will help children during this stage of growth. At this stage, they explore their environment and learn to trust their senses. They must leave the lap and the crib and explore their world in order to develop their intelligence, their sense of self, and their ability to do things.

Affirmations for Doing

- You can explore and experiment, and I will support and protect you.
- You can use all of your senses when you explore.
- You can do things as many times as you need to.
- You can know what you know.
- You can be interested in everything.
- I like to watch you initiate and grow and learn.
- I love you when you are active and when you are quiet.

You *give* these affirming messages by the way you interact with your child and by providing a safe environment in which the child can move about freely. You can also *say* or sing the affirmations. Children seem to understand, perhaps from your tone of voice and your caring actions, what they mean.

Of course, you have to believe the affirmations yourself or they will come off as confusing or conflicting messages. In order for your child to believe them, it must be truly important to you that your child try things, initiate things, explore things, and be curious and intuitive. Also, you must be happy with your child because she is unique and not because of the little tricks that children learn. If children believe that they don't have to be cute or clever or sad or mad or scared or amusing or smart or delicate or macho or fragile for you to love them, they are encouraged to grow. They can learn to trust their senses, to believe in their own ability to learn, and to understand the environment and themselves.

Since we never outgrow the need for these health-giving messages, children continue to need the Being affirmations, which are about the right to exist and have needs. Remember, it is never too late for you to start giving these affirmations. (See "Affirmations for Growth—Being.")

When you discover additional affirmations that your child needs, write them down and give them to your child.

Jean Illsley Clarke

Doing
—Six to eighteen months and ever after—

You can explore and experiment and I will support and protect you.

You can use all of your senses when you explore.

You can do things as many times as you need to.

You can know what you know.

You can be interested in everything.

I like to watch you initiate and grow and learn.

I love you when you are active and when you are quiet.

**Copy these ovals and color them orange.
Post them for daily reading.**

Parents of Toddlers Get Another Chance—Recycling

Parents of toddlers have an important, sometimes exhausting job—caring for their busy explorers. As we explained in "Parents Get Another Chance—Recycling," parents of children this age get a chance to experience their worlds anew through the eyes and antics of their child; they can recycle their own need to see things in new and exciting ways.

Recycling the Exploratory Tasks

Parents, especially if they have been at home full time with an infant, often experience renewed energy and a heightened interest in "doing something" around the time the child reaches six or seven months. Because of this urge to reach out for different experiences and activities, the parent often seems more alert and suddenly restless.

Parents can use this energy to find new things to explore. They may renew activities that they had dropped during their child's infancy. Sometimes they take up a new hobby or sport, or they take some time away from that busy toddler for lessons they have been promising themselves for years. By doing this, parents increase their own ability to explore the adult world.

The affirmations that are helpful to our children are also healthy for us. (See the affirmations listed in the previous section.) Because many of us decided when we were young not to believe some of those healthy messages or only to believe them partly, this is an ideal time to accept those messages for ourselves and to claim more of our ability to be whole, healthy, joyful adults. If you didn't get the affirmations you needed the first time around, you can take them now as you offer them to your children.

Jean Illsley Clarke

Common Pitfalls

Sometimes as children go about their developmental tasks, they do things that are misinterpreted by parents who may be overly severe or hurtful in an attempt to stop or control these normal behaviors. Parents may believe that they are "disciplining," but when they punish their children for doing what is developmentally correct and normal, children are hurt physically or emotionally.

The following behaviors of children this age are frequently misunderstood:

- *The toddler should be learning to explore and to trust his or her environment.* Adults who misinterpret this activity as "getting into my things" or "deliberately breaking things" or "messing up the place" may become inappropriately angry or even violent. Parents of toddlers can learn to cope by saying "Messy is beautiful" when their children are at this stage. Also, the environment should be changed when children are this age. Anything the parents value highly should be stored away from the baby's areas for these few months. It is developmentally inappropriate to teach "don't touch" this early.

- *Children at this age are active and curious,* and supervising them is physically tiring to an adult. Tired adults are more likely to act and speak abusively in spite of their best intentions. Parents can cope by getting enough sleep and rest.

- *Children this age are beginning to want some time and space away from others* to develop their separateness. Caring adults sometimes respond by feeling rejected and then may reject the child emotionally. Parents can remember to refrain from interrupting the child whenever possible.

• As the *child starts to become mobile*, it is possible to think of him as someone who will fulfill the parent's dreams. Asking the child, through words or actions, to live out a parent's dream hampers the child's development of his sense of self.

Christine Ternand, M.D.

Keeping Toddlers Safe

Explorers need especially careful supervision for safety. Parents who do not abuse or neglect their children keep them safe by doing the following:

- Childproofing their homes. One effective way to evaluate the safety in every room the child can enter is to lie on your stomach and see the exciting environment from the child's point of view. Remove or secure all dangerous attractions, especially cords and outlets, household chemicals, soaps, and medications.

- Carefully adding solids to their diets. New foods should be added slowly so that unusual reactions can be more easily noted. Food should be cut into very small pieces to prevent choking. Grapes and hot dogs are two of the most frequent causes of choking in children of this age.

- Refusing to allow children this age to eat nuts. If choked on, nuts can cause serious lung damage.

- Refraining from using walkers. The American Academy of Pediatrics recommends that walkers not be used because of the high number of accidents they cause.

- Carefully supervising play with older children, who sometimes hit or bite a younger sibling who is exploring their favorite possessions.

- Removing fragile, breakable objects from the explorer's environment for these few months.

- Refusing to leave a child alone in a house or car.

- Carefully supervising a child in a shopping cart.

- Always using a car seat when traveling with a child in a car.

- Using caring, nonsexual touch when changing the active child's diapers. Children learn about the acceptability of their genitalia by having the genitalia cleaned in a gentle, nonstimulating way. Touching a child in a sexually stimulating way is always wrong.

- Safely, caringly changing diapers. Children this age would prefer to explore than quietly cooperate with diapering. It is important that they be in a safe spot where they can't squirm and harm themselves and that parents use only nurturing and nonviolent touch when changing these squirming, active little ones.

- Making certain that other adults who care for the child know how to support the child's need to explore. Ask them to think from a child's point of view and to figure out ways to protect the child without hitting the child or using harsh words.

- Allowing the child to be around water only with constant adult supervision. Toddlers have drowned in toilets or buckets of water while parents answered a "quick phone call."

- Monitoring outside play with very careful structure for the safety of these active explorers.

If you suspect abuse of any kind, find a way to protect your child. Get help if you need it. Report the abuser to the child protection service in your area. (See "Where to Go for Additional Support," "Common Pitfalls," and "Signs of Abuse and Neglect."

Christine Ternand, M.D.

Chapter 12

The Nature of the Toddler

89. My seven-month-old does not crawl yet. I'm worried.

- Don't worry! Children develop at their own rate.

- Provide lots of chances for the baby to be on her tummy on the floor.

- To ease your worry, ask your physician or public health nurse to see if your child's development is normal. Most children at this age don't crawl, but they do act alert and roll over.

- Read a book about developmental stages—for example, Brazelton's *Infants and Mothers* or Leach's *Your Baby and Child*. (See "Resources.")

- Don't be in a hurry to advance your child to a new stage of development.

- Be sure her clothes are loose and comfortable; also allow her to be naked for short periods.

- Don't get hooked by what relatives or friends say *their* children did.

- Put something interesting or entrancing just out of reach when she is on her tummy.

- Relax and enjoy. She will take off soon enough.

(See also question 164.)

Thanks to Backyard Center Parents,
Suggestion Circle from Yakima, Washington

90. How can I feel better about my child's not being ready to share? He is fourteen months old.

- A fourteen-month-old may hand things to another child, but sharing is a very mature concept. Lots of adults don't do it well, either.

- Play games that encourage him to pass things back and forth.

- My children didn't share well until after kindergarten.

- Have enough toys and pots and pans for all the toddlers.

- Avoid taking the child to places where he needs to share.

- Children this age play *near* each other, not *with* each other. Read *Baby Learning Through Baby Play,* by Ira Gordon. (See "Resources.")

- Don't expect him to share a favorite toy yet. He's too young.

- Help him get ready for sharing by letting him pass the cookies when there are enough for everyone.

- Remember, at his age asking him to share is like asking you to open your bank account to a friend. You probably wouldn't like that.

(See also question 117.)

Thanks to Backyard Center Parents,
Suggestion Circle from Yakima, Washington

91. What should I do when my thirteen-month-old pokes, pushes, and pulls on playmates?

- Say, "That hurts. If you want to pull on something, you can pull on this," and offer something acceptable like a pillow.

- Touch both children and talk to them calmly. The book *Infancy and Caregiving*, by Gonzalez-Mena and Eyer, tells how to do this. (See "Resources.")

- Say, "Here are two things you can poke."

- A favorite game for this age is "investigating faces"—especially poking at eyes and mouth. Guide her hand as she touches your eyes and say, "Gently, gently." Refer to Segal and Adcock's book, *Your Child at Play: From One to Two Years*. (See "Resources.")

- Remember, she's not hurting the other child "on purpose." She needs time to learn what "gently" means.

- Don't interfere unless the other child is upset or in danger of being injured.

(See also questions 115, 118, and 151.)

Thanks to Backyard Center Parents,
Suggestion Circle from Yakima, Washington

92. My son gets upset when Mom or Grandma holds another child or directs her attention elsewhere. He throws himself down on the floor and cries.

- Give him a teddy bear to hold while you hold the other child.

- Act bored with his tantrum.

- Remember that it is normal at his age not to want to share his mom.

- At another time, rock your son and say, "There is enough holding for you."

- Make sure Mom or Grandma has special time with him later that day.

- Have Grandma continue to hold the other child while you move closer to your son. Just be there by him.

- Before the problem arises, encourage your son to join in singing a song to the child being held, perhaps a funny song.

- Don't make fun of your son or shame him.

- Tell him it is OK for him to feel the way he does and that you will pay attention to him next, and he must wait.

- Get a rocking chair that is big enough to hold both of them at once.

- Say, "When you want to be held, I expect you to reach out with your arms."

(See also question 128.)

Thanks to Backyard Center Parents,
Suggestion Circle from Yakima, Washington

93. When should I start reading to my baby, and what should I read? She doesn't pay attention to anything for very long.

- Start today.

- Look at a simple picture book together each day.

- Pick books that have one large picture per page, pictures that are good for naming and pointing to objects.

- Include the baby when you're reading to your older child.

- Read a few sentences out loud from whatever you are reading: recipes, newspapers, or magazine articles.

- Allow your child to play with and even mangle some adult books.

- You can expect a very short attention span at this age. She may stay interested for two minutes or less.

- Provide cloth books that your child can chew on and crumple.

- Make story time a special time for physical closeness with your baby, cuddling her when she allows it.

- Repeat favorite nursery rhymes throughout the day while bathing, diapering, or riding in the car. Occasionally show her nursery-rhyme books.

- Use very stiff board books. The baby may rather open and close the book than be read to.

- Give her old magazines to look at and tear up.

Thanks to Backyard Center Parents,
Suggestion Circle from Yakima, Washington

94. There is so much talk lately about sex-role stereotyping. How can I avoid stereotyping with my fifteen-month-old son?

- Teach your child to feel good about his own gender. Say, "I'm glad you are a boy," and "I surely do love you, son."

- When both spouses work around the house, doing all kinds of chores and taking care of children, your son will see that both men and women do many things.

- Offer him a variety of toys such as blocks, pull toys, and dolls.

- Take him to a woman doctor.

- Don't limit the father-son interaction to roughhousing.

- Don't be afraid of your boy child playing house with dolls. He needs to practice nurturing skills.

- Follow your child's interests. Let him do what he wants, regardless of gender.

- Be sure to hug, love, and cuddle both little boys and little girls, and let your son see you do it.

- Give your son lots of hugging and touching.

- Take a look at the decor of his bedroom. Does it suggest that he should play football or hunt? Or is it a colorful room that reflects children at play?

- Don't handle him more roughly than you would a girl, and don't tell him that boys don't cry.

(See also questions 165 and 173.)

Thanks to Backyard Center Parents,
Suggestion Circle from Yakima, Washington

95. My baby will be walking soon. What should I know about selecting shoes for her?

- Choose tennis shoes or shoes with soft soles for warmth and safety out of doors.

- Bare feet and booties are OK for indoors.

- Take her with you when you are buying her shoes to see that she gets a good fit.

- Select shoes with treads. They're safer.

- Feel the inside of the shoe to be sure it doesn't have rough edges.

- Many learning-to-walk babies like to go barefoot. They have better balance that way.

- Look for shoes with a good, firm arch.

- Get straps or laces to keep the shoes on.

- It's OK to use shoes another child has used if the shoes are worn evenly and fit properly.

Thanks to Backyard Center Parents,
Suggestion Circle from Yakima, Washington

96. What are some things I can do when I'm "stuck in one place" with my explorer?

- Bring several plastic eggs or small paper bags filled with favorite toys and various snacks like raisins, Cheerios, or fish crackers.

- Bring along a favorite book of nursery rhymes.

- Play peekaboo and patty-cake, sing songs and do finger plays, or name and touch parts of the child's body.

- Keep a pencil and a pad of paper in your purse.

- Bring along a straw to blow "soft breezes" on arms, legs, and tummy.

- Fill a special sack or purse with toys used only for "going out" times. Consider including a soft ball.

- Before heading out, visualize yourself as having lots of patience. Be in the right mood!

- Find a "feely" book for your child to touch, like *Pat the Bunny,* by Dorothy Kunhardt. (See "Resources.")

- Toys that stack work well and take little space.

- When you can, choose a family-oriented place to be "stuck in."

(See also questions 126 and 135.)

Thanks to Yakima Valley Community College,
Suggestion Circle from Cooperative Preschool Parents,
Yakima, Washington

97. How can I prepare my child for being in a baby-sitter's care or at day care?

- Practice separation at home in the early months. Tell your child when you are going into another room, and then come back quickly.

- Play games like peekaboo and "guess which hand" to assure your child that things do exist even though she can't see them.

- Being afraid of strangers is normal at this stage, so exchange sitting with friends for a while rather than leave your daughter with strangers.

- Tell your child where you are going and who will be with her. Let her help pack a snack.

- Tell the sitter about any special fears or preferences your explorer has and the best ways to comfort her when she cries.

- Before you go away for the first time, pay the baby-sitter to come while you are there.

- Establish a ritual at home for getting ready (packing favorite toys or blanket).

- Stay with the child the first time. Then leave for short periods, gradually increasing the time you are away.

- Pack a T-shirt you've worn for her to nap with. Your scent will be familiar and comforting.

(See also questions 172 and 177.)

Thanks to Backyard Center Parents,
Suggestion Circle from Yakima, Washington

Chapter 13

Now I Lay Me Down to Sleep

98. How can I get my baby on a schedule?

- Try keeping the same *sequence* of activities instead of worrying about a specific time schedule.

- Follow your child's own natural "schedule." Set a schedule that is based on her rhythms.

- Play or sing the same soothing lullaby each time you put her to bed.

- See if establishing a bedtime ritual, such as a warm bath or warm bottle, will "cue" your baby that it is bedtime.

- When your baby begins to eat solids and finger foods, aim for regular mealtimes.

- Be aware that some babies go on schedules more easily than others.

- When you realize that the schedule is for your own convenience rather than for the baby, you will see that you need to find time for yourself *and* fit into the baby's rhythms.

- If you sometimes change the baby's bedtime to suit you, don't expect her to go back on schedule automatically.

(See also questions 100 and 157.)

Thanks to Yakima Valley College,
Suggestion Circle from Cooperative Preschool Parents,
Yakima, Washington

99. My thirteen-month-old wakes up two or three times during the night. What can I do?

- Be patient. It may just be his age. New walkers sometimes move their legs as though walking during light sleep. He may be waking himself up with all this activity.

- He could be teething and having more pain and pressure in his mouth when he is prone. Try a pillow.

- Take him to bed with you.

- Listen to the sleep tape, *Infant and Toddler Sleep Disruptions*, by Saul L. Brown, M.D., and Helen Reid. (See "Resources.")

- Leave a humidifier or radio on softly for "white" noise.

- Go in, lay him down, pat his back, tell him you love him, and then leave. Don't go back into his room until he wakes the next time.

- Leave him at home with grandparents for a night. Check into a motel and get some sleep.

- Nap during the day when he naps. (Take the phone off the hook.)

- Try feeding him solids before bedtime.

- Try a pacifier. Don't play with him.

- Keep him awake during the morning and early evening so he doesn't sleep more than five hours during the day.

- Avoid rigorous play just before bedtime.

  (See also questions 158 and 159.)

Thanks to Ellen Peterson,
Suggestion Circle from Orinda, California

100. How can I get my baby to go to sleep without nursing her?

- Very calmly give her a warm bath just before bed.

- Offer her a pacifier.

- Rock your daughter in her room and sing to her.

- Put on a record of the same soothing music every night just before bedtime.

- Give her a drink of milk from a cup just before bed.

- If *you* want to continue nursing at bedtime, why not?

- See that she has a bottle of water.

- Establish a nice bedtime ritual, with lots of cuddling and soothing talk.

- Mom can be part of the early ritual, but someone else can put the baby into bed.

- Don't get discouraged. Your daughter has been nursing all her life. It may take days or even weeks for her to get used to the new routine.

(See also questions 98, 105, and 106.)

Thanks to Backyard Center Parents,
Suggestion Circle from Yakima, Washington

101. My sixteen-month-old screams so hard at bedtime that he has a bowel movement. If he falls asleep on the couch, he wakes up and screams when moved. My doctor and my sister are warning me to let him cry it out. I feel terrible about that.

- Hum with him. Walk, sway, and use a low voice. Calm him down.

- Turn off the light. Hold him, sway, and rock.

- Establish a routine as to who carries him to bed, saying good night to everyone. Talk quietly to him.

- Don't blame yourself.

- If his stools are hard or blood streaked, tell your physician.

- When you are sure he is cared for, let him cry for ten minutes for three nights. See if that works.

- Remember that your physician is a *medical* specialist and doesn't have to listen to your child's screams. Trust your own feelings.

- Stay in your son's room. Talk quietly to him so he knows you are there. Each night, stand farther from the crib.

- Ask your physician to examine your child to be sure he doesn't have something wrong with his bowels.

(See also questions 98, 100, 102, 128, and 147.)

Thanks to Ellen Peterson,
Suggestion Circle from Orinda, California

102. Our seventeen-month-old used to be a good "napper." Now all of a sudden she cries and fusses and fights taking a nap.

- Take her for a walk in the fresh air just before she takes a nap.

- Try adjusting nap time to an hour later than usual, and shorten the time she is down.

- Lie down with your baby. You deserve some rest, too.

- Establish a routine. Say the same "time to nap" words or play a lullaby record as you put her to bed.

- Make the room dark and quiet. Turn the lights and TV off. Pull the shades down.

- Read a story to cue the child to quiet down. If she doesn't seem to fall asleep after that, let her quietly look at some stiff board books in her crib.

- Sing quietly to the baby for several minutes. Then leave the room.

- Rock her for a while before nap time.

- Gently massage her before you lay her down.

- Babies need less sleep as they grow older. Maybe she is ready to choose whether she will nap or have a quiet time.

(See also questions 101 and 104.)

Thanks to Sue Hansen,
Suggestion Circle from Bellevue, Washington

103. How can I get my son to go into his crib while he is still awake? I always end up rocking him to sleep.

- Decide on a certain amount of time to rock him (five to ten minutes) and then put him to bed. Decrease the time a little each night.

- Just make up your mind that you'll put him to bed while he's still awake and then follow through. Babies can sense if you are unsure about your decision.

- Use a flannel sheet for warmth, or give him a special blanket or toy he can become attached to and use for comfort.

- Allow at least three nights of crying before you expect a change.

- Get a cradle that rocks automatically, and let it rock him to sleep.

- Tape the noise of a vacuum cleaner and play the tape before putting him to bed. Or use soft music or a clock.

- Remember that some babies do not need as much sleep as others and will have a more difficult time dozing off.

- Put your most used piece of clothing, like a T-shirt or nightgown, into the baby's crib so he will be reassured by your scent.

- Read *Crying Baby, Sleepless Nights,* by Sandy Jones. (See "Resources.")

  (See also questions 102 and 104.)

Thanks to Backyard Center Parents,
Suggestion Circle from Yakima, Washington

104. How do you handle a child who has just learned to climb out of her crib?

- Stand outside her door. When she begins to crawl out, say firmly, "Go back to bed."

- If she can't get down safely, figure out a way to keep her safe so she doesn't fall on her head.

- Put her back in bed *every time* she climbs out.

- Lay the mattress on the floor.

- Tell her, "I like the way you stay in bed" every time she is staying there.

- Try a youth bed.

- See if there is a lower adjustment level for the mattress, and drop the mattress down a few inches.

- Switch to a twin-size bed with a portable side railing.

Thanks to Nancy Bergerson,
Suggestion Circle from Minnetonka, Minnesota

Chapter 14

Nursing, Feeding, and Weaning

105. My baby is six months old. I want to continue nursing, but I'm all worn out.

- The important emotional nurturing you are providing is an investment in your baby's future. Try to nap or go to bed early at least every other day.

- Check your diet. Often strains or impatience come from lack of energy.

- See your doctor and ask for help with feeling better.

- Decide not to do so much. Don't take on additional responsibilities.

- Go for walks; sunshine increases vitamin D. It helps your skin and your outlook.

- Call another nursing mom and compare ideas.

- Decide if you want to continue, and then be OK with your decision.

- Nursing allows a portable baby.

- Pamper yourself. Go out to dinner.

- Trade off baby-sitting to get some time just for yourself.

(See also questions 158 and 159.)

Thanks to La Leche League,
Suggestion Circle from Yakima, Washington

106. I'm trying to get my seven-month-old baby to take a bottle instead of nursing all the time. He doesn't want anything to do with the bottle. Do you have any ideas?

- Use a nipple shield on your breast to get him used to the feel of the nipple.

- See if using different formulas will help.

- Give him time to get used to the bottle. It is a big change for both of you.

- Try different nipples for bottles, and adjust the size of the holes.

- Cuddle him closely when you give him the bottle.

- Pump your breast. Offer only the expressed milk in the bottle for a while.

- Ask your husband to give your son the bottle. You may want to leave the room or even leave the house.

- That's a big transition for your little one and for you, too. Neither one of you has to hurry!

- He may adjust better to a cup than to a bottle.

- Your baby might like some of the new bottles on the market, especially the ones with the Disney characters.

- See what the hospital nursery staff or your doctor can offer in the way of suggestions.

(See also questions 100 and 107.)

Thanks to Backyard Center Parents,
Suggestion Circle from Yakima, Washington

107. My explorer is fifteen months old, and she still wants her bottle. How can I get her off the bottle?

- Put your child's favorite drinks in a cup.

- Find her a fun cup that has pictures on the bottom or maybe a built-in straw.

- Offer your explorer beverages in her cup several times a day, when you take a coffee break.

- Don't rush. Let the child choose the right time.

- Put only water in the bottle.

- Make a place mat with outline drawings of a plate, cup, and silverware. Your child's cup then will have its own special spot.

- Allow both of you to have fun while you're feeding her solids and using a cup! Babies sometimes miss the closeness and attention more than the bottle.

- Think about why you want her off the bottle. We all have oral needs. Some of us smoke or chew gum.

- Rock your child and sing to her instead of giving her a bottle.

- My physician explained that water in a bottle is OK as long as the baby wants it. Sugared fluids like milk and juice may cause cavities.

(See also question 106.)

Thanks to Backyard Center Parents,
Suggestion Circle from Yakima, Washington

108. My baby bites me when nursing. How can I get him to stop?

- When he bites, stop nursing immediately.

- Stick your finger into the baby's mouth to relieve the suction.

- Explain that it hurts. Say, "No, that hurts."

- If your child is teething, offer him something else to bite.

- Change your position. Maybe lie down.

- Try the football hold to change your baby's position: hold your baby close to your body with his head in your hand, his body on your forearm, and his feet between your upper arm and body.

- Pull down on his chin and say firmly, "Don't bite." Wait a few seconds and return to nursing.

- Decide if your child is really hungry. If he's not serious about nursing, don't let him dawdle.

- Watch his expression. Maybe you can anticipate the bite.

(See also question 125.)

Thanks to La Leche League,
Suggestion Circle from Yakima, Washington

109. My seven-month-old baby won't let go of me while she is nursing. She holds onto my arm so tight that she bruises it. What can I do?

- Hold her hand during nursing.

- Position your child so you can give her your finger to hold.

- See that she is in a comfortable position with secure support under her.

- Stroke her arm to help her relax, and sing to her.

- Talk to her gently and look into her eyes. Make nursing a special time together.

- Don't let her bruise you. Take her hand gently away, and give her a soft toy to hold.

- Try a pad of some kind under your arm so she can't get hold of your skin.

- Get in a different position for nursing. Try lying down with her beside you, keeping her head slightly elevated.

Thanks to Nat Houtz,
Suggestion Circle from Seattle, Washington

110. I've been nursing my baby for seven months, and I'm constantly questioned as to when I'm going to stop. People say, "Are you *still* nursing?"

- Give them a date. Say, "I plan to nurse at least ten months."

- Say, "Yes, isn't it wonderful? My doctor is so proud of me!"

- Join a nursing mothers' support group. They have terrific answers to questions like this.

- State that closeness is good for babies, and this is one way to give it.

- Say, "Yes," in a factual, nonemotional, I-have-no-more-to-say tone.

- This gives you the chance to teach them all about immunity, closeness, touching, and the baby's need to suck.

- Tell them to read *Touching*, by Ashley Montagu. It tells why babies need lots of touch. (See "Resources.")

- Stress that nursing is a personal relationship between you and your child and that it helps the baby bond with you.

- Tell them he will only be a baby once, and if he is going to be nursed, he has to get it now.

- Say, "Yes, this is one thing his father can't do."

- Say, "Why do you ask?" and then decide whether you want to respond further or not.

(See also questions 147 and 175.)

Thanks to La Leche League,
Suggestion Circle from Yakima, Washington

111. I can't get my seven-month-old baby to eat baby food. Should I be concerned?

- Concerned, yes; tense, no. Children go on food spurts. Don't worry.

- Feed her what she likes. Don't be concerned about preferences at this age.

- Don't force her to eat.

- Try introducing small amounts of food at different times during the day.

- Notice the time when your child is in her best mood, and try some baby food then.

- Watch for allergies. Try only one food for a few days at a time until you find one she likes.

- Ask your doctor if vitamins are needed to supplement her diet.

- Try making your own baby food rather than buying the commercial brands. Just put your unsalted table foods into a blender.

- If you are nursing, don't worry about it yet. Breast milk is a good diet for your baby if you are eating well.

- Let your child put her hands in the food so she can lick her fingers.

- If your child isn't underweight, don't make a mountain out of a spoonful of beans.

(See also question 112.)

Thanks to Backyard Center Parents,
Suggestion Circle from Yakima, Washington

112. My baby has been eating solids for quite a few months, and now he won't eat baby cereals.

- Trust him. Perhaps he has a slight allergy to cereal.

- Try a different type of cereal.

- Omit cereal for a while and try again later.

- Put finger treats on his tray, like puffed wheat or Cheerios.

- Give your child the grains he needs in other ways— through muffins or cornbread, for instance.

- See if he would like some old-fashioned cream of wheat or oatmeal instead of "pasty" baby cereal. Perhaps baby cereal is boring to him now.

- Make edible play dough out of whole wheat flour, water, and instant rice, and let him play with it.

- Don't wheedle, scold, or force.

(See also question 111.)

Thanks to Backyard Center Parents,
Suggestion Circle from Yakima, Washington

113. My baby is starting to eat finger food, and now I'm concerned about her protein intake.

- Try frozen chicken or fish sticks cut into finger-size pieces.

- Do you know that a one-inch cube of cheese equals one-half cup of milk?

- You might get a small tabletop grinder, and then grind foods for the baby right at the table. She'll love to watch it being ground and may be more interested in trying it.

- In *Your Baby and Child*, Penelope Leach says that an average-size ten-month-old needs about twenty grams of protein. So if the baby takes one pint of milk, that takes care of sixteen grams already. (See "Resources.")

- My kids love yogurt, especially yogurt pops and cottage cheese with fruit mixed in.

- Try grilled cheese sandwich strips, French toast squares, quiche cubes, and peanut butter toast.

- Offer your child a variety of food from all four food groups, and then relax. My doctor says the typical American diet contains too much protein.

- Babies know how much they need to eat. Just make sure that what you give her is nutritious and not junk food.

- Put some soybean in her food. Soybean protein is almost a perfect substitute for animal protein.

(See also question 114.)

Thanks to Backyard Center Parents,
Suggestion Circle from Yakima, Washington

114. I want my fourteen-month-old baby to eat ground meats or baby meats, but he just spits them out. I'm worried about him getting a balanced diet. What do you recommend?

- Try baby-food chicken or beef sticks. They look like Vienna sausages but are not spicy.

- Make spaghetti with hamburger or baby meats in it.

- Avoid red meats for a few months. Offer chicken or turkey.

- Mix the meat with rice, bread, or anything he does like.

- Look for substitute foods that have similar mineral and vitamin content, such as cheese, fish, or lentil soup.

- This is probably a phase that will pass. Perhaps he doesn't like the texture.

- Buy wafer-thin sliced meat and cut it into small pieces.

- Try cheese or cottage cheese.

- Let him see you grind the meat especially for him in a blender or in a small hand grinder.

- If your baby is getting a balanced diet, you could avoid meats for a while.

- Don't talk with your child about it. He is not a bad person for not wanting meats.

(See also question 113.)

Thanks to Backyard Center Parents,
Suggestion Circle from Yakima, Washington

Chapter 15

Siblings and Such

115. How can I keep my explorer out of my older girl's toys?

- Tell your daughter to keep her special toys in her own room. Keep the baby out.

- Use an actual physical barrier (by using a gate or fence) to keep the children separate for short periods.

- Ask your daughter which toys she wants to share, and keep those in the family room. "Separate" toys can be kept in other places.

- Tell your girl to put away her special toys when she is done playing with them.

- Let your daughter know it is OK to have "private" toys.

- Get your older child a little chest with a combination lock.

- Help your older daughter find a hideaway where she can play without being disturbed.

- Divert the younger child with a basket of special toys.

- Have special time with the young one during the time your daughter is playing with personal toys or projects.

- Sometimes put the baby in a high chair with Cheerios or other finger foods.

(See also questions 91, 117, and 136.)

Thanks to Ellen Peterson,
Suggestion Circle from Walnut Creek, California

116. How can I give my second child as much attention and as many opportunities as I did my first child?

- Realistically, there isn't as much time for the second child as there was for the first. I would plan for special time with the younger child—quality instead of quantity.

- Family activities with your explorer can make up for lots of things you did individually with the first child.

- Look into starting a neighborhood play group for your older child. When the group is at another family's home, use this time to do special things with your explorer.

- Constantly trying to keep everything "even-Steven" makes for very competitive kids. Also it can be wearing. Your needs are important, too, so take care of your own spiritual and intellectual needs.

- Schedule naps at different times so both children have individual time with you.

- Ask your older child to do some special activities with your explorer for short periods of time.

- Hire an older youngster in the neighborhood to come over a couple of times a week to play with one of them while you spend time with the other.

- Look at the experiences your explorer is getting that your preschooler didn't get. Your second child is learning a lot from his big brother.

(See also questions 119 and 171.)

Thanks to Marilyn Grevstad,
Suggestion Circle from Seattle, Washington

117. My three-year-old constantly grabs toys away from the baby—ones that aren't even his. What can I do to stop this?

- Spend special time daily with the three-year-old without interruption.

- Watch. When the older child shows signs of sharing, praise him.

- Pay more positive attention to the three-year-old.

- Encourage the older child to tell you when he offers a toy to the baby, and then praise him.

- Say, "I expect you to find things for you to do and to let the baby have his toys."

- Have certain toys just for the baby, and let the three-year-old do some things that the baby can't do.

- Make some time when you keep the baby out of the three-year-old's projects.

- Catch the three-year-old being good. Praise him when he hasn't grabbed toys away from the baby.

- Buy some items for the baby only and some for the three-year-old only.

  (See also questions 90, 115, and 118.)

Thanks to Backyard Center Parents,
Suggestion Circle from Yakima, Washington

118. My two-and-a-half-year-old nephew takes toys away and hits my one-year-old son whenever we have family gatherings. I need suggestions on what to do so I can enjoy these outings without worrying about protecting my son.

- Decide when it is critical for safety reasons to intervene and when you can let the children work it out. Read *Infants and Mothers* or *Toddlers and Parents*, by Brazelton. (See "Resources.")

- Ask your brother and sister-in-law to split the time of watching the children with you.

- Consider leaving the baby at home with a sitter.

- Tell the older child he is not to hit the baby, and give him something else to hit instead.

- Give the older child a doll or teddy bear of his own to practice being gentle with.

- Do whatever you need to do to stop the hitting. It's not OK to hit people.

- It is OK to protect the baby yourself. Keep your son out of your nephew's reach.

- Your child needs protection. One way you can lessen your worry is to take a competent baby-sitter with you to protect your child.

- Tell his parents how you feel. Ask them to be in charge of their son's behavior.

(See also questions 117 and 163.)

Thanks to Backyard Center Parents,
Suggestion Circle from Yakima, Washington

119. How can I get my three-year-old daughter to be more positively involved with the baby?

- Tell your daughter stories about her when she was tiny. This helps her realize how special she is.

- When you can, give extra special time to your daughter so she won't view the new baby as a threat. It's even fun to splash through a mud puddle together.

- Catch your daughter being good with the baby. Comment on her helpfulness.

- Show your three-year-old how to behave and how to handle and play gently with the younger child. You could buy a doll for her to practice with.

- Allow the older child to help you in taking care of the younger one.

- Watch what you say. She may not understand "Be nice." Saying "Be gentle" or "Touch softly," while you demonstrate it, tells her what to do.

- Talk with your daughter about her feelings—that some days she may be jealous and not always "like" the baby and that her feelings are OK.

- While your three-year-old is within earshot, tell the baby how lucky he is to have such a helpful big sister.

(See also question 116.)

Thanks to Backyard Center Parents,
Suggestion Circle from Yakima, Washington

120. With only two bedrooms in our home, should the baby sleep in our room or in her brother's room?

- One solution is moving, but if you can't, don't put her in your bedroom. You need to sleep. Put the baby in the living room, and she won't bother your other child. When the baby starts to sleep for longer periods of time, put her in with her brother.

- It is difficult to remove your child from your bedroom once you start letting her sleep there. Your baby will sleep through more interruptions if exposed to household activities and noises.

- *The Family Bed*, by Tine Thevenin, has lots of suggestions. Having your baby in the room with you is convenient, and then you can nurse the baby in bed. (See "Resources.")

- Look for a solution that fits your needs, the baby's needs, and your spouse's needs.

- If you take the baby to your room, use your intuition as to when to move the baby, so she doesn't stay in your room too long.

- If your baby is sleeping through the night most of the time, let her join her brother.

- Ask your three-year-old to help prepare a spot for the baby in his room.

- You may really like having your baby sleep next to your bed.

- Don't have sexual intercourse while the baby is in the room.

Thanks to Mary Paananen,
Suggestion Circle from Seattle, Washington

121. We're considering having another baby. What do you think about spacing kids?

- The ideal for me was to have one child out of diapers before I had another.

- Read Burton White's *The First Three Years of Life*. He says the ideal is to space children at least three years apart. (See "Resources.")

- Four or five years is even better because the older child has her own world at school.

- There is no right or wrong. There are difficulties with any age spread.

- At three, the sibling is more independent and has less need of Mom's attention than earlier. The child understands more about Mom's having a baby and can express herself.

- I know of a family where the children are sixteen months apart. Right now it is very hard on both Mom and children.

- If you have your children close together to get it over with, you may not have enough time for each one.

- Space them at least two and a half to three years apart.

- If you wait seven to ten years between children, it extends parenting for a long time and keeps you young longer.

- Perhaps consider only one. I was an only child and found it a positive experience, as there wasn't any competition or jealousy.

Thanks to Backyard Center Parents,
Suggestion Circle from Yakima, Washington

Chapter 16

Coping with the Explorer

122. How can I keep my son from turning into a wrestler every time I change his diapers?

- Use diversionary tactics. Try dangling toys from your mouth to catch his attention.

- Use some musical toys on the changing table. Switch to different toys or a different table for variety.

- Hold your child calmly for a few moments and tell him you love him before you start to change him.

- Save special toys to keep him occupied during diaper changing.

- Keep a firm grip and say calmly, "Lie still. Stay here." Make sure the firm grip is not abusive.

- The book *Infancy and Caregiving*, by Gonzalez-Mena and Eyer, tells how to talk to the baby, telling him what you are doing and getting his cooperation every step of the way. (See "Resources.")

- Wind up a music box, and both of you can sing along while you change his diapers.

- Play the body-parts game, "show me your ears," and teach him new parts during changing time.

Thanks to Backyard Center Parents,
Suggestion Circle from Yakima, Washington

123. My daughter is seventeen months old, and I have a terrible battle washing her hair. Any suggestions?

- A few times wash her hair without soap and see if that helps.

- Make sure the water is not too hot or cold, and don't rush her.

- Tell her favorite stories with lots of expression during the shampoo.

- To stop water from running into her eyes at shampoo time, lay her on the counter and place a folded washcloth on her forehead. Tell her to look up and ask her what she sees. Make it a game.

- Use washcloth shampoos for a while. She might be afraid of water splashing in her nose and mouth.

- Give her plenty of water playtime *before* the shampoo.

- Remember you are a good parent even when you don't wash her hair every single day!

- Use a shampoo that doesn't sting the eyes.

- Let her choose how she wants her hair washed—in the tub or lying on her back on the counter by the sink.

- My boys enjoyed hair washing lots more after I let them wash my hair first.

Thanks to Backyard Center Parents,
Suggestion Circle from Yakima, Washington

124. Give me some hints for cutting my son's finger-nails without drawing blood.

- Cut them while he is asleep.

- Have Dad cut them while your son nurses.

- Cut them with blunt-end scissors that are especially made for babies.

- Trim your son's fingernails while he is on your lap. Talk to him, and hold his hand out in front of you.

- Do the task when he is at his best physically. Also make certain that you are not tired or in a hurry.

- Don't cut them too short.

- Have someone else keep your son busy looking at something while you trim. Sing while you cut.

- Play a game in which each finger has a special name.

Thanks to Backyard Center Parents,
Suggestion Circle from Yakima, Washington

125. My fourteen-month-old bites me when I am holding her. What can I do to stop her?

- Put your daughter down when she does it, and pick her up later.

- Hold her away from you and say, "Ouch!" Let her know you hurt.

- Say, "Stop it!" in a very stern voice.

- Use a startling voice.

- Make eye contact with her and say firmly, "No biting!"

- Offer her something that is OK to bite on. Then demonstrate by putting a wooden spoon or a plastic toy in your mouth.

- Put safe things into her mouth.

- Tell her, "People are not for biting."

- Your child may be trying to imitate kissing and perhaps is confused about how to kiss. Show her how to purse her lips.

- She may be teething. Massage her jaw or give her a rubber toy, a bagel, or a frozen banana to chew on.

- Snap a teething ring on a short ribbon to the shoulder of her sleeper.

(See also questions 108 and 131.)

Thanks to Nancy Drake and Ellen Peterson,
Suggestion Circle from Walnut Creek, California

126. We're going on a long car trip. What can we do to entertain our sixteen-month-old?

- Take drinks and finger foods that are easy to eat.

- Leave during the night or at regular nap time.

- Make a cassette tape of songs and rhymes to play during travel.

- Keep formula prepared in a thermos or stop to nurse him when needed.

- Stop every hour and let the baby crawl or run.

- Take things to keep the child busy—books, games, and so on. Buy a few things ahead of time at a garage sale so he has some toys he hasn't seen before.

- Make the car seat comfortable with soft padding.

- Decide beforehand that you are going to have fun.

- Make sure one adult on the trip is responsible for driving and the other for taking care of kids.

- Realize you may have fussy times but that they will pass.

(See also questions 96 and 135.)

Thanks to Backyard Center Parents,
Suggestion Circle from Yakima, Washington

127. My son, fourteen months old, won't keep his hands off the TV and stereo dials. What should I do?

- Take his hands off firmly and say, "TV is not to play with." Keep removing him gently.

- Be very consistent in not permitting him to play with the TV!

- Make a cover to put over the TV when not in use.

- Give him something else with lots of knobs to play with when he goes for the TV set.

- Try to find someone—like a grandpa—who will make a "knobby" box.

- Place the TV and stereo out of reach during this stage, so you can cut down on the no's.

- Put masking tape over the knobs.

- We decided his exploring was more important than the TV show, and let him do it until he got bored, which was soon after we stopped reacting.

- Buy a toy TV with knobs, and have him play with that instead of the real one.

- Take the knobs off the TV. Use them only for on/off and volume control.

Thanks to Backyard Center Parents,
Suggestion Circle from Yakima, Washington

128. What can I do about my baby's tantrums? She is twelve months old. She cries, hits me, and even bangs her head, and that scares me.

- Physicians say there is danger in head bumping. Get a helmet.

- Don't get angry yourself.

- Stay with your baby, hold her so she can't hit you, talk to her calmly, and let her know you love her even when she is angry.

- Think about changing your expectations of what you will get done during the day; perhaps your baby is feeling too pushed.

- Put your baby into her crib, and then leave her alone for a short time (two or three minutes).

- Don't give her attention for tantrums.

- Let your child know you are not afraid of her anger as you gently but firmly keep her from hitting you.

- Look at the before-tantrum times. See if there is something that seems to bring the tantrums on that you could adjust.

- Touch your baby, cuddle her, rock her lots when she is not having a tantrum.

- She seems young for this. Perhaps you could talk with a counselor about your fears.

(See also questions 92 and 101.)

Thanks to Ellen Peterson,
Suggestion Circle from Lafayette, California

129. What can I do instead of hitting the baby when I'm exhausted?

- Get a sitter, get away, and give yourself a rest.

- Put the child in a safe place, go into the bathroom, close the door, and scream.

- Call a friend.

- Figure out some ways not to get so tired.

- Take a deep breath and count to ten.

- Hit a pillow.

- Read an old favorite letter or reread a list you had written earlier of ways in which you are a good parent.

- Get your feelings out so the child can see you are angry, but don't threaten, scare, or hit or shake him.

- Go out and walk around the house (if the baby is in a safe place).

- Move away from your child and start whispering instead of yelling.

- Put the child in his crib for four or five minutes so you can have time out for yourself.

- This is the time to use the playpen.

- Put some calm, flowing music on the stereo, and fix yourself a cup of tea.

- Learn and practice some meditation or relaxation exercises.

(See also questions 130, 157, and 159.)

Thanks to Carole Gesme,
Suggestion Circle from Minnetonka, Minnesota

130. At our house, 4:00 to 7:30 P.M. is pandemonium time. How can I calm it down?

- Fix a casserole for dinner early in the morning, or use a Crockpot. Then you can play with the kids at this time and not feel pulled about by needing to fix dinner.

- Feed the children earlier sometimes.

- Listen to soft or danceable music during this time. Dance. Look at a book with the kids.

- Give the older kids jobs like setting the table to help get dinner ready.

- Go to the park for part of this time.

- See if an older neighbor child can come in to entertain your child (or children) for part of the time.

- Hire a sitter to come in every day from 4:00 to 5:00 P.M. Then do whatever you need or want to for yourself.

- Feed the children some fruit at 4:00 P.M. and have some yourself.

- When your mom asks when she can help, ask her to come between 4:00 and 7:30 P.M. one day a week.

- Take turns with your spouse. One takes the kids for a walk while the other gets dinner ready.

- Keep frozen dinners in the freezer for days when the pandemonium is worse than usual.

Thanks to Pearl Noreen,
Suggestion Circle from Seattle, Washington

131. The fifteen-month-old daughter of a male friend of mine bites and hits me when I'm with her father. What shall I do?

- Learn the Being affirmations and say them to her gently.

- Remove her hand and say, "No, I can't let you hit me."

- Don't bite or hit her back. Show her how to be gentle.

- Plan an activity that you will both enjoy when you are with the child.

- Write or find affirmations for yourself, and say them before you are with the child.

- Ask her father to hold her firmly but gently and say, "No biting or hitting."

- Stop the biting now, but look for good qualities in the little girl.

- Get the biting and hitting stopped for everybody's sake. Sounds like this little one is distressed and may be threatened by her dad's caring for you. Give her time.
- Get down on the floor and play with her.

(See also questions 125, 128, and 163.)

(See also questions 125, 128, and 163.)

Thanks to Sandra Sittko,
Suggestion Circle from Saint Paul, Minnesota

132. I need options for physical exercises that I can do and still have my toddler with me.

- Set a routine for taking a brisk walk while your child comes along in a backpack, rides a pedal or push toy, or is pulled in a wagon.
- Take advantage of the family and preschool swim programs at local recreation centers.
- "Mom and Me" exercise classes are offered through recreation programs.
- Try recorded disco or aerobic music in your own living room, and both of you dance.
- Look for folk dance groups that include children in classes.
- Invest in a child seat for your bicycle and a child's helmet, and enjoy the bike trails in the area.
- Some roller rinks have child care available.
- Try jumping rope at home.
- If you like running, form a joggers' baby-sitting co-op, and map out a route that goes past each member's home.
- If you can run at a park or school, take a baby-sitter along.
- Try a cross-country ski trip with the baby in a backpack.

Thanks to Gail Davenport,
Suggestion Circle from Seattle, Washington

133. What can I do when my child is screaming and the telephone is ringing?

- Choose not to answer the phone. Attend to the child.
- Let it ring.
- If this is an ongoing problem, answer the call on an extension phone in another room, and make the call short—really short!
- Ask another adult to take care of the child.
- Pick up the child, answer the phone, and ask if you can return the call later.
- Get an answering machine for your phone, and call back later.
- This may be a time for a brief playpen interlude for your baby.

    (See also question 162.)

Thanks to Backyard Center Parents,
Suggestion Circle from Yakima, Washington

134. I need options for arranging child care so we can get some time alone as a couple. Please include any ideas for overnight, evening, or daytime care.

- Ask relatives to baby-sit.
- Set it up with grandparents to keep the children at your house or theirs.
- See if you can trade child care with a neighbor.
- Set up a monthly baby-sitting exchange with another family that has children matching yours in age. You can use the time together as a couple even if you choose to stay home.

- Make use of recreation facilities that offer child care, such as bowling alleys and swimming pools.

- Set up a baby-sitting co-op that exchanges hours. Small co-ops can work just as well as larger twenty- to fifty-member co-ops. (See "How to Set up a Child-Care Co-op.")

- Contact the Girl Scouts for referrals of teenage sitters who have had some training.

- Contact home economics teachers at the junior and senior high schools for referrals of reliable sitters.

- Connect with a licensed family day-care home that accepts part-time and drop-in children.

- Drop-in child care is available at some YWCAs and YMCAs. Check it out.

(See also question 177 and "How to Start a Backyard Center.")

Thanks to Gail Davenport,
Suggestion Circle from Alderwood, Washington

Chapter 17

Keeping Them Safe

135. How can I get my one-year-old daughter to get into and stay in the car seat without a big fuss?

- Keep a fire fighter's hat for her to wear just for car time.

- Congratulations for starting at this early age! It becomes a habit and may save her life someday.

- Our car won't start until our child gets into the seat and is buckled in.

- Practice consistency. Don't deviate, not even once. Insist on using the car seat for *all* travel, not just in your car.

- Save special toys and books for your child to use only while she is in her car seat.

- Our child checks to see if I'm using my seat belt, and then I check to see if she is buckled into her car seat.

- When you advance your daughter to a toddler seat, wrap it up and make it a special gift for her.

- As you buckle her up, play an imitation game where you do something like tapping your chin, and then she does the same.

- We say favorite nursery rhymes and sing songs as we buckle up in our car.

- Place a sticker on her car seat that she can look at or peel off.

- Recite, "I love you too much to let you out of your car seat; I want you safe," as long as necessary when the going gets rough.

(See also questions 96 and 126.)

Thanks to Backyard Center Parents,
Suggestion Circle from Yakima, Washington

136. What can I do to keep my fourteen-month-old in the playpen?

- Arrange so he doesn't stay in it too long, like five to ten minutes.
- Give your child something safe and soft to have in the playpen with him.
- Play a special record he likes, if you have to put him in.
- Save the playpen for emergency or safety times only.
- My daughter never did stay in her playpen. She was too busy, and her frustration wasn't worth it. Don't put any toys in that she could use to climb out.
- Put the playpen out where the rest of the family is. Use it only for safety, *not* convenience.
- Put the playpen next to the table where you're working.
- When you're exhausted and the baby doesn't object, putting him "in the pen" for ten minutes is a good idea— it's a rest period for you.

Thanks to Samara Kemp,
Suggestion Circle from Modesto, California

137. My daughter wants to stand up in the bathtub, and I'm afraid she will fall. What can I do?

- Put a plastic laundry basket inside the tub. Allow her to stand in the basket while you hold on.

- Use a suction seat.

- Mount a bathtub hammock and let her hang onto that.

- Take a bath with her.

- Those molded, sponge baby tubs work really well.

- See if showering with her works.

- Use a firm grip and say, "Please sit down."

- Use a bath mat to cut down on slippage.

- When she stands, say "No" firmly and sit her down. If she stands again, take her out of the tub and end the bath.

Thanks to Backyard Center Parents,
Suggestion Circle from Yakima, Washington

138. My toddler gets into the silverware in the dishwasher. What should I do?

- Put plastic containers and other safe things into a drawer. Open that drawer for the toddler to play in while you do the dishes.

- It's a good thing that you are being careful. Children can break glass in the dishwasher.

- Place plastic plates and wooden spoons and forks in the dishwasher just for him. He can help by putting these in and taking them out.

- Keep spoons in the basket in the dishwasher for your toddler to play with. Then put forks and knives in later.

- Do the dishes when the child is occupied somewhere else. The corners of the dishwasher are sharp.

- If you let him play with the dishwasher, be sure that there is no detergent in it!

- I keep a stock of empty cans (coffee cans and such) for my son to stack in the dishwasher or bang on or roll on the floor. Be sure the cans have no sharp edges.

- Fill one bottom drawer in your kitchen with fun stuff for your toddler to empty out: clean dust cloths, empty grocery sacks, sponges, whatever. He'll love it!

- I wonder if our kids will enjoy doing dishes when we want them to?

Thanks to Melinda Scott,
Suggestion Circle from Walnut Creek, California

139. My sixteen-month-old screams and stiffens when I try to put her into the grocery cart, and she runs the other way when I let her out. She hurt herself by running smack into a gum machine because she was so intent on getting away that she didn't look where she was going.

- Leave your daughter at home with someone to care for her.

- Use a day-care center or ask neighbors for child care when you need to do the grocery shopping.

- Let her ride on the bottom of the cart.

- Give her a job to do—carry bananas or hold the grocery list for you.

- See to it that you take a favorite toy.

- Keep in mind that this, too, will pass. This may be a way for your daughter to begin to establish her independence.

- Bring along a snack.

- Stop at the park on your way to the store. Tell your toddler this is her time to run.

- Avoid shopping trips at nap times. Shop early in the day when you and she are both rested.

- Play a game, helping her identify familiar objects in the store. Let her choose a safe one to hold.

(See also questions 128 and 135.)

Thanks to Nat Houtz,
Suggestion Circle from Edmonds, Washington

140. Grandma's house is not babyproofed. How can I deal with this?

- Call your mother before you leave for your visit to give her a chance to prepare.

- Pick up valuables and put them in a safe place when you first arrive.

- Ask Grandma to look for safe, interesting objects to put into a special drawer, like plastic spoons and containers, metal lids, and coffee cans.

- Ask Grandma to visit in your home and lovingly explain why.

- Make visits short, and don't plan to stay overnight.

- Explain to her that your son can learn the difference between a crystal ashtray and a margarine tub later, after he has had plenty of chances to explore how things feel and stack.

- Affirm yourself for not wanting to say no all the time!

- Babyproof one room in Grandma's house. Get socket covers and safety locks. Use heavy rubber bands to lock cabinet doors. Bring them with you when you visit.

- Bring a special box of toys with you to keep your child busy.

Thanks to Backyard Center Parents,
Suggestion Circle from Yakima, Washington

141. Christmas is coming soon. We really want to have a tree, but how can I make it safe?

- Put your tree up on a table.

- Place your tree in the playpen.

- Don't decorate the tree. Just enjoy the fragrance of pine.

- Block off the tree so your child can't reach it, but be sure your child can still see the tree.

- Show your child how to touch, not grab, the tree.

- Use a living tree, which will be in the house for a short time with unbreakable ornaments and no lights.

- Have a tree as you normally do, but keep the breakable ornaments near the top. You can use lights to teach the meaning of "hot."

- Tie the tree to the ceiling and floor. Place the valuable ornaments at the top. Put safe ornaments at the bottom.

- Let your toddler have her own tiny tree with unbreakable ornaments that she can put on and take off the tree.

Thanks to Backyard Center Parents,
Suggestion Circle from Yakima, Washington

142. How can I safeguard my toddler from abduction?

- Never leave your child alone in the car.
- Discuss safety rules with your sitter about opening the door, going for walks, and answering the phone.
- Always stay beside your child in public!
- Use a stroller strap or a backpack when you are shopping.
- Choose sitters with care. (See question 177.)
- Don't let your toddler wear a T-shirt with her name on it.
- Investigate your local police or Red Cross fingerprint program.
- Be consistent with your child in insisting that she stay with you.
- Trust your feelings about people who approach your child.
- Read *Jenny's New Game,* by Laurella Cross, a book on how to prevent people from stealing your child. (See "Resources.")

  (See also question 143.)

Thanks to Backyard Center Parents,
Suggestion Circle from Yakima, Washington

143. I'm hearing so much about sexual abuse, and it worries me. How can I protect my child?

- It's up to you to be really careful about who he's around.
- Don't force him to kiss or hug relatives.
- It's the parents' job to screen sitters carefully.
- Tell your kids, "Nobody touches you there but Mommy and the doctor."
- Be aware of any changes in his genital area.

- When a child cringes from a neighbor or doesn't want to go to someone's house or be near someone, *wonder why.*

- It's a good idea to teach your children that you have "surprises," *not* "secrets" in your family.

- Read him the book, *It's My Body,* by Lory Freeman. (See "Resources.")

  (See also question 142 and "Keeping Toddlers Safe.")

Thanks to Educational Service District 105 Staff,
Suggestion Circle from Yakima, Washington

Chapter 18

Who Raises the Kids?

144. How can I handle grandparents who favor one of my kids over the others?

- Express your concerns by describing what they do and telling them what you want them to do.

- Say it as you see it, directly to *them.*

- Let them see only one kid at a time.

- Grandparents must be made aware of their behavior. Having the parents try to make up for it to the neglected child doesn't work. The child knows full well what is happening.

- Point out that favoritism is a heavy burden for the favored child.

- You could stand up to the grandparents and tell them they can't come to your house without comparable presents for both children.

- Show the grandparents things they could do to favor all the children.

- I remind my parents often. They claim they are making up for *my* favoring one over the other. I wonder if they're right?

- Remind them that all children are born equal as far as needing grandparents is concerned. Ask how you can help them treat each one as a favorite.

- Tell them you know that they have enough love for all the grandchildren.

(See also question 164.)

Thanks to Backyard Center Parents,
Suggestion Circle from Yakima, Washington

145. How do we help grandparents not to feel rejected when our explorer doesn't want to be held and cuddled?

- If the grandparents and a parent sit together when the child is quiet, they can all get used to each other.

- Reassure them that parents can feel rejected, too.

- Say, "Mom, he's busy exploring now. He'll need loving later."

- Give each of them a chance to rock the baby to sleep and snuggle when he is sleeping.

- Give them the chance to bottle-feed or read a story to your toddler.

- Tell them that after this age of depending on Mom, there will come an age when he'll want to be with grandparents.

- Remind grandparents to explore *with* him by getting down on the floor and playing, stacking blocks and such.

- I suggest to my folks that they not pick him up immediately but first give him "warm-up" time to get reacquainted.

- It's kind of you to care about your parents' feelings, but remember it's up to them *not* to feel hurt.

- Share Clarke's tape, *The Wonderful Busy Ones*, with them. (See "Resources.")

Thanks to Backyard Center Grandparents,
Suggestion Circle from Yakima, Washington

146. My explorer loves to grab her grandpa's glasses. What shall we do to protect life and lens?

- Advise your father to take his glasses off when holding the baby.

- Insist that grabbing glasses is a no-no.

- Tell Grandpa to take the baby's finger and push it gently against the nosepiece each time she makes a grab. This really works!

- Buy a pair of toy glasses for your little one.

- Warn people with glasses that kids do make passes!

- This is a passing curiosity. In a few months, glasses will be safe.

- Offer the child something else to play with while she is being held by a "glasses" person.

- Has Grandpa tried contact lenses?

- Be sure that all your grandfolks with lenses know about explorers and their curiosity. The toddlers aren't being purposefully naughty!

- Make a "poncho" for Grandpa to wear to distract your baby. Make one out of a terry-cloth towel with a hole cut out of the center for his head. Sew a variety of toys on it.

Thanks to Backyard Center Parents,
Suggestion Circle from Yakima, Washington

147. The grandparents object to my picking up our six-month-old when he cries. They say he should cry it out. What can I do?

- Say, "I'd rather pick him up now than wait until his screaming reaches a desperate pitch, which would teach him that he has to be desperate to get my attention."

- You and your husband should present a united front, stating, "We decided to meet our baby's needs in this way and at this age."

- Say, "We want to build the baby's self-esteem by acknowledging him when he calls us."

- Crying is how a baby communicates.

- Tell them, "I am building my child's trust in me and the other adults who care for him."

- Turn the situation around and ask, "If you were crying, wouldn't you like me to comfort you?"

- Remind them that the family is the first place to teach your child that his needs are important. This teaches him to get his needs met later on.

- Remember that it is OK to stay with your values and beliefs, even when your parents disagree.

- See if you can get them to read the chapter on crying and spoiling in *The First Three Years of Life*, by Burton White, and then ask them what they think. White says you can't spoil a baby under eight months old. (See "Resources.")

(See also questions 101, 110, and 174.)

Thanks to Backyard Center Parents,
Suggestion Circle from Yakima, Washington

148. How should I handle the visiting grandparent who brings soda pop and candy for my explorer? We don't approve.

- Just ask your parents not to bring candy. Tell them that your child isn't allowed to eat candy.

- Get your child a T-shirt that says, "Please don't feed me candy."

- Say, "Please bring stickers instead of candy. The baby loves them."

- Ask them to bring fruit.

- Suggest that Grandma bake something special and healthful instead of bringing candy.

- Tell them hugs and kisses help kids grow better than sweets do.

- Suggest some little picture books or inexpensive toys they could bring instead of candy.

- Have them bring fruit juice instead of pop.

- Limit sweets to one day a week. If grandparents come on that day, the kids can eat sweets.

> *Thanks to Yakima Valley Community College*
> *Cooperative Preschool, Eisenhower Parents,*
> *Suggestion Circle from Yakima, Washington*

149. My mom is pressuring me to toilet train my seventeen-month-old. He is not ready and neither am I. What can I do and say about this?

- Explain that most kids this age don't have enough awareness of how their bodies work to begin toilet training.

- Say, "It goes faster and easier when you train a child who is two and a half or so because the sphincter muscles are ready then."

- Explain that you don't feel he is ready. Then don't let yourself be pressured.

- Say, "Mom, I'm sorry, but we don't agree on this issue. Let's talk about something else."

- Find a way to remind Mom that it will be your decision and that you don't feel he is ready.

- Show her medical books that give reasons not to push an "unready" child, or ask her to talk to your physician.

- Say, "Relax, Mom, I don't mind the diapers."

- Say, "I know you were expected to train us early. I'm so glad that rule has changed."

- Say no, and then don't do or say anything else.

- Assure her that there is lots of time and that he won't be carrying a diaper bag to school.

(See also questions 110 and 147.)

Thanks to Yakima Valley Community College
Cooperative Preschool, Central Lutheran Parents,
Suggestion Circle from Yakima, Washington

150. So many adults we know, and even some strangers, want to kiss our ten-month-old on the lips. What should I do to discourage this?

- Say, "It bothers me when you kiss my baby on the lips."

- Explain to the adult that your baby likes to be hugged.

- Make a game of touching in other ways, like an "Eskimo kiss."

- Be assertive and say, "Please kiss her on the cheek."

- Tell them you are trying to teach your child to turn her cheek.

- If all else fails, have your baby teethe on garlic buds!

- Show by example how to give and accept kisses on the cheek.

- Ask the person to play a small game or sing a song to the child instead.

Thanks to Backyard Center, Community-at-Large Grandparents, Suggestion Circle from Yakima, Washington

151. My friend brings her explorer to play with mine and just lets her run wild. What should I do?

- Set down some simple rules at the beginning of the visit.

- Direct suggestions to the mother, like "Doris, I expect you to keep Jenny in this room. I have not childproofed the back rooms."

- Don't invite them back until the kids are in college.

- Establish a safe, childproofed room, and let the explorer loose.

- Try meeting your friend and her explorer someplace else besides your house, where you won't worry about your special things.

- Talk with your friend before she comes over, and let her know your concern.

- This may be the time to make a "tent" with a blanket and chairs for the explorers.

- Gather together some safe toys that your explorers can play with in the same room with you.

- Get adults together in the evening, when the kids aren't around.

- If your friend won't take charge of her own explorer, it's up to you.

(See also questions 131 and 163.)

Thanks to Backyard Center Parents, Suggestion Circle from Yakima, Washington

152. My husband didn't handle a situation with our toddler as I thought he should have. What can I do?

- Say, "This disturbs me. When can we talk about it?"

- Say, "Our kid is important. I think he needs a dad who does. . ."

- Both of you have different opinions. If it's not harmful to the child, let the disagreement slide.

- Choose a calm time, and then tell your husband you are upset. Give him examples of what you would like him to do instead and why.

- Write him a note that says you don't have all the answers but that you want to talk about the incident and how you feel about it.

- Say, "It's your right to choose, but I want you to know my feelings about. . ."

- Compliment your spouse when you like what he does.

- Read child development articles pertaining to your baby's stage of development, and show the articles to your husband. Let him know you are still learning, too, or ask *him* to read the article or book and discuss it afterward.

- I don't think it hurts kids to have parents disagree about little things. They'll sort it out.

- Take a parenting class together to help you decide on mutual goals.

(See also questions 153, 154, and 165.)

Thanks to Backyard Center Grandparents,
Suggestion Circle from Yakima, Washington

153. My ex-husband doesn't know very much about kids, but now he wants to have our daughter every weekend. What should I do?

- Ask him how he plans to take care of her and what he knows about the needs of explorers.

- What are his visitation rights? Do you think you need to challenge them? Call your lawyer.

- Send along your daughter's schedule and a list of food choices.

- Suggest that he take a parenting course to learn how to care for her.

- Ask him to take care of the baby for a couple of hours while you're away. This will help to break him in.

- Perhaps his mom could help out.

- It's OK for you to be concerned about your daughter's welfare. Find ways to see that she's protected. Call your local child protection service for ideas.

- Write a list of tips for making the weekend fun and safe. Include your child's favorite activities. Mention mannerisms that can aid him—for example, "She pulls on her right earlobe when she is tired."

- Be straight with your ex-husband. Let him know that you expect him to be responsible.

(See also questions 152 and 154.)

Thanks to Gail Nordeman,
Suggestion Circle from Cincinnati, Ohio

154. Sometimes my wife does things with our kid that I don't like. What should I do?

- Ignore it, but let her know when she does something you do like.

- Tell her what a good mother she is and how much you love her. Then say, "I didn't like the way you did this because. . . "

- Say, "I think it would have worked better if you had. . . "

- I'd express my view, want to know what my wife's views were, then come up with a compromise on how to handle it next time.

- Tell her.

- Have a weekly meeting to discuss how to deal with the kids.

- Excuse yourself and your wife from the child quietly. Plan a united front, and present it to the child that way.

- Be consistent with limits previously set up. If a situation arises that you didn't anticipate, play it by ear at that moment, and decide later what the policy from then on will be.

- Tell your wife why you want her to do it another way.

- Read *The Father's Almanac,* by S. Adams Sullivan. (See "Resources.")

(See also questions 152 and 153.)

Thanks to Backyard CenterParents,
Suggestion Circle from Yakima, Washington

Chapter 19

Parents Have Needs
and Problems, Too

155. I thought a baby would make our marriage even better, but now we never seem to have any time together. What are some tips to renew us as a couple?

- Set an appointed time one day each week to get away.

- Take several short (five-minute) times during the day to pay attention to each other.

- From as early an age as possible, set an early bedtime for the child so you can be alone.

- Don't forget that little things like love notes and presents are the spice of life.

- Switch baby-sitting with another couple once a week to have a night alone at home, or get a sitter and go out.

- Think of three ways to make your sex life more exciting.

- Put the baby in a front or back carrier, and walk and talk together.

- See if you can help each other with the housework. After each job, take fifteen or twenty minutes to talk or snuggle.

- Keep a sense of humor.

- Get problems out in the open. Listen to each other and help each other.

- Start a hobby together.

  (See also questions 134, 156, and 159.)

  Thanks to Backyard Center Parents,
  Suggestion Circle from Yakima, Washington

156. I'm so tired I don't feel like having sex. What can I do about this?

- Have a baby-sitter come in one hour per day or even just once or twice a week. Do *whatever* you want to do—clean a closet, read a magazine, rest.

- Tell your husband how tired you are, and ask him to help solve this problem.

- Tell your husband that you really love him and that you are too tired to have sex tonight. Consider having sex in the mornings sometimes.

- See if your husband can come home during the baby's nap time, if you have more energy then.

- Hire help for housework.

- Nap with your child.

- At least every two weeks, go out with your husband. Be consistent about doing this.

- Have a regular, early bedtime for your baby so you can have more time with your spouse.

- Be sure you are getting enough vitamins for extra energy.

- Have your hemoglobin level checked.

- Agree with your husband on which days you will skip the housework and keep that energy for loving.

- Are you nursing? Many women are not as interested in sex while they are nursing.

(See also question 158.)

Thanks to Nat Houtz,
Suggestion Circle from Seattle, Washington

157. I feel like I'm all "boxed in." I no longer do the things I used to do for fun. How can I find time for myself?

- Put your baby in front of a mirror or in a swing, and have a good supply of reading material close by to "take you away" for ten minutes or so.

- Do fun things during your baby's nap time. The cobwebs can wait.

- Join a baby-sitting co-op, or ask Grandma to watch your child.

- Plan and schedule a once-a-week appointment with a sitter so that you will be sure to go out and it won't be just an "option."

- Get your baby into the routine of an early bedtime.

- Get up earlier while your baby is still sleeping.

- On weekends, take turns with your spouse taking care of the baby. Read Sandy Jones's *Crying Baby, Sleepless Nights.* (See "Resources.")

- Ask your librarian for a time-management book or article that will help you find shortcuts for what you need to do.

- Unplug the phone.

- Make a list of priorities and put yourself near the top. Remember, it is OK to take care of yourself.

(See also question 124.)

Thanks to Judy Popp,
Suggestion Circle from Yakima, Washington

158. I'm pregnant with my second child. With my explorer still waking up at night and my having to run after him in the daytime, how can I get more rest?

- Be sure to nap when your explorer naps. Let housework wait.

- Alternate with your husband in getting up at night.

- Take "minibreaks" for five to ten minutes. Put your feet up, play soothing music, read.

- Give yourself permission to ask a friend to watch your explorer when you need help.

- Encourage Dad to take the explorer for a twenty-minute walk or a ride every day. Relax while they are gone.

- On weekends, take turns with your husband sleeping in.

- On your spouse's night to get up with the explorer, sleep in another part of the house so you'll sleep through the night.

- Exchange baby-sitting with a friend who also needs more rest. You take the 1:00 to 2:30 P.M. shift while she rests. You rest from 2:30 to 4:00 P.M. while she watches the kids.

- Save the playpen for times when you are physically exhausted. Put the baby in it and curl up nearby for a few minutes without sleeping.

(See also questions 99 and 156.)

Thanks to Backyard Center Parents,
Suggestion Circle from Yakima, Washington

159. How can I get enough rest? I have two kids under two years old.

- As soon as both children go down for a nap, leave the housework and go to bed yourself.

- Let housework slide a little. Reevaluate your priorities.

- Take advantage of any help. You are worth it!

- Swap sitting with a friend so you have one afternoon a week to yourself.

- Get help. Make lists of resources and use them.

- Keep meals simple. Use convenience foods.

- Use disposable diapers or a diaper service.

- Remember, you don't need to be perfect to be a good parent.

- Have Grandma take the kids once a week while you sleep.

- Get a sitter to come in for one hour every day after school. Lie down or listen to a relaxing tape.

(See also questions 99, 134, 156, and 158.)

Thanks to Backyard Center Parents,
Suggestion Circle from Yakima, Washington

160. As a single parent, I spend all my time with my little girl. How can I find some other grown-ups to be with?

- Join Parents Without Partners or a child-care co-op (see "How to Set up a Child-Care Co-op"), or start a Backyard Center group (see "How to Start a Backyard Center").

- Take your little girl to visit some folks in a nursing home. Often they are hungry to see children and will talk with both of you.

- Call a Tupperware lady and ask to be invited to a party.

- Join a church where there's an adult Sunday school class for you and a nursery for your little girl.

- Look in the Sunday supplement for classes that offer baby-sitting or "Mom's day out" ads.

- A coed sports activity, like volleyball, might be a lot of fun!

- You could trade baby-sitting with a friend so you have the time to get out and do things.

- Sell Shaklee, Amway, Avon, or one of those products, and go to the meetings.

- Take a class at the community college. And don't be in a hurry to leave the minute the class is over.

- Go to story hour at the library. Other parents will be there, too.

(See also question 132.)

Thanks to Backyard Center Parents,
Suggestion Circle from Yakima, Washington

161. I feel guilty that my seventeen-month-old doesn't mind me better. How can I handle this?

- Remove as many items as you can that you don't want her to get into. Then you don't have to say no as often.

- Tell your baby that she's doing a good job of exploring the world. That's her job right now, and she'll be at the "minding" stage soon.

- Read the chapter about six- to eighteen-month-olds in Clarke's book, *Self-Esteem: A Family Affair.* (See "Resources.")

- Buy a doll or teddy bear for yourself—one that will "mind you."

- Find ways to spend less time with the people who help you feel guilty.

- It sounds as if you're feeling guilty about spending so much time feeling guilty! Could you be expecting too much of both you and your explorer?

- Check out some other seventeen-month-old children, and relax a bit.
- Remember that at seventeen months your child will still need you to provide a safe environment.
- Join a support group for parents of toddlers.

(See also question 162 and "Ages and Stages.")

Thanks to Backyard Center Parents,
Suggestion Circle from Yakima, Washington

162. Whenever I'm on the telephone, my toddler gets into everything. How can I talk on the phone without feeling so frustrated?

- Pick up your child while you talk on the phone.
- Sit on the floor with him while you're talking.
- Get a play phone, and have him use it at the same time.
- Limit your phone calls to five minutes.
- Put a collection of toys into a basket that the child is not allowed to play with unless you are on the phone.
- Hold your toddler in your lap, and let him play with something special.
- Ask the caller if you may call back during nap time.
- If the call is an emergency, put the child into the crib.
- Expect him to play near you and give you a few minutes of time. Have chalk and a chalkboard near the phone.
- Put your child in a high chair, and talk on the phone while he uses crayons and paper.

(See also questions 133 and 161.)

Thanks to Backyard Center Parents,
Suggestion Circle from Yakima, Washington

163. What are some ideas for correcting another child in my home when her parents are not acting on the problem?

- State the problem without piling on any judgment. "If I see your child getting into something unsafe or inappropriate to play with, I'll go ahead and take care of it."

- Say to the child, "In our family, we don't play with the TV dials, but you can turn the dials on this busy box." Find something the child can do instead when she does something inappropriate.

- Give a house tour to the parent, pointing out areas that are off-limits and those in which the children can play.

- Make sure there are toys, boxes, blocks, and other interesting and safe things to play with.

- Invite the parents over without the kids, or just don't have the family over until the children are older.

- Move yourselves into the childproofed area so you can watch the kids.

- Avoid the problem by visiting with your guest on the couch. Pull the couch far enough away from the wall so that the child can play behind it in her own special spot. Give her some interesting and safe toys or kitchen gadgets.

- Put a sheet over a card table so the child will have a hideaway.

(See also questions 131 and 151.)

Thanks to Backyard Center Parents,
Suggestion Circle from Yakima, Washington

164. My brother's baby and mine were born six days apart. Now they are already being compared at seven months. What can I do to discourage this?

- Give your brother Brazelton's *Infants and Mothers* to show him the range of *normal* development. (See "Resources.")

- Redirect the conversation. Don't talk about your baby's achievements.

- Tell your brother that you are not into competition. Then don't get caught up yourself by comparing.

- Children deserve the right to grow without being compared.

- Ask your brother and his wife to practice enjoying each child as if he were the only one.

- Tell the adults to compete with other adults instead of setting up competition between babies.

- Stress differences in "normal" children. Each body grows at its own rate. By the time children are eighteen years old, nobody will care who was first, unless you make a big deal of it.

- Be "tactfully blunt" and ask the person to stop comparing.

- Try to befriend your nephew despite the competitive atmosphere.

- Tell a story of when you were compared as a child and how you didn't like it.

(See also questions 89 and 144.)

Thanks to Backyard Center Parents,
Suggestion Circle from Yakima, Washington

165. How can I get my husband to spend more time with our baby?

- Tell him the baby deserves to know her dad. Tell him babies react with dads in ways they don't react with moms and that your baby deserves both experiences.

- Reinforce the positive interaction your husband already has with the baby.

- It is not your responsibility. It is *his* responsibility.

- If you want Dad to interact with the baby, show Dad what he's doing right, not just what he's doing wrong.

- Let the father be alone with the child.

- Children take one-half of their rearing from each parent. Ask him if he wants his half to be blank.

- Buy a copy of Greenberg's *The Birth of a Father*. (See "Resources.")

- Tell him you wish he would hold the baby more often.

- If he doesn't know how to be with a baby, tell him to go ahead and practice.

(See also questions 152, 154, and 173.)

Thanks to Backyard Center Parents,
Suggestion Circle from Yakima, Washington

166. The doctor just told me my baby is handicapped and said that she may need to be institutionalized. I feel terrible.

- I'm sorry.

- Get a second opinion.

- Share your grief with someone.

- Join a support group. Your doctor can probably tell you about one.

- Do whatever you need to do to learn not to blame yourself.

- Get support and information from at least one other parent whose child has the same handicap.

- Write "Dear Abby" and find out if there is a national support group for parents with a child like yours.

- Check and see if your area has a Parent-to-Parent Program that will match you with a family that has a similarly handicapped child and has been through it. Call your local public health department.

- Get some counseling. Talk about how you feel as many times as you need to.

Thanks to Backyard Center Parents,
Suggestion Circle from Yakima, Washington

167. How do I know whether to bring my sick baby to our church nursery or friend's home?

- Check with your physician *first* to see what the child has and if it is contagious.

- Don't bring your child if she is running a temperature.

- Don't bring your child if her nose is running.

- Don't bring your child if she has a visible rash.

- If you must bring your child, keep her and her things separate and at a distance from other children. Realize that it takes only one toy from a sick child to spread infection.

- Leave your baby with a sitter.

- Ask if there are any guidelines for bringing ill children to your play group or nursery.

- Establish guidelines with your friends as to when and where not to bring sick children when you are visiting one another.

- You probably wouldn't want your child to be exposed unnecessarily to illness. Show the same courtesy to others.

Thanks to Backyard Center Parents, Suggestion Circle from
Yakima, Washington

168. My baby and I are just out of a drug recovery house and trying to build a new way of life. My family does everything in the old, destructive, codependent ways. How can we survive and stay sober?

- Believe in yourself and take your time.

- Get all of the outside help that you can for the next year.

- Ask for help from your AA group—find one that works for you.

- Study the whole series of affirmations and offer them to yourself visually and verbally every day.

- Build new support networks that will reinforce your new way of life. Go to church, exercise classes, and parenting groups.

- One day at a time, practice your own new, strong behavior that is self-protective.

- Share your feelings and needs honestly with your family, without being judgmental.

- Keep your sense of humor.

- Record your successes in a journal.

- Strive for independence. Plan for further education or job training if you need it.

Thanks to Riel House Parents,
Suggestion Circle from Yakima, Washington

169. The baby is a year old now, and I thought his father would marry me, but I'm not even sure he'll be around much longer. What should I do?

- Find a time when the two of you can talk seriously about the baby's future. Avoid blaming and trying to make him feel guilty—focus on what the child needs.

- Both of you are responsible for the quality of this baby's life. Can you talk about that together?

- Take some time each day to grieve about your own dreams and hopes in all of this until you feel calm about it.

- Build some support systems—family, church, clubs. Babies need a lot of caring adults in their lives.

- Be *sure* that you don't get pregnant again while you are trying to figure this out.

- Think about all the support your son needs in the next eighteen years—emotional, financial, building values, just being there for him. Figure out together how he is to get those things.

- Expect that your son's father does love and want to care for him. Talk with him about his own childhood and what he received or didn't receive from his father. (See "Resources" for books on fathering.)

- Be sure to care for yourself. If you're about to become a single mother, you need to care for your own self-esteem.

Thanks to Riel House Parents,
Suggestion Circle from Yakima, Washington

Chapter 20

Working Parents

170. How can I get everything done and get to work on time?

- Shower the night before. Have your clothes and baby's clothes all laid out.

- Get your spouse to share the duty of transporting the baby to the sitter.

- Pack the diaper bag at night with an extra set of clothes.

- Ask your baby-sitter if your baby can arrive with his sleeper still on and have breakfast at her house.

- Find a quality sitter who will come to your house in the mornings.

- Ask your boss if you can start your work half an hour later and then stay later.

- Think about the things that absolutely have to be done. For instance, try leaving your bed unmade.

- Try making your own breakfast simple, like a liquid protein drink.

- Supply your sitter with an extra set of clothes, food items, disposable diapers, and so on so that you're only packing supplies once or twice a week.

- Share morning duties with your spouse so that one person isn't burdened with all the nitty-gritty details of getting out of the house.

- Forgive yourself for what doesn't get done, and go to work peacefully.

Thanks to Backyard Center Parents,
Suggestion Circle from Yakima, Washington

171. How can I have more time with my baby when I work full time?

- Keep dinners simple. Stock up on high-protein snacks, and buy frozen entrées.

- Eat out occasionally. Use paper plates when you don't.

- Visit the baby during your lunch hour.

- Use a diaper service in your area.

- Hire a high school student or a cleaning service to clean house once a week.

- Fold diapers only as you need them, and use disposable diapers.

- For dirty dishes, put them in the sink to soak in the morning. Wash them just once a day, or buy a dishwasher.

- Ask other working moms how they cut corners.

- Start a movement at your office for an employees' day-care center right there!

- Remember that verse about "the cobwebs can wait!"

- Read *2001 Hints for Working Mothers,* by Gloria Mayer. (See "Resources.")

Thanks to Backyard Center Parents,
Suggestion Circle from Yakima, Washington

172. What can I do about our daughter crying every day when I leave her at the sitter's?

- Remember, this can be a normal phase at this age. Don't feel guilty.

- Leave something of yours (a glove, a hankie) with her to keep until you come back.

- Always let your child see you leave. Don't sneak away to avoid her crying.

- Prepare a "surprise bag" with different things for her to play with each day.

- If it happens all the time, try another sitter, or make arrangements for one to come to your house.

- Have your husband take her to the sitter. Maybe that will make a difference.

- Help your child start an enjoyable activity before you leave.

- Give your daughter a chance to be upset while you stay calm.

- Establish a good-bye ritual, like a kiss on each cheek and your saying, "I love you, and I'll be back after work."

- Affirm your child's feelings. Say, "I'm sorry you're sad about my going, but I need to go! See you soon, special kid."

(See also questions 97, 170, 177, and "Keeping Toddlers Safe.")

Thanks to Yakima Valley Community College Preschool Cooperative Parents, Suggestion Circle from Yakima, Washington

173. How can I get my husband to share more of the household responsibilities?

- Find some ways to share with him the ideas in Letty Pogrebin's *Family Politics*. (See "Resources.")

- Sit down and explain your needs. Get your feelings out.

- Ask for help. Make a list of things that you need help with.

- Have your husband take full care of the baby and do all the household chores for a day. This will make him aware of how much needs to be done.

- Together list all the chores that need to be done on squares of paper. Put the slips of paper in a basket, and have each partner draw one until they're all gone. Then do the ones you draw!

- Working on the jobs together makes them take less time. Then you can plan an outing or just plain cuddle.

- At our house my husband usually does the outdoor chores, like mowing the lawn, hauling wood, and fixing the car. Sometimes we trade chores or work together.

- Say, "I need help! Should I quit work, get a cleaning person, or will you agree to divide the chores?"

(See also questions 152, 154, and 165.)

Thanks to Backyard Center Parents,
Suggestion Circle from Yakima, Washington

174. My mother thinks I should stay home with the baby, but I want to pursue my career.

- Find good care for your child with a person who shares your values, and then reassure your mother.

- Point out some benefits your working has for your family.

- Remember that wanting to pursue your career doesn't mean you love your child less.

- If you need the income, tell your mom that. Expect her to trust your decision to work.

- Invite your mom to help with child care as much as she'd like, if you are willing for her to do that.

- Trust your own feelings about wanting to pursue your career.

- Hug your mom. Let her know you appreciate her concern but that you need to follow your own decision.

- Perhaps your mom needs reassurance that you feel she was a good mother even though she didn't have a career.

- This can be a good time for both of you to realize that you can disagree about something important and still love and value each other.

- Consider her reasons. Consider yours. Consider the baby's welfare. Then decide.

(See also questions 110, 147, and 175.)

Thanks to Melanie Weiss,
Suggestion Circle from Bellevue, Washington

175. My husband is pressuring me to go to work, but I want to stay home.

- Stay home if you can. Kids are little only once!

- Find a part-time job that you will enjoy!

- Find a job you can do at home, like telephone sales, typing, ironing, or sewing.

- Start your own day-care center.

- Read and share with your husband Burton White's *The First Three Years of Life*, page 247, where he encourages moms to stay home for the first three years.

- Rank your family's needs. Perhaps you can give up some material things in order to afford to stay home.

- Set time-limited goals, such as work for a year to save money and then quit.

- Borrow money now; pay it back when the child is older.

- Collect data about moms and working from books like Selma Fraiberg's *The Magic Years*. (See "Resources.")

- Plan a time when the two of you can sit down and really talk about what you want, such as quality of life as well as quantity of material things.

- This is a time when a counselor or perhaps your minister can help you both sort out your goals. If your husband won't go with you, you can still see a counselor yourself.

(See also question 174.)

Thanks to Backyard Center Parents,
Suggestion Circle from Yakima, Washington

176. How do I deal with my guilt about going back to work?

- If you can, cut down your work hours. If you can't, leave thoughts about your job at your workplace, and make the most of at-home time.

- Go home for lunch.

- Work when your spouse can watch the child.

- Find the very best child care you can.

- Join a working parents' support group.

- Celebrate your child's milestones—first steps, waving bye-bye, first word—instead of feeling guilty about things missed.

- Remember that past generations seldom were able to be full-time parents. So enjoy your provider role and your mothering one, too.

- Allow yourself twenty minutes a day to feel really guilty. Then spend the rest of the time knowing you're a very energetic and interesting person, who's a better parent because you work.

- Have a special, sacred time each day that you spend with your child. Don't allow interruptions, not even phone calls!

- Use some of those hard-earned bucks for a cleaning person. It's worth it, and you'll have more time to spend with your child—guilt-free! (See also question 175.)

Thanks to Backyard Center Parents,
Suggestion Circle from Yakima, Washington

177. What do I look for in a quality day-care provider?

- Find someone who enjoys and values time with children. Look for someone who has some activities planned for each day.

- Find someone who is comfortable with you and will tell you things as they are.

- Look for clues at the end of the day, like a play area that is neither too disarrayed nor super neat.

- Drop in unexpectedly to get a "feel" for things. Watch how discipline, crises, and routines are handled.

- Look at the ages and numbers of kids being cared for. One adult is needed for every two or three explorers.

- Look for someone whose feelings on discipline and child care are similar to yours.

- Ask for recommendations from friends. Then go with what feels right to you, trusting your "gut."

- Choose a provider who *does* use car seats but *can't* stand playpens (as a regular thing).

- Look for a provider who is licensed by the state and can offer references. Also set up your own standards for safety, hygiene, routines, and learning ideas.

- See how your child feels about this place and person and how he reacts to going back there.

(See "How to Set up a Child-Care Co-op.")

Thanks to Backyard Center Parents,
Suggestion Circle from Yakima, Washington

Moving On from Toddlers to the Terrific Twos

When your children are about a year and a half old, you have cause to celebrate. As parents, you have seen your offspring through the first two important stages of development. You have nurtured your children and taught them that their needs are important, that they don't have to hurry to grow up, that being a boy or being a girl is equally wonderful, and that the world is a safe and comfortable place in which to learn and explore. Along the way, you have also met many of your own needs for nurturing and exploring.

For the next eighteen months or so, as your child begins to think for himself, you will need to continue to offer positive messages for being and doing, and you will focus on encouraging your child's thinking skills. You'll describe his behavior for him, supplying him with words to build his vocabulary, and you'll accept and affirm his need to become a separate person. You'll set limits lovingly and offer choices: "Skipping quiet time is not a choice, but do you want your doll or your teddy bear?"

As his skills in thinking grow, your child will need you to affirm his ability to think and feel at the same time. He will begin learning that his choices have an effect on the world around him. You can view his contrariness as an effort to separate from you, and you will let him know that he is a "terrific two."

Almost miraculously, you will relearn these same lessons of independent thinking in your adult relationships, because as your children grow through each age and stage, you, as parents, have the opportunity to recycle and relearn. In the next section of this book, you can read about the joys and challenges of parenting growing toddlers and terrific twos.

Darlene Montz

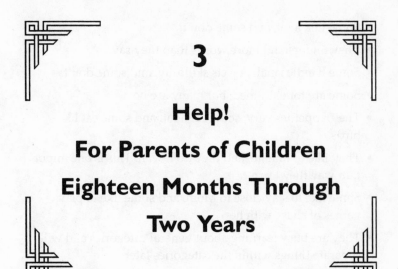

3

Help!
For Parents of Children
Eighteen Months Through
Two Years

Ages and Stages

I have known more than 350 children this age. What I know about these children, who are beginning the important task of separating from parents so they can become independent, is this:

- They don't cooperate.

- They are often angry, and they try out many ways of showing it. Some of them have lots of tantrums, and some just fuss.

- They are practicing saying no, but they shouldn't be held to it at this stage.

- They test limits.

- Sometimes they are independent, and sometimes they are not.

- Some talk a lot, and some don't.

- They understand more words than they say.

- Some handle small objects skillfully, and some don't.

- Some are toilet trained, but many are not.

- Their appetites vary; some eat a lot, and some eat like birds.

- They like to imitate, and they do it well. This is one important way they learn.

- Some like to stay close to Mom, and some like to play games of chase with her.

- They are busy learning about general categories and will separate things within the categories later.

- They are starting to understand "after lunch" but don't understand "in fifteen minutes."

- Routines and rituals are important to help these children understand time and sequence and learn about expected and responsible behavior.

- They develop their memories by insisting that you repeat the same stories and songs over and over.

- They understand one-step commands or requests (like "get your coat") but lose it if you ask them to do two or three things at a time.

- They try out whining and screaming and continue these behaviors for a long time if adults respond to them.

- They learn to walk and fall down and climb and turn in dizzy circles and walk backwards.

- They climb up and down stairs early and easily, if their legs are long enough and they have stairs to practice on and a patient adult to guide them.

- They need adults to provide safe places for them to "grow" their climbing muscles because they will climb anywhere.

- They like to fit little things into little holes, so watch that they don't put beans in little noses or magic markers in little ears.

- They can help clean up the many spills that result from their poor aim and their fascination with liquids.

- They are wonderful, exciting, interesting people.

I like being with two-year-olds. I know that parents sometimes tire of children's whining. Some parents don't understand that children are not powerless but, in fact, are doing what they need to do at this age to prepare themselves to grow up successfully and become loving, caring, responsible people.

Parents need to provide the structure—that is, the environment, the safety, the security, the rules and rituals, and the love—that will give these children the freedom to grow.

Gail Davenport

Affirmations for Growth—Thinking

Here are some special affirming messages that will help children during this stage, when they need to become separate, learn to think for themselves, explore anger and resistance, and learn cause-and-effect thinking.

Affirmations for Thinking

- I'm glad you are starting to think for yourself.
- It's OK for you to be angry, and I won't let you hurt yourself or others.
- You can say no and push and test limits as much as you need to.
- You can learn to think for yourself, and I will think for myself.
- You can think and feel at the same time.
- You can know what you need and ask for help.
- You can become separate from me, and I will continue to love you.

You give these affirming messages by the way you *interact* with the child, by the way you accept the child's no's and resistance yet still enforce your rules for safety and family welfare. You can also *say* these affirmations directly in a supportive, loving way.

Of course, you have to believe the messages yourself, or they come off as confusing or conflicting messages. If you don't understand or believe an affirmation, don't give that one until you do. Do whatever you need to do for yourself to allow your child the essential experiences he needs to help him move toward independence and responsibility. When children believe that you love them as they are and that you will consistently set clear, firm limits, they can go about the important job of learning to think for themselves and trusting their ability to do so.

Since we never outgrow the need for these health-giving messages, children at this age continue to need the Being and Doing messages from earlier stages as well. (See the Being and Doing affirmations.)

Children who decided not to believe all these messages at a younger age have another chance to incorporate them now. Remember, it is never too late for you to start giving these affirmations.

When you identify additional affirmations that your child needs, write them in this book and give them to your child.

Jean Illsley Clarke

Thinking
—Eighteen months through two years and ever after—

I'm glad you are starting to think for yourself.

It's OK for you to be angry and I won't let you hurt yourself or others.

You can say no and push and test limits as much as you need to.

You can learn to think for yourself and I will think for myself.

You can think and feel at the same time.

You can know what you need and ask for help.

You can become separate from me and I will continue to love you.

Copy these ovals and color them yellow.
Post them for daily reading.

Parents of Two-Year-Olds Get
Another Chance—Recycling

Parents of a young child who is separating and practicing saying no and starting to think for herself sometimes feel pushed and frustrated. One of the side benefits of this period of children's growth is that parents get a chance to rework or recycle their own tasks of being separate, of thinking clearly, and of handling their anger in appropriate and healthful ways. (See "Parents Get Another Chance—Recycling," in Part One.)

Recycling the Tasks of Becoming
Separate and Thinking

Parents of children who are separating by resisting, saying no, and being angry often feel angry and want to say no themselves. This is an excellent time for parents to think about and practice their own ability to say no clearly. They can do that by saying no directly when they enforce the (few) rules that their child must observe.

They can also do it by saying no clearly in other parts of their lives: "I agree that the need you describe is important, but I can't add the work of being on that committee right now. I must say no." "No, I can't add that extra work and get it done during regular hours. I could work overtime, or we can get extra help or give it to someone else."

Often as adults practice the clear thinking needed to say appropriate no's, they also discover that they have less anger and that they handle it better.

The affirmations that are helpful to our children are also healthy for us. (Read through the affirmations in the previous section again now.) Because many of us never received or decided not to believe some of those healthy messages (or we only believe them partly), this is an ideal time to accept those messages for ourselves and to claim more of our ability to be whole, healthy, joyful adults. If you didn't get the affirmations you needed the first time around, you can take them now as you offer them to your children.

Jean Illsley Clarke

Common Pitfalls

Sometimes, as children go about their developmental tasks, they do things that are misinterpreted by adults. Parents may believe that they are "disciplining," but if they punish their children for doing what is developmentally correct and normal, children are hurt physically or emotionally. Sometimes, too, parents who do not understand what level of responsibility a child is ready for may overindulge the child and thus delay the child's growth.

The following behaviors of children this age are frequently misunderstood:

- *Resisting using the toilet.* Some children this age may be ready for toilet training, and some may not. Some parents may forget that children are in charge of their own bodies and, in an effort to help their children learn toilet habits, may become abusive. Both the child and adult will benefit and have much happier lives if the adult acknowledges that the child is in charge of his own body and should initiate toilet-training activities himself rather than when the parents or the neighbor's children say it is time to start.

- *Becoming separate and saying no.* When adults are fearful for a child's safety or misunderstand his need to resist and become separate, they may respond to normal two-year-old contrariness with anger or even violence. This may teach the child to feel powerless or that big people can be violent. On the other hand, giving in to tantrums teaches the child to get what he wants by bullying. Whenever possible, ignore tantrums.

- *Learning about how they are unique, separate individuals.* When parents are fearful that the child is "too separate" and not fulfilling their dreams, adults may coerce the child into being what the adults want instead of allowing the child to be who he is; this happens, for example, when parents want a naturally quiet child to be active.

Christine Ternand, M.D.

Keeping Two-Year-Olds Safe

The methods of protecting children this age are a continuation of "Keeping Toddlers Safe." Because children this age are developing their thinking skills, it is important for parents to *explain why* they are keeping the child safe. Remember to add the "why" when you set limits for your child.

Christine Ternand, M.D.

Chapter 21

The Nature of the Two-Year-Old

178. How can I encourage my two-year-old to use words? She whines a lot.

- Whining can come before words. When she's whining say, "Use words."

- Use "I" statements. Say, "I want you to tell me in your regular voice." Model how to use a regular voice.

- Wait for her to ask—don't anticipate her needs. Listen to how other people in the family talk. If one of them whines, stop leaning on the two-year-old.

- Remind her she can think and tell you what she needs.

- As she begins to use words, have her point at what she is talking about, and then you repeat her words.

- Put a sticker on her shirt that says, "Words." Touch the sticker each time she does use words.

- Remember to notice when she uses words and respond to them.

- Keep a list on the refrigerator of the words she uses. Update the list when you notice better pronunciation, as when "teetee" becomes "kitty."

- Sing a lot, use rhymes, and pause so she can fill in the word you leave out.

- Read the language development book, *Teach Your Child to Talk*, by David Pushaw. (See "Resources.")

Thanks to Marilyn Grevstad,
Suggestion Circle from Seattle, Washington

179. How can I encourage my son to play by himself? He always wants me to play with him.

- He may not be able to play alone yet. He will outgrow his need to be with you all the time; my child did.

- If you want time for yourself say, "For ten minutes I'll play with you; then I'm going to do something else."

- Say, "I have something to do. Here is something to play with so we can be together in this room."

- Use a timer. Set the timer for only a few minutes at the beginning, and tell him that when the bell goes off he can come and get you.

- Give him safe jobs to help you with, like dusting, polishing windows, and putting the silverware away.

- Invite a neighbor child to come and play.

- Make the environment safe so he can play alone for a while without getting hurt, and then expect him to do that.

- Set aside a box of a few toys that he can play with when you want time alone.

- Have "alone time" at the same time. Say, "We'll each have fifteen minutes (half of 'Mister Rogers' time) of 'alone time.' When the timer goes off, we'll both come out of our rooms and be together."

(See also questions 191 and 256.)

Thanks to Joyce Portigal,
Suggestion Circle from Calgary, Alberta, Canada

180. How do you handle two-year-old no's?

- Don't give her choices unless you mean it.

- There are many types of no. Sometimes just sit back and listen, because she might have a valid point.

- Sometimes when she says no, she means yes.

- Enjoy them. This is a natural time for her to learn to say no.

- Make a list of all the things you need to be able to say no to and visualize her your age, saying no clearly and easily. Tell her you are glad she is learning to say no.

- Don't hold her to her no's. That will come later. Right now let her practice.

- During a time when she isn't resisting you, have fun together trading no's back and forth.

- Ask questions that expect no for an answer. "Would you like me to eat your ice cream for you?" Then compliment her on saying no well.

- Listen to the tape, *The Terrific Twos*, by Jean Illsley Clarke. (See "Resources.") It explains why children say no and how to set limits.

(See also question 187.)

Thanks to Judi Salts,
Suggestion Circle from Yakima, Washington

181. I am ready for my child, who is almost three, to give up his pacifier, but he isn't willing to. What can I do?

- Change your expectations.
- Let him take the lead.
- When it wears out, replace it with a different style nipple.

- Limit its use to rest or nap time.
- Give the child the responsibility of keeping track of his pacifier.
- See if he would be willing to trade the pacifier for a special new toy or book.
- Let him keep it as long as he wants. But tell him he can't take it to kindergarten.
- Notice when your child wants to use his pacifier. You may find that he's drawn to it when he's tired, tense, or bored. Decide how you can help him through these daily situations.
- Decide together how you are going to solve this. If people in your family smoke or sip beverages all day, leave him alone.

Thanks to Gail Nordeman,
Suggestion Circle from Cincinnati, Ohio

182. How can I encourage my two-and-a-half-year-old to think about what will happen if she breaks a rule at our house?

- Get her to think by saying, "What is the rule about this?"
- Ask her, "What happens if. . . ?"
- Use puppets with her to play out rules, cooperation, and consequences.
- Make a star chart on which she can put stars when she remembers and follows the rules.
- If she breaks a rule, have her take a "time-out" on a chair to think about what the rule is. After one minute, ask her to tell you the rule. (See the section in this book entitled "Time-Out.")
- Make sure you don't have too many rules for her to follow at this age. Six or seven are probably plenty.

- Support cause-and-effect thinking in general with pop-up toys and simple toys that require a series of two or three steps to make them work. (Save the electric train for age eight.)

(See also questions 183, 237, and 241.)

Thanks to Jean Clarke,
Suggestion Circle from Minneapolis, Minnesota

183. How can I find out what is reasonable to expect from a two-year-old?

- Join a play group with children the same age as yours, and talk to the other parents.
- Take a child development class.
- Join a co-op preschool that has parent education.
- Ask people with two-year-olds how theirs act.
- Ask people with kids a little older what age two was like.
- Get a sitter; then visit a nursery school and observe.
- Trade child-care hours with a friend who has a two-year-old.
- Go to the biggest bookstore around and ask what books about two-year-olds folks are buying.
- Listen to Clarke's *Terrific Twos* tape. (See "Resources.")
- Ask your doctor or public health nurse for guidelines.
- Read *Your Two-Year-Old,* by Ames and Ilg, and then pretend to be two for about ten minutes. (See "Resources.") Also read "Ages and Stages."

(See also questions 182, 184, 185, 186, and 241.)

Thanks to Ellen Peterson,
Suggestion Circle from Lafayette, California

Chapter 22

Tantrums and Other Power Struggles

184. My two-year-old has tantrums. What can I do?

- Remember that tantrums are normal for this age.

- Think about whether the child is using tantrums to control or whether she is responding to big stresses in her life. If she's responding to stress, do what you can to relieve it.

- Go on with your activity. Don't reward the behavior. Tell her she can finish her mad behavior.

- Say, "You are really mad. What else can you do to use up your mad feelings?"

- Practice acting bored.

- Give her the Thinking affirmations when she's not having a tantrum. (See "Affirmations for Growth—Thinking.")

- Make sure that she is in a safe place so she won't hurt herself or damage things. Then ignore the tantrum.

- Don't leave the room. Let her know you won't leave her just because she is mad.

- Tell her that it is OK for her to be mad, that you won't change your mind, and that you will be available when she is finished.

- Compliment yourself on running a family where your two-year-old can have her tantrums at home.

• Give her lots of loving.

(See also questions 180, 183, and 185.)

Thanks to Gail Davenport,
Suggestion Circle from Seattle, Washington

185. What is OK for two-year-olds to do when they get mad?

• Stomp their feet.

• Yell.

• Hit a mattress or pillow.

• Roll on the floor.

• Make faces.

• Say, "I'm mad!"

• Growl.

• Kick a pillow.

• Hit a punching toy.

• Scribble.

• Use a loud mad voice.

• Put their hands on their hips.

• Get out the hammering toys.

(See also questions 183 and 186.)

Thanks to Nat Houtz,
Suggestion Circle from Seattle, Washington

186. What should I do when my two-year-old starts screaming or acting up in public?

- Take the child away from the scene to a quiet place for some one-on-one quiet talk.

- Tell him, "Stop, or we'll leave." Follow through, even if it is inconvenient.

- Kneel to be at the child's level. Tell him to stop screaming and to use his indoor voice or you will both leave. Then do.

- Tell him, "When you stop screaming, we'll continue with our plans to go to do _____ [something he's eager to do]."

- Realize that everybody's kids act up and that yours will, too—not because you are a bad parent, but because they are kids.

- Be reassured that lots of people understand and empathize with your situation. Don't worry about those who don't.

- Get some perspective first. Ask yourself how you will feel about this in five years. Then decide calmly what to do.

- Figure out how many minutes of total public embarrassment you are willing to endure, and then give yourself that much time.

- As long as your child can scream without hurting himself, others, or property, go on with what you were doing. Ignore it!

(See also question 230.)

Thanks to Nat Houtz,
Suggestion Circle from Alderwood, Washington

187. What can I do instead of yelling and spanking my two-and-a-half-year-old when she is being defiant and I am at the end of my rope?

- Put her in her room and say calmly, "When you are ready to cooperate and remember the rule about _____, you can come out." Then turn up the radio and sing loudly with it.

- Count to ten backwards, slowly, and think of what you really want your child to learn from this.

- Tell her what you want her to do: "Stop playing and put your toys on the shelf now."

- Go in the bathroom and wash your face. Then come back and deal with the child calmly.

- Have your spouse take the kids off to a park while you call three people you want to say no to.

- Take a break. When I expect too much of my child, it is often because I am expecting too much of myself.

- If it is a safety issue, put your child in a safe place and both of you take a one-minute time-out.

- Make an A-to-Z list for yourself of things to do instead of hitting. There is a list like that on page 145 of *Self-Esteem: A Family Affair,* by Jean Illsley Clarke. (See "Resources.")

- Watch for times when your child is cooperating, and hug her.

(See also questions 180, 183, 188, and 194.)

Thanks to Nat Houtz,
Suggestion Circle from Alderwood, Washington

188. My child says, "I hate you!" if he doesn't get to do what he wants. Sometimes he says he will run away. I need ideas for coping with this.

- Acknowledge your child's anger, and then show him how to hit a pillow or a soft toy.

- Say, "Yes, I guess you do hate me right now."

- Say, "All children get mad at their parents sometimes, but you are not to run away."

- Say, "I see you are upset," then reassure your child that it is OK to be mad.

- Remember that children this age are experimenting with their anger and your response to it. Calmly let him know that you hear his anger, that you are not afraid of it, and that you love him even when he is mad.

- Ignore his hate. Be bored with it.

- Realize that *his* understanding of "hate" and yours are probably quite different. "Hate" may be the strongest word he can think of to express his displeasure. Stay calm and honor his feelings. Let him know that you won't abandon him.

- Say, "You are not to run away. This is your family and you must learn to get along here."

(See also questions 180, 187, and 237.)

Thanks to Pearl Noreen,
Suggestion Circle from Seattle, Washington

189. How can I deal with my two-year-old, who hates to take baths and screams in the bathtub?

- Take a bath or shower with her.

- Allow her to make some choices about her bath. For example, say, "Do you want to take a tub bath, or shall we take a shower?"

- Give her some soap crayons to draw on herself and the tub, or use a soap mitten or soap sock.

- Sing, "This is the way we wash our hair," and so on. Practice this song often outside of the tub, so she can have fun with the words and actions while bathing.

- Give her an occasional rest from taking tub baths; sponge her down instead.

- Pick some special interesting bath toys from the kitchen, like an eggbeater, a baster, or funnels.

- Play music during bath time.

- Be sure the water isn't too hot or too cold.

- Take her to a swimming pool, and let her just watch if she doesn't want to go in. Then let her wear a swimsuit in the tub to practice "swimming."

- Occasionally give her a bath in a different container, like the sink, an infant tub, or a small inflatable pool.

- Keep the problem in perspective. Find a short-term solution till your child grows out of it.

Thanks to Pearl Noreen,
Suggestion Circle from Seattle, Washington

190. My son, two and a half years old, doesn't want to change from pajamas to play clothes in the morning. I have to dress him because he can't go to his day care in pajamas. He fights it. What can I do?

- Distract his thoughts from pajamas to something more fun like getting dressed under the dining table.

- Go to day care in pajamas and change there.

- When he's dressed, give him a special sticker or stars.

- Give him a choice between you dressing him or your spouse dressing him.

- Dress him in clean clothes at night so he's ready in the morning when he wakes up.

- Tell him he can put his pajamas back on as soon as he gets home from day care.

- Ride it out—be firm but not angry as you dress him anyway.

- Let him wear his pajama top to day care as a shirt.

- Read *Prescriptions for Parenting*, by Carolyn Meeks, for tips and techniques for ending power struggles. (See "Resources.")

Thanks to Susan Duke,
Suggestion Circle from Seattle, Washington

191. I need help with my eighteen-month-old daughter who is throwing temper tantrums to get my attention. It happens when her dad gets home and starts talking to me, or when we are visiting, or when I am talking to a friend.

- When your husband comes home, have a big "sandwich" hug with your daughter in the middle. Play with her a bit, and then if she has a tantrum, ignore it.

- When my daughter is having a tantrum, I take on the attitude of "What else is new?" and act bored.

- Get a sitter so you can go out with your friend and talk all afternoon sometimes.

- Soothe her and stay close, maybe holding or touching her, but don't expect her to listen to reason when she is caught up in a rage.

- Move to another part of the room and continue your conversation.

- Warn her in advance that your attention will soon be directed elsewhere, and provide some special toys for her.

- Tantrums are normal. This will pass.

- See that you give her lots of attention just before your husband gets home.

- When my daughter was having a tantrum, I'd put some soft rock-and-roll music on. The rhythmic beat calmed her.

  (See also questions 179, 184, 186, and 256.)

Thanks to Gail Davenport,
Suggestion Circle from Lynnwood, Washington

192. My son is almost two. He deliberately hits, bites, or scratches me, sometimes in play but other times when he's angry. He doesn't do this with his dad. What can I do?

- Tell him, "People are not for hurting!"

- Hold him at arm's length and say, "STOP! I won't let you do that to me." If he tries to continue, leave the room temporarily.

- Explain to him that hitting, biting, and scratching hurt.

- Don't put up with it. Give him a time-out in his room. (See "Time-Out.")

- Say "STOP! You're hurting Mommy." Use a sharp tone of voice and be firm.

- Make sure his dad also tells him to stop and then insists that he does.

- Say no, then leave for a few minutes.

- Help him tell the difference between playful feelings and angry feelings. Pretend you are playful, then angry, and have him say which is which.

- I went through it, too. You and your husband should show him OK ways to touch and OK ways to be mad.

- Hitting, biting, and scratching are *not* playful. Get them stopped.

(See also questions 185, 191, and 198.)

Thanks to Gail Davenport,
Suggestion Circle from Edmonds, Washington

193. Whenever I set a limit and say "don't" or "stop," my two-and-a-half-year-old screams and yells. Help me deal with this!

- When you tell her to stop, be available to follow through. If she doesn't stop by the count of five, stop her yourself.

- Keep rules to a minimum.

- Tell her that the consequence of screaming is a time-out, and then follow through. (See "Time-Out.")

- Make a place where it is OK to yell and stomp.

- Make sure she is getting enough love and positive attention—play with her at least fifteen minutes a day, letting her take the lead.

- Tell her that you are not afraid of her anger, and use your size to remove her if necessary.

- Make up a game for being loud together at a different time during the day.

- Remember that kids this age must learn to say no in their own way.

- Get some time away for yourself during this phase.

- Tell her that people can tell how they feel in their regular voices.

- Visualize her being able to do what you say without yelling. She will get there soon.

- Tell her what she can do instead. Say, "Use your indoor voice instead of yelling."

(See also questions 180, 185, and 227.)

Thanks to Maggie Lawrence,
Suggestion Circle from Edmonds, Washington

Chapter 23

Toward Cooperation

194. My son (almost three) has a mind of his own. When I tell him to pick up his toys, he says, "I don't know how, I don't want to, and you can't make me." How can I get him to cooperate?

- Try saying, "When you are finished putting your toys away, then we'll do. . . " In other words, reward the cooperative behavior with something he enjoys.

- Offer a choice of two or three things, and avoid direct confrontation. Say, "Will you pick up the books or the blocks first?"

- Contrary behavior is typical at this age. Be sure that you are getting your *own* needs met so you can handle these episodes without getting angry or giving away your power as the parent.

- If it is a power struggle, get out of it by ignoring his defiance, and then allow him to live with the consequence of his behavior.

- Use a puppet; let the puppet give directions instead of you.

- Consider how important each of these confrontations really is. Let him win sometimes.

- Examine your expectations of your child. Perhaps he is not developmentally ready for some of the responsibilities you are asking him to take on.

- "Clean your room" is overwhelming and vague for a two-and-a-half-year-old. Tell him, "Put this on the shelf. I will help you, one thing at a time."

(See also questions 183, 187, 188, and 227.)

Thanks to Nat Houtz,
Suggestion Circle from Alderwood, Washington

195. How can I encourage my child, almost three, to share toys when friends come over to play?

- Have her select a few favorite toys that she won't have to share. Help her hide them.

- Explain that when she has friends over, you expect her to let other kids play with her toys.

- If the children can resolve the problem themselves, stay out of the situation.

- Help her learn how. Model the behavior. Practice with adults and with her. Use words like *share, take turns, wait, all done, your turn,* and so on.

- Respect her possessions and put away her favorites.

- Say, "Wait for her to be done with it, then you take a turn."

- Buy two of several popular toys.

- Get her to show another child how a toy works.

- Bring out a fun activity (like drawing with crayons) that offers enough toys for everyone.

- Take the children to a stream, where everyone can throw rocks in the water.

- First teach the difference between sharing and giving.

(See also question 197.)

Thanks to Lyn Dillman,
Suggestion Circle from Seattle, Washington

196. When a friend and I get together, our two-year-olds fight. What can we do?

- Be direct about it. Say to the other parent that this doesn't work.

- Avoid being together with your children. For instance, don't sign the kids up for the same swim class.

- If the relationship with the adult isn't that important, cool it.

- Each of you focus on supervising your child.

- See if inviting a third child over to play will help.

- Invite an older child to play with them.

- Take the children to a neutral place like a playground.

- Tell the other parent, "The children are going through a stage where they don't get along well. Let's get together again in a month or two."

- Plan a "grown-ups only" outing that would be really fun.

- Plan a child-centered get-together that would be fun for moms, too.

- Give the children lots of attention each time you see them cooperate or play together well (and not just when their play becomes disruptive).

(See also questions 195 and 197.)

Thanks to Marilyn Grevstad,
Suggestion Circle from Seattle, Washington

197. The children in our play group are all two-year-olds. I need suggestions for handling them when they are fighting over a toy.

- Two is pretty little. Help them work it out.

- If they are not hurting each other, give them a chance to end it themselves.
- Say, "Hang onto the broom, Adam. Ray, when Adam is finished, you can play with it."
- Join their play for a few minutes.
- Offer another favorite toy!
- Start an activity that they can all get involved in.
- Have them take turns with the toy. Call out their names and keep track of whose turn is next.
- Invent a game to keep them all occupied.
- Suggest that each child bring a toy of his own that he does not have to share.
- Give them each some extra loving.

  (See also questions 195 and 196.)

Thanks to Lyn Dillman,
Suggestion Circle from Seattle, Washington

198. My twenty-month-old daughter bites other kids when she's mad. How do I stop her?

- Tell your child, "Don't bite people. Biting hurts!"
- Stay close by when she's playing with other kids.
- Learn your child's warning signs so you'll know when to step in before she bites.
- Intervene before she gets too mad. Move near and touch the other children to reassure them that you are there for protection.
- Show her other things to do when she is angry, like yelling or stomping.
- Don't bite her.

- Find a soft rubber toy for her to bite on.
- Look around the room to see if any other children need comforting or reassurance.
- Teach the other children to say, "No! STOP!" if your child tries to bite. Stay close to coach them through any struggles.
- Don't kick yourself because your two-year-old bites. Keep on being a good mother.

(See also question 192.)

Thanks to Nat Houtz,
Suggestion Circle from Lynnwood, Washington

199. How do you get two-year-old twins to be quiet during the evening news?

- Hire a sitter to take them for a walk.
- It is as *unnatural* to keep a two-year-old quiet as it is to walk a cat on a leash.
- Tape the news on a VCR and play it after they are in bed.
- Watch the late edition of the news.
- Take turns with your spouse bathing the twins during news time.
- Listen to the news on headphones.
- Try putting the TV in your bedroom.
- Spend some time with them right before news time—reading stories and so on. Then tell them, "Now you can look at books while I listen to the news."

Thanks to Nancy Delin,
Suggestion Circle from Chaska, Minnesota

200. My two-year-old resists getting into her car seat, and she takes forever even if she is willing. I could use some suggestions.

- Don't expect her to do it on her own if you are in a rush or feeling impatient; lift her in yourself. Be sure you have placed the car seat where you can reach it easily.

- Teach her to put the straps on herself. This involves her in the process.

- Start to leave earlier so there is time for her to do it herself. Remember she is only two.

- If she is fooling around, start the motor of your car to let her know it's time to go. But don't leave until she's all buckled in.

- Keep a favorite toy in the car for her to play with after she's got her straps on.

- Let her try doing some of the buckling.

- Talk about where you are going so the focus is not on the car seat and her cooperation.

- Have her pack a snack or a collection of toys in a lunch pail, and tell her that she can open the pail only after she is buckled in.

- Have a favorite song to sing after you are both buckled in.

(See also question 232.)

Thanks to Gail Davenport,
Suggestion Circle from Lynnwood, Washington

Chapter 24

Good Night, Sleep Tight

201. Our two-and-a-half-year-old child is getting in bed with us in the middle of the night, and we don't want her to. What can we do?

- Place a camp cot in your room for her.

- Rest in her bed a while and then go back to your own bed.

- Put her back firmly and calmly.

- Insist on her staying in her own bed. If she's feeling lonely, provide a soft toy for her to hug.

- Ride it out. This could be a stage of bad dreams that will pass.

- Set up an intercom in your child's room so that you can hear her cry out. Sometimes tired parents don't hear their child call, so she wanders into their room to get their attention.

- *The Family Bed,* by Tine Thevenin, gives reasons to let the kids sleep with you. You might be interested in it. (See "Resources.")

- Pretend to be little, and try "sleeping" in your child's bed. You might discover a reason why she doesn't like sleeping in her bed, like a drafty window or scary shadows in the corner.

- Have her checked for allergies. If she has bronchial allergies, she may be allergic to something in her room.

- Make up a story about a little girl who is growing up and learning to stay in her own bed all night.

(See also questions 202 and 203.)

Thanks to Joyce Portigal,
Suggestion Circle from Calgary, Alberta, Canada

202. I am a single parent. My two-and-a-half-year-old gets out of his crib and comes into bed with me. I need ways to encourage him to stay in his crib.

- He might be ready for a bigger bed. You can introduce it in steps by sliding a floor mattress partway under the crib and using it for naps.

- To change this behavior, you'll have to put him back to bed many times. Keep doing it firmly but without getting mad.

- Make yourself a bed beside his crib. When he gets up, go in and sleep beside him. Rather than touching him, use your voice to assure him that you are there. The tape *Infant and Toddler Sleep Disruptions,* by Saul Brown and Helen Reid, tells more about how to do this. (See "Resources.")

- Tell him that you expect him to stay in his bed. Reward that.

- Show him how to use a special lovey doll for comfort instead of coming into your bed.

- Make time during the day to cuddle him on your bed instead of doing it at night.

- Prepare yourself by resting, deciding what to do, and getting support before you start to change this behavior.

- If your separation is recent, either let him sleep with you or increase the amount of comfort you give him.

(See also questions 201, 203, and 204.)

Thanks to Maggie Lawrence,
Suggestion Circle from Edmonds, Washington

203. My daughter (twenty months old) wakes up five times each night and only needs a pat from me to go back to sleep. How can we end my getting up so often?

- See if leaving a night-light on in her room makes a difference.
- Wean her gradually from the pats to a security object, such as a teddy bear or blanket.
- Leave a radio on at low volume in her room.
- Bring her to bed with you.
- Look for any new insecurities or stresses in her life, and try to relieve them.
- Ask your spouse to go in and do the patting.
- Try talking to her from outside her room to reassure her that you are near.
- Be real uninteresting when you go in to pat her.
- Have a doctor make sure she doesn't have an ear infection.
- Try not going in; let her settle it herself.
- Fix a place for you to sleep in her room. Each time she wakes, say, "I am here. Go to sleep," and don't touch her. Try that for three or four nights.

(See also questions 201, 202, and 204.)

Thanks to Gail Davenport,
Suggestion Circle from Lynnwood, Washington

204. How can I get my two-and-a-half-year-old to go to bed at bedtime and stay in bed?

- His sleep needs may have changed. If you don't expect him to nap every day, he may be more willing to go to bed at night.

- Offer him books or quiet toys to play with in his bed at bedtime.

- Perhaps the child needs less sleep. Tell him he must stay in bed even if he is not going to sleep.

- Explain to your child that your grown-up time begins after his bedtime, so he has to stay in bed.

- Play a story or lullabies on cassette tape in his room.

- Bathe him before dinner. Have no loud or active play between dinner and bedtime, and do things the same way every night.

- Let your child know that it is OK with you if he doesn't like to go to bed; he still has to go to bed and stay there.

- Try limiting his nap to an hour and see if it makes a difference.

- Snatch a few minutes of quiet time for yourself before you start the evening routine.

- You are in charge of when your child goes to bed. Put him in bed and expect him to stay there.

- Establish a routine. First put Teddy Bear to bed, shut the drapes, turn on the night-light, and sing a special song. Let him lead you through it after he is familiar with it.

Thanks to Craig Halverson,
Suggestion Circle from Coon Rapids, Minnesota

205. My two-and-a-half-year-old has a strong preference for his mommy at bedtime. How can I (the dad) get into the act when I'm not always home at bedtime?

- Make a deal with your wife so she's gone at bedtime a couple of times a week. Stick with it for a month or so.

- Say, "Mommy is busy right now. Daddy will do it." Don't give the child a choice.

- To strengthen your bond, set up some routine that only you and your son do regularly so he will trust you to put him to bed.

- Accept the condition as temporary, and be accommodating to your child when possible.

- When you are home, say, "I really like putting you to bed."

- Once a week, take your child out for a treat and then home to bed, making it a special event.

- Take your child to a bookstore and choose a wonderful child's bedtime story, like *Goodnight Moon,* by Margaret W. Brown, or *Close Your Eyes,* by Jean Marzollo. Make it Dad's book only to read. (See "Resources.")

- Give yourself plenty of time to let this relationship unfold. He might not like it at first, but hang in there.

Thanks to Mary Lou Rozdilsky,
Suggestion Circle from Edmonds, Washington

Chapter 25

Toilet Training

206. I'm thinking of beginning to toilet train my two-year-old. What are some tips?

- Have a lot of training pants on hand.

- As your child becomes more responsible for his toileting, remind yourself that your job is only to coach him.

- Reward his use of the toilet with something you are comfortable with—for example, a hug, jelly beans, stars, or fancy underwear.

- Make the potty very familiar—have it sitting in the bathroom long before you expect him to use it properly.

- Stay out of power struggles—the child should be in charge of his own going to the bathroom.

- Take advantage of imitation by letting your child see others going to the bathroom.

- Do not expect immediate results from a person who is only two years old. Most kids' sphincter muscles aren't ready till they are almost three.

- Read the chapter about toilet learning in *Your Toddler*, by Johnson and Johnson. (See "Resources.")

- Toilet training is a gradual process; remind yourself of this, and don't be hurried. Remember to take good care of yourself during this time.

Thanks to Betty Beach,
Suggestion Circle from Minneapolis, Minnesota

207. I lose my temper when my thirty-two-month-old child won't use the pot and has accidents. What should I do?

- Read *Toilet Learning,* by Alison Mack. (See "Resources.")
- Keep your reaction low-key, and let her wear diapers if she wants to.
- Remember that it's a trial-and-error process at this age.
- Separate your own self-esteem from her diapers.
- Instead of getting angry, give her a ho-hum reaction to soiled britches.
- Remember that this is pretty typical behavior for a child her age. You don't need to get so mad.
- Ask yourself if maybe you are really mad about something else, and if you are, take care of that. Cool it. I got locked in a power struggle with my child, and it took a long time to finish toilet training.
- Remember, this, too, will pass.

Thanks to Deane Gradous,
Suggestion Circle from Minneapolis, Minnesota

208. I thought he was toilet trained, and now he's not. He's thirty-four months old and wetting the bed at nap time at his day-care home.

- Have the day-care people monitor how much he drinks before his nap.

- Encourage him to use the potty before his nap.

- Think about what has been going on at home and at day care. Is he under stress?

- Don't insist that he take a nap every day.

- Take him in for a medical checkup.

- Ask him what he needs to help him stay dry.

- Ask him how much longer he thinks he will be wetting the bed.

- Don't make a big deal of it. Act bored.

- Don't drop the nap because he has wet the bed. Protect the mattress with a rubber sheet. Expect him to rest.

- Show him in lots of ways when you are together that you love him.

- Remember that he is not even three years old yet.

  (See also question 209.)

  Thanks to Nat Houtz,
  Suggestion Circle from Alderwood, Washington

209. My almost three-year-old will only use the potty when she initiates it. If I suggest it, she won't, or she urinates in her pants. What can I do that will help her to be potty trained?

- Don't suggest it, even if she looks like she really has to go.

- Back off. It is a power struggle you can't win, because you cannot force a child to be potty trained.

- Offer rewards like gum, stickers, or pennies in a jar when she successfully uses the potty.

- Have her help clean up accidents. Give her a sponge, and show her where to put soiled pants.

- Go to a potty-training workshop, or read a good book about it. (See "Resources.")

- Try telling her that it's time for one of her stuffed animals to go potty while she watches. Then tell her that the stuffed animal will watch while *she* goes.

- Buy a potty chair that sits on the floor, and let her wear elastic-waist pants that she can manage to pull down herself. Then let her be in charge.

- Don't yell at her when she has an accident. Treat it matter-of-factly.

(See also question 208.)

Thanks to Judy Popp,
Suggestion Circle from Yakima, Washington

210. My daughter loves to fill up the toilet with toilet paper. What can I do?

- Have her help you clean it up.

- Tell her not to play in the toilet.

- Imagine what would be fun about doing that if you were her age. Then find another way for her to have that kind of fun.

- Give her the end of a roll of toilet paper, and let her stuff the tissue into a box or can.

- Set up water play with containers to fill and empty.

- Keep the bathroom door shut, and use doorknob safety gadgets to prevent her from going in unsupervised.

- Put rubber bands around the roll of toilet paper. It's a nuisance, but it will work until she learns to take the bands off.

- Put the toilet paper up high.

- Teach her how to measure out a certain amount, like an arm's length of tissue.

- Don't let her play in the bathroom alone.

- Show her some acceptable ways to play in the water—the sink, tub, wading pool, and so on.

Thanks to Carol Goss,
Suggestion Circle from Seattle, Washington

Chapter 26

Nursing, Eating, and Weaning

211. I want to wean my two-year-old from his juice bottle. What are some ideas to get me started?

- Buy a special, decorated cup, and keep it within his reach for sipping.

- Teach him to come to you for a hug when he wants comforting.

- Eliminate his juice bottle in the car first.

- Do wean him. Bottles with sugary fluids can cause terrible cavities.

- If you smoke, let him have the bottle.

- Have fun with a cup. Say, "Cheers!" Make a toast for each drink to encourage the feeling that using a cup is fun and OK.

- Put the drink he likes least in his bottle and the one he likes best in a cup.

- Try straws.

- Let him keep the two or three bottles of milk each day that he needs for sucking and comfort.

- Take off the nipple and screw-on top and let him drink from an open bottle. Make sure he gets lots of love and hugs for comforting.

- Read about weaning in *Your Baby and Child,* by Penelope Leach. (See "Resources.")

Thanks to Gail Davenport,
Suggestion Circle from Lynnwood, Washington

212. I have been using nursing to comfort my child whenever she wants it. I'm getting tired and want to stop this. What can I do?

- Put your hand on your chest and say, "No nursing now." Then comfort your child with hugging.

- Offer her a bottle.

- Give her a cozy blanket or favorite stuffed animal with a cup or bottle when she wants comfort.

- Gradually switch to a cup but continue to hold her for comforting.

- Rock and sing instead.

- Read *Mothering Your Nursing Toddler,* by Norma J. Bumgarner. (See "Resources.")

- Contact La Leche League.

- Make a list of all the ways you can comfort your child; then post it and use it. Also, limit nursing to only one chair at home.

Thanks to Gail Davenport,
Suggestion Circle from Lynnwood, Washington

213. My child is twenty months old and very active. During mealtimes he throws food on the floor, which is carpeted. I need some ideas for dealing with this every day.

- Put a plastic shower curtain under his high chair as a drop cloth, and ignore the throwing.

- Put his chair on a linoleum floor.

- Put an area rug or beach towel under his chair.

- Feed him in the kitchen by himself.

- Only offer him two bites at a time on his tray.

- Take the food away when he throws it.

- Tell him he is big enough to keep food on the table now.

- Be sure he is hungry at mealtime and that he doesn't eat for an hour before each meal.

- Let him throw other things. Take him to the lake where you can both throw rocks in the water.

Thanks to Pearl Noreen,
Suggestion Circle from Seattle, Washington

214. My two-year-old is pouring juice into her cereal, and there is a lot of spilling. She knows I don't like it. What can I do?

- Take her down from the table, and tell her that she has to do her playing somewhere else. Then dump the cereal.

- Ignore it. I did, and after a week or so she stopped.

- Take it away and say, "When you pour, I know you are through eating."

- Show her how to help clean up the floor, but don't make it a big deal.

- Provide lots of pouring play. Give her cups in the tub.

- Give her more attention when she is doing things you like.

- Teach her to say, "All done," when she is finished, so she won't have time to start playing with her food.

- Say, "Not to play with or I'll take it away" as a warning. If she keeps messing with the cereal, follow through and remove her bowl.

- Pouring is natural at this age. Find out why you get so upset, and get what you need so you can let her be messy.

(See also questions 207 and 218.)

Thanks to Gail Davenport,
Suggestion Circle from Edmonds, Washington

215. My child (twenty months old) is a picky eater. I need some new ideas for dinner.

- If his height and weight are fine, don't fret about it.

- Try tortillas with melted cheese or refried beans.

- Keep homemade chicken potpies in the freezer.

- Serve vegetables blended in casseroles.

- Offer breakfast foods for his dinner menu.

- Fix pasta in lots of different shapes so he can finger-feed himself.

- Spaghetti is a favorite.

- Increase the nutritional value of favorite foods, like peanut butter and eggs and cheese, by adding brewer's yeast, wheat germ, powdered milk, or grated carrots.

- Let him have cheese and tuna over and over if that's what he likes.

- Dipping can be fun and nutritious. Mix up yogurt or cottage cheese dips for crackers, fruit, or vegetables.

- Minimeatballs go over big at our house.

- Fish sticks are a hit with my toddler, and they are easy to fix.

- Buy a cookbook that features kids' favorite foods. I like Vicki Lansky's *Feed Me! I'm Yours.* (See "Resources.")

- Call your extension office of the county health department and ask for available brochures.

Thanks to Gail Davenport,
Suggestion Circle from Edmonds, Washington

216. Our two-and-a-half-year-old wakes up in the morning whiny and demanding, and she can't decide what to eat for breakfast. This is hard for me to handle. How can I make our mornings more pleasant?

- Give her some special attention in the morning.

- Give her an easy job to do, such as getting out the spoons.

- Watch "Sesame Street" with her in the morning.

- Give her a manageable choice: two choices of cereal instead of only one or as many as five.

- Say, "I will listen when you talk with your regular voice."

- Being indecisive is part of a two-year-old's development. Tell her how well she is doing her two-year-old work.

- Ignore it.

- Put her to bed earlier.

• Sounds as if she is too young for this choice. You make the breakfast and serve it.

Thanks to Nat Houtz,
Suggestion Circle from Edmonds, Washington

217. I can't get my two-and-a-half-year-old son to eat solids at home. He will eat solids for his day-care provider. What can I do?

• Let him help you cube the cheese and cut the banana.

• Let him choose one of three. Say, "Johnny, which of these will you choose for lunch?"

• Place solids in front of him but not much to drink, and avoid negative statements.

• Provide foods for a few days that are nutritious but not solid.

• Take him to the grocery store and have *him* choose some solid foods.

• Have little friends over to eat with him.

• Give him lots of loving messages, but don't push him and don't bribe him.

• Provide nutritious, wholesome food only—no junk food. When he is hungry, he will eat.

(See also question 215.)

Thanks to Sandra Sittko,
Suggestion Circle from Saint Paul, Minnesota

218. My two-and-a-half-year-old insists on pouring her own milk. She cannot do it well yet and makes a big mess. What can I do?

- Help the child do it herself but on a smaller scale; use a small pitcher.

- Praise her when she does pour carefully.

- Have her help clean up the mess—buy lots of sponges.

- Don't hover over her. Stay away and let her practice, which is the only way she'll improve.

- Buy little cartons of milk for her to pour from.

- Be sure she gets lots of opportunities to play with water: in puddles, wading pools, and the sink, and with squirt bottles and sprinklers.

- Spread a plastic tablecloth on the floor and let her practice pouring dry things, like puffed wheat or dry rice. She'll soon be better at pouring.

- Start out by giving her only a tablespoon or so to pour. It's easier to clean up than a full cup.

- Two-year-olds are supposed to be pouring, and it's bound to be messy at first.

- Praise her for trying something on her own.

- Have her watch you pouring things, and talk about the ways you are being careful.

(See also question 214.)

Thanks to Celia Osenton,
Suggestion Circle from Calgary, Alberta, Canada

219. Do you continue to cater to the eating wishes of an almost three-year-old?

- No.

- Let him eat on his own—not necessarily with family.

- No. Offer healthy options with no preparation on Mom's part.

- No. Trust his hunger to solve the problem.

- Don't punish—encourage him to eat with you.

- Offer small meals plus snacks—make no big deal out of eating.

- Yes. Don't fight about food.

- Kids eat only a little at this age—don't expect him to eat big amounts.

- Know that kids usually choose a variety of food over a two- or three-week period—keep track if you want to know for sure.

- Most kids this age are picky eaters. They usually outgrow it.

(See also question 215.)

Thanks to Mary Lou Rozdilsky,
Suggestion Circle from Edmonds, Washington

Chapter 27

Brothers, Sisters, and Playmates

220. How can I prepare my two-and-a-half-year-old for the birth of our second child?

- Tell her that she will soon have a baby brother or sister. Let her touch your belly to feel the baby kick and move.

- Look for children's books like *On Mother's Lap*, by Ann Scott, and *That New Baby*, by Sara Stein. (See "Resources.")

- Get a doll the size of the newborn, and give it to your child before the time of your birthing.

- Let her see a real infant, if you can.

- Give her lots of loving messages, but expect some static even if she's well prepared.

- Spend time together looking at your two-and-a-half-year-old's newborn pictures, clothes, toys, and so on. Pick some things for her to keep and some to pass on to the baby.

- Tell her own newborn stories to her often.

- Take your child with you to your prenatal checkups. Ask the doctor to let her listen to the baby's heartbeat.

- Arrange for her to practice staying with the folks who will care for her during the birthing.

- Don't tell her that the reason you are having another baby is because you love her so much.

- Don't tell her she will have a new playmate.

- Don't tell her she is going to love the baby; remember, she may love the baby *sometimes*.

(See also question 221.)

Thanks to Charlotte Newport,
Suggestion Circle from Bellevue, Washington

221. How can we handle our two-year-old to avoid jealousy with the new baby?

- Let him help you if he shows interest in the new baby's care.
- Get him a doll, and let him practice doing the same things you are doing with the baby.
- Tell him that even though he is a big brother, he's still your little boy.
- Give him a lot of attention.
- Let him touch the baby.
- Don't tell him he should love the baby.
- Accept his feelings. Remember that jealousy is a natural feeling.
- Don't expect him to figure out how to play safely with an infant. When he shows interest in the baby, show him what infants like to watch, listen to, and feel.
- Show him the pictures in Karen Hendrickson's *Baby and I Can Play*. (See "Resources.")

(See also question 220.)

Thanks to Nancy Delin,
Suggestion Circle from Chaska, Minnesota

222. Our daughter, age four, wants to roughhouse with our eighteen-month-old son, who is not walking yet. He gets hurt. Can you help me with this?

- Act as a coach—teach her how to play gently.

- Talk to the older child; tell her to settle down when she is with him.

- Limit the activity. Give them some structure and rules and enforce them.

- Teach her how to play appropriately with an eighteen-month-old. Say, for example, "Four-year-olds are good at building tall towers, but your brother is good at knocking them down. Toddlers also like to drop blocks into a can. We'll find something safe for you to do with him."

- Check and see if either child is getting hurt; realize that children may not be hurt when they scream.

- Pay a lot more attention to the kids when you see them playing together well.

- Decide with whom, where, and when rough-and-tumble play is OK. Protect your little one from possible injuries.

- *You* roughhouse with her instead.

- Let her listen to Jason and Jenny on the *Terrific Twos* tape, by Jean Illsley Clarke, to find out what kids that age are like. (See "Resources.")

- Give her lots of loving at other times.

  (See also question 221.)

Thanks to Harold Nordeman,
Suggestion Circle from Cincinnati, Ohio

223. A twenty-two-month-old in the neighborhood, who comes over to play with my son, pushes and scratches. What can I do to correct his behavior?

- Separate the children and give them a time-out. (See "Time-Out.")

- Show him some gloves. Explain that scratching hurts, and if he scratches, he will have to wear the gloves until he can remember.

- Tell the child's mother and father what is happening when he comes to play and that his behavior is not acceptable. Tell them you will have the child take time-outs when he behaves in unacceptable ways.

- Ask the child's mother to take her child home when he scratches. Set up several practice visits when the mother stays so she can immediately take the child home when his behavior is not appropriate.

- Observe when the scratching and pushing happens. Is the child tired or overstimulated? Are the children fighting over toys?

- Tell him, "If you scratch, you must go home." Then make sure you follow through.

- Teach the child an alternate form of behavior. Say, "No, don't push Jacob. Push this chair when you feel like pushing."

(See also questions 196 and 197.)

Thanks to Meg Murray,
Suggestion Circle from Lafayette, California

224. What can I do with a child who hugs too hard?

- Give him a soft hug and then a hard, but not hurtful, hug to teach him the difference.

- Stay close to him and restrain him when he starts to do it.

- Explain that other kids don't like it.

- Tell him, "Don't hug hard because it hurts. Hug softly instead."

- Show him how to give pats instead.

- Say, "Ouch, that hurts people. Hug gently, please."

- Give him something else to hug, like a stuffed animal.

Thanks to Pearl Noreen,
Suggestion Circle from Seattle, Washington

Chapter 28

Coping

225. My friend provides child care for my two-year-old daughter. When I get off work and go to pick her up, my daughter greets me. She is eager to nurse, but then she doesn't want to leave. I'd like some suggestions.

- Start talking to her about how she can help you fix dinner when you get home.

- Spend some time together at the sitter's finding out about her day.

- Tell her that it is time to finish what she is doing. Offer to help her finish.

- Have something in the car to look forward to, like a snack or a doll.

- Establish a routine so she knows it is time to go after she is done nursing.

- Be prepared to handle the transition differently every day of the week. You can be spontaneous and successful.

- If lingering at the sitter's is not OK with you, be clear about leaving, and let her be angry if she wants to be.

- Acknowledge the child's desires; then say that you don't have time today to stay.

- Let your child know that you won't be staying when you arrive. Plan a time soon when you can stay a while.

- Help her tell her favorite people and toys good-bye until tomorrow. Do this each time you leave.
- Give the child a set time limit in which to get ready to leave—only two to five minutes.

Thanks to Gail Davenport,
Suggestion Circle from Alderwood, Washington

226. How should I respond to my two-year-old when he takes his clothes off at inappropriate times?

- Have a special time, like right after his bath, for the child to run around nude.
- Comment on how neat his body is.
- If you are uncomfortable with it, let him know your feeling, and tell him to stop.
- Decide what your comfort level is, and set limits within it.
- Tell him he may not run outside nude because many adults think children should wear clothes outside.
- Say, "I'm happy to see you are learning how to take off your clothes. Neato! Can you put them back on, or do you want me to help you?"
- Check to see that his clothes fit. Maybe they are uncomfortably tight.

Thanks to Judi Salts,
Suggestion Circle from Yakima, Washington

227. My child throws toys. If I motion for her to stop, she leaves the toy and runs and screams. How should I stop the throwing?

- Be sure your motion is not seen by her as a threat.

- Go over to her and gently hold her arms as you say, "Don't throw toys."

- Tell her, "You can throw balls outside, but you can't throw toys in the house."

- Show her how to throw beanbags in a box.

- Set aside specific times for playing chase games or throwing games together.

- Instead of only motioning for her to stop, tell her and go over to her, too. You *can* make her stop.

(See also questions 187 and 193.)

Thanks to Maggie Lawrence,
Suggestion Circle from Lynnwood, Washington

228. Our family was eating in a restaurant and the waiter had a severe birthmark on his face. Our three-year-old kept saying, "Look at him—he looks like a monkey!" We could see how she thought that. We couldn't hush her and were terribly embarrassed. What could we have done?

- Take her to the rest room until the food is served.

- Apologize to the waiter.

- Say, "People are not monkeys. That is a birthmark like the one on my knee, only bigger."

- One of you take her for a walk.

- Don't blame yourself for having an observant child.

- Show your child the book called *People,* by Peter Spier. (See "Resources.")

- I don't know what you could have done then, but now you can begin to teach her about how people are different. Later you can teach her about embarrassment.

Thanks to Jean Clarke,
Suggestion Circle from Bloomington, Minnesota

229. What can I do when I need to answer the phone or complete a phone call and my twenty-month-old is demanding my attention?

- Set him up in a room or his crib with some toys or a fun activity.

- Get another adult or an older child to play with him.

- Let him play in the kitchen sink if you use a phone in the kitchen. Fill the sink with water, suds, and utensils.

- Have a notepad and pencils by the phone for him to play with.

- Offer him a new toy, like crayons or Play-Doh. Let him know you can watch him while you talk.

- Save a collection of novel toys just for phone calls.

- Say, "While I'm on the phone, I need you to be quieter." Expect to repeat the message several times before it takes.

- Call the person back.

- Give him juice and a book, and sit him in your lap.

- Keep Band-Aids or transparent tape by the phone, and let him stick them all over himself.

- Have a toy phone or disconnected phone for him to use.

- Remember that twenty-month-olds are as important as the people on the phone. Honor both of them.

- Hang this list of things to do by your telephone.

Thanks to Carol Goss,
Suggestion Circle from Seattle, Washington

230. My nineteen-month-old daughter screams and cries and clings to my leg when I leave her with someone. What can I do?

- Don't sneak out.

- Tell her when you will return in terms of the events of her day, like "before lunch," not "at 11:30."

- Tell her you will come back.

- Tell her you know she is unhappy and you will come back.

- Try calling her just before you return to pick her up.

- Play peekaboo a lot.

- Pick her up, hug her, and say, "I am going to hug you and kiss you and then hand you to Mrs. Lamb." Then do it.

- Give her more hugs and cuddles at other times.

- Reassure yourself by asking the sitter how long she cried after you left. Most kids quiet right down.

- Remind yourself that *you* trust the sitter you are leaving her with. If you have any questions about the sitter's ability, get a new one.

(See also questions 179 and 186.)

Thanks to Sue Hansen,
Suggestion Circle from Medina, Washington

231. My nineteen-month-old son has figured out how to open the refrigerator door. I can't always be there, and he loves the eggs. What can I do?

- Look for refrigerator locks in baby specialty shops.

- Put a plastic container inside with appropriate snacks, and teach him to get a snack out of the "snack box."

- Use electrician's tape to keep the refrigerator shut.

- Keep the eggs in a carton at the back of the refrigerator.

- Put a Bungie stretch cord around the refrigerator. You can buy them at outdoor equipment stores, or make one your own length.

- Have him help break the eggs for scrambled eggs or French toast as many mornings as possible until the fascination with eggs wears down.

- Refrigerators in boats and campers have simple pin locks. Check hardware, marine supply, and camping equipment stores.

- Calmly and firmly tell him, "No, get Mommy first so I can watch you open the door." But don't respond with too much enthusiasm, or your behavior could encourage him to try again just to get attention.

- Give him other things to open and shut.

Thanks to Mary Paananen,
Suggestion Circle from Medina, Washington

232. I will be traveling soon with my two-year-old daughter. I would like some travel tips.

- Take along a lunch pail filled with little toys, a puppet, paper and pencil, and bubbles.

- Listen to cassette tapes of kids' songs and stories.

- Bring along snacks like string cheese and oriental rice cakes, which are not too messy.

- Wrap up some of the small toys you take along, and let your child open the "presents."

- Request a bulkhead seat if you are flying. There's more room there for kids to play on the floor.

- Take along a new toy airplane, and enjoy pretending about the trip.

- Make a tape recording of the trip.

- Try to avoid the busiest flights.

- Break a long car trip into short parts by making frequent stops.

- AAA will map a route with rest stops for a trip by car.

- Check with your physician about how to prepare your child for motion sickness.

- If she has an ear infection, don't fly until it's cleared up. Give her a bottle during takeoff and landing to prevent ear-aches.

- Make sure you both get enough rest the day or two before the trip.

(See also question 200.)

Thanks to Gail Davenport,
Suggestion Circle from Alderwood, Washington

233. I need options for exercise that include my child.

- Go for a walk with your child while he rides a riding toy or is pulled in a wagon.

- Play together by going to preschool swim programs or "Mom and Me" exercise classes at the recreation center.

- Look for child care available at skating rinks, bowling alleys, racquetball courts, swimming pools, or private fitness clubs.

- Play records and dance with your child.

- Look for a folk dance class that includes children.

- Get helmets and a child seat for your bicycle, and enjoy the bike trails in your area.

- Try jumping rope at home.

- Form a joggers' baby-sitting co-op and map out a route around each member's home. (See "How to Set up a Child-Care Co-op.")

- In the winter, pull your toddler in a laundry basket that's strapped to a sled.

- Get a Mickey Mouse disco record.

- Form an exercise club. Moms and kids meet at one house. Half the moms exercise while the other half tend the kids; then switch.

Thanks to Gail Davenport,
Suggestion Circle from Lynnwood, Washington

Chapter 29

Keeping Them Safe

234. I'm reading and hearing on TV that it is important to teach my child to be cautious of strangers. How do I do that? My daughter is two and a half.

- Help your child learn about this in very small steps.

- This is not a child's problem. This is an adult's problem. We not only need to protect our kids; we really need to do something to change the adults who hurt kids.

- Remember that it is still your job to protect her at this age.

- Educate yourself. Read *It's My Body*, by Lory Freeman, to your child now, and read *Safety Zone*, by Linda Meyer, to know what to say when your child is a little older. (See "Resources.")

- Decide what you want to say to her, and then practice saying it over and over to yourself and to another adult to get used to talking about it.

- Teach your child that her body is important.

- With all safety issues, it takes time for the child to "get it," and adults must take responsibility for the child's safety for years.

- Look at some of the new picture books for kids on this subject.

- Be sure you are teaching by example—don't automatically open your door to someone you don't know, for instance.

- Have your child fingerprinted.

Thanks to Jean Clarke,
Suggestion Circle from Plymouth, Minnesota

235. My mother keeps bleach, dishwasher soap, and drain stuff under her sink. I worry about my twenty-month-old son's safety when I visit her. What can I do?

- Ask her to put these poisons away in a high, locked cupboard for a few years.

- Take a portable gate to put across the kitchen door.

- Install childproof latches on those cupboards.

- Hold your conversations in the kitchen with your chair braced against the cupboard doors.

- Whenever you visit, *you* put the poisons up on a shelf out of reach.

- Tell Grandma how damaging these things are to a child. (Call the local poison control center for information.)

- If Grandma won't cooperate, have her visit at your house until your child is older.

- Continue to protect your son—a child his age is supposed to be curious and is too young to know how dangerous that stuff is.

Thanks to Carole Gesme,
Suggestion Circle from Minneapolis, Minnesota

236. How can I teach my two-year-old that there are some things not to climb on or play with?

- Show her where she can and can't play. When you tell her no, be sure to tell her what she can do instead.

- Explain in child's words why she can't.

- Praise her cleverness in doing things by herself, and be clear about out-of-bounds areas.

- Do another round of childproofing so you can say no to fewer things.

- Make sure that every room has a safe space that she can be in.

- Use a key phrase like "remember the rule" to remind her that your family has a climbing rule to think about and follow.

- Provide something safe to climb on, and tell her what is not safe to climb on.

- When she's touching fragile things, teach her to touch with one finger so she learns to be careful.

- She may be climbing out of curiosity; carry your child and give her a guided tour of the top half of each room.

- Praise her when she follows the rules.

Thanks to Nat Houtz,
Suggestion Circle from Edmonds, Washington

237. My two-year-old runs away from me, and this is becoming a safety issue in parking lots, when we go shopping, and when we are near streets. What could I try doing?

- Show him that you are upset. Do not smile or tell other adults about his running as if it were cute.

- Use a stroller.

- Do some prevention work. Practice walking near cars. Tell him clearly what he is expected to do and why.

- Use and enforce the "hold-hands rule" in parking lots and near streets.

- Use a backpack.

- Rent a stroller at the malls.

- Seat him in front of a three-way mirror when possible, and let him practice staying near you while you browse.

- Children get easier to take with you when they are closer to three years old.

(See also questions 182 and 188.)

Thanks to Gail Davenport,
Suggestion Circle from Edmonds, Washington

238. Both of my children, who are twenty-four months and ten months old, are playing with the plugs and electrical outlets. How can I manage this problem?

- Place heavy furniture in front of the outlets.

- Use the outlet caps that insert into the socket, but experiment with several brands to find one that fits tightly.

- Control the outlet with a boxlike cover that screws over the outlet. (You can buy them at hardware stores.) The cover has two notches that let the cords hang out.

- Your two-year-old might want more one-on-one time with you if she is doing it to get your attention.

- Show the young one something else to divert her attention.

- Move the children away from the outlets, and tell them touching them will hurt. Keep at it, and before long they will lose interest.

- Two-year-olds like to poke things in holes. Provide her with objects or toys that are similar to cords and plugs— latches, yarn, threading spools, and so on.

- Mount an unwired outlet on a board and provide a cord with a plug. Then insist that the children play only with "their" (safe) plugger.

Thanks to Gail Davenport,
Suggestion Circle from Lynnwood, Washington

239. My two-year-old is terrified of people in masks and costumes. With Halloween coming up, I need suggestions on how to help him deal with the "spooks" coming to the door.

- Get a mask or two for him to play with and explore.

- Play peekaboo games with him with a single homemade paper bag mask. (You put it on your face.)

- Take him to see clowns or other costumed creatures at a supermarket or shopping mall. Let him approach them, if he wishes, from the safety of your arms. Don't insist. (This can work for Santa Claus, too.)

- Have someone distract him when trick-or-treaters come to the door.

- Let him watch in a mirror while you paint his face (if he will let you), and talk to him about pretending.

- Take him to or have a neighborhood Halloween party with other small children and parents—just costumes, no masks.

- Try putting a mask on a puppet and then have the puppet pretend to be someone else.

- He is too young to sort this out. You protect him from people in masks until he is older—four or five, maybe.

Thanks to Nat Houtz,
Suggestion Circle from Edmonds, Washington

Chapter 30

Parents Are in Charge

240. How can I find quality day care for my child?

- Check out the local day-care association. Find out what day care is available, how to see and interview day-care providers, and how to see and interview parents of children at each day-care center.

- Form a child-care co-op. (See "How to Set up a Child-Care Co-op.")

- Check with local churches for names of responsible teenage baby-sitters or day-care providers.

- Call the local high school's home economics department for referrals.

- See if your city park department or YMCA has baby-sitter classes, and ask for lists of recommended graduates.

- Call the county department responsible for licensing day-care centers. Get names of people in the area and call them.

- Talk to friends and neighbors who might have day-care experience with their kids. If those places are full, ask them for recommendations.

- Visit centers and day-care homes in person with a list of criteria, and interview the providers.

- Call an early childhood education department at a local college for information on what to look for.

- For little ones, arrange day care with a friend until they are older and ready for group day care.

Thanks to Melanie Weiss,
Suggestion Circle from Bellevue, Washington

241. How can I decide on a few sensible rules?

- Consider your child's safety, and set limits that will allow her to be somewhat independent while being protected.

- Think about what kind of behavior you are unwilling to tolerate; decide if your child is developmentally able to cope with these expectations, and expect your limits to be tested many times.

- Trust yourself. Choose rules that fit your family.

- Take a look at a developmental chart to learn what you can expect of your child. See *Without Spanking or Spoiling,* by Elizabeth Crary. (See "Resources.")

- Be sure you are willing to enforce the rules you choose.

- Two-year-olds are pretty little. Don't expect too much.

- Remember, a "few" rules means less than ten.

- Choose rules that the child can understand and follow.

- Try out a few rules, and change them if they don't work.

  (See also question 183.)

Thanks to Craig Halverson,
Suggestion Circle from Coon Rapids, Minnesota

242. What's the difference between discipline and punishment?

- Discipline says, "Stop. Do something else instead." Punishment says, "You did something wrong, and you are bad!"

- Discipline sets the child up for success next time. Punishment focuses on failure.

- If there is physical hurt, it is punishment.

- Discipline is something that shows consequences but is not as severe as punishment.

- Discipline does not expect more than a child this age can do. Punishment often does.

- Discipline is learning the right and wrong of life. Punishment is the negative side of discipline.

- Discipline addresses the *act* as wrong. Punishment addresses the *person* as wrong.

- Discipline has a good chance of being effective. The results of punishment are unpredictable.

- Discipline comes from thought, and punishment comes from anger.

- Punishment is being disciplined without knowing what's expected of you.

- If the parent feels gleeful or vengeful, it's punishment.

Thanks to Marilyn Grevstad,
Suggestion Circle from Seattle, Washington

243. What should I do when my child (almost three) says, "I need my dad—where's Dad?" whenever I am giving directions that he doesn't want to hear?

- Say, "He's at work."

- Tell him, "I'm in charge now," and then return to what you expect.

- Say, "I wish Daddy could be here, but he is not."

- Tell him where Dad is, and when he's coming home, that he will see him then, and now it's time to do what you told him to do.

- Ignore it.

- Don't get hooked by this. Go ahead and be the mom.

- Don't give more than one direction at once, and be sure it is one he can do. He may be wanting help because the directions are too complicated.

(See also question 241.)

Thanks to Carole Gesme,
Suggestion Circle from Minnetonka, Minnesota

244. I am a single parent. I spend a lot of time at my parents' house, where my dad watches lots of violent TV that I don't want my two-year-old son to watch. What can I do?

- Spend more time at your home and less with your folks.

- Invite friends to your home more.

- Look for other places where you and your child are comfortable spending time.

- Offer alternative programs on a different TV set, if one is available, and watch these shows with your son.

- Examine your values regarding TV, and then establish priorities. Set some limits for your child, and negotiate them with your family.

- Ask for your dad's help.

- Be frank about your uncomfortable feelings with TV violence.

- Ask your dad to involve himself with your two-year-old. Offer some suggestions for activities or games they can play together.

- Try to time your visits when the TV is unlikely to be on.

- Read the chapter about TV in *The New Read-Aloud Handbook,* by Jim Trelease. (See "Resources.")

- Ask your dad what you could trade so he won't watch boxing when his grandson is there.

(See also question 250.)

Thanks to Nat Houtz,
Suggestion Circle from Edmonds, Washington

245. How do I teach my two-and-a-half-year-old to deal with criticism from other adults?

- This is too complicated for a child that age. You protect your child.

- Give him lots of good strokes that will build self-esteem.

- Play the game, "Who loves Jonathan? Mommy loves Jonathan, Daddy loves Jonathan, Grandma loves Jonathan, kitty loves Jonathan," and so on, eight times a day.

- Apologize for the other adult. Say, "I'm sorry that person did that. It wasn't nice."

- Teach him to listen for behavior clues. If they say, "You are a bad boy," teach him to ignore it. If they say, "You make too much noise," tell him that is a clue to be quiet.

- Tell the adults to stop it.

- Show him how to ignore it, and tell him that is what you are doing.

- Tell him to say, "Ouch, that hurts!"

(See also question 249.)

Thanks to Deane Gradous,
Suggestion Circle from Wayzata, Minnesota

246. I have the opportunity to go to Europe in September. How do I make my departure easier for my two-year-old?

- Be sure that she has stayed with others before you go on this longer trip.

- If at all possible, have her cared for in your own home while you are gone so she is surrounded by familiar objects.

- Two-year-olds are supposed to be separating from their parents. When parents leave for a long time, it can interfere with that process. Could you go to Europe later?

- Be sure her sitter is familiar with your daily routine and knows the importance of sticking to it.

- Plan to call her while you are away and to write letters that can be read to her.

- Tell her you are leaving, and reassure her that you will be returning.

- Make a tape of your voice so she can hear it while you are gone.

- Don't go now. Wait until your child is older.

- Make a calendar with your picture on the day you return, and leave stickers for your child to put on each day that you're away.

- Make your trip as short as possible.

- Have a plastic-covered picture of yourself for her to look at, hold, or carry around.

- Expect her to need some time to warm up to you when you return.

Thanks to Carole Gesme,
Suggestion Circle from Minneapolis, Minnesota

247. My toddler's father is away in the military service. How can I keep the two of them "in touch" so that our son doesn't forget his dad?

- Be sure to have a BIG picture of Dad on display, and talk to the picture several times a day.

- Point to Dad or let your son point when you are looking at snapshots.

- Keep in regular phone contact if you can so that your child can hear his dad's voice frequently.

- My friend's husband sent audiotapes and sometimes videos, too, so that his children wouldn't forget him.

- Always talk about what you are sending Dad, writing to him, and so forth. Let your son mark a paper to send along.

- When you play specific games, say, "Daddy will play this with you when he gets home."

- Be joyous when you talk about Dad. Don't let your child always associate conversations about Dad with your being tearful and lonely.

- Regularly read storybooks that have fathers in them, and refer to your son's dad during the stories and activities.

Thanks to Darlene Montz,
Suggestion Circle from Yakima, Washington

Chapter 31

Hassles with Other Adults

248. My husband was supposed to be watching our nineteen-month-old son. When I came home, I found the child playing in our busy street. What shall I do?

- Get with it and insist that your husband take responsibility for his son's safety.

- Parents should discuss and agree about mutual expectations. Each of you has a need for time away from your child and a need for shared parenting.

- Send a clear message about how you feel. Hang in there until the two of you establish responsibility for his safety.

- You and your husband decide where your child may and may not play, regardless of who looks after him.

- Fire him.

- State your expectations, and let your husband choose whether he wants to meet them or hire a baby-sitter.

- Explicitly tell him how you feel. Resolve the issue with him.

(See also question 257.)

Thanks to Laurie Perchaluk,
Suggestion Circle from Calgary, Alberta, Canada

249. How do I respond to other adults when they criticize my two-year-old in front of her?

- Say, "She is special and has many unique ways of expressing herself."

- Don't respond to the adult. Protect the child. Explain to the child what is going on.

- Give this message to the adult: "It sounds as if you have a hard time with that behavior."

- Reaffirm the positive part of the criticized behavior. Change "She is a bossy little miss!" to "She is learning to be assertive. She'll polish it later."

- Say, "Will you tell me what you would like her to do instead?"

- First, provide *immediate* nurturing attention to your child. Then respond to the adult.

- Be a model. Reword the criticism to be a positive message or a "you-can-do-better" statement for your child. Read Chapters One and Four of Clarke's *Self-Esteem: A Family Affair*. (See "Resources.")

- Say, "Thank you for your input."

- Say, "Don't say that. She is too young."

- Say, "I appreciate that you care about her."

(See also question 245.)

Thanks to Sandra Sittko,
Suggestion Circle from Saint Paul, Minnesota

250. I'd like some ideas on how I can limit the TV my son is watching. He is two and a half. My husband watches a lot.

- Tell your son which programs he can watch today. Then enforce these limits.

- Move the TV to your husband's room so your son can't watch.

- You and your husband judge which programs are not good for a two-and-a-half-year-old to watch. Find some programs for your husband to watch with his son.

- Sell the TV.

- Create a list of things to do instead of watching TV. Use it.

- Make a rule that your child must ask your permission to watch TV.

- Position the TV so it can't be seen from the doorway, and use a gate.

- Hammer out rules about how much TV your child should watch. Expect your husband to act as a father and an adult.

- Discuss buying VCR equipment and recording programs a two-and-a-half-year-old shouldn't watch. Then your husband can watch them after your child is in bed or when your son is outside.

(See also question 244.)

Thanks to Lyn Dillman,
Suggestion Circle from Seattle, Washington

251. What can I do? My ex-husband won't visit my girls (two and a half and four), and they miss him.

- Sit with the children and let them dictate a letter to their father.

- When you talk with him, ask him which day he wants to see the children.

- If he chooses not to visit, be clear with your children that they are worthy of love; it is his problem to work out, not theirs.

- You can't be responsible for him; take good care of yourself and your kids.

- When they want to see him, put them on the phone with him.

- Say, "I see that you sometimes feel lonely for Daddy since he is gone, but I expect sometimes it is a relief to have the fighting stopped."

- There are other people dealing with this; get support and advice from groups like Parents Without Partners. (See "Resources.")

- Say to yourself, "This isn't how I wanted it to be, but I can build a new life."

- Ask your ex-husband to join you for several sessions with a mediator or counselor to solve this problem.

- If he does "drop out" of their lives, get support for yourself so you can help them through the loss.

- Find other loving grown men for them to relate to: a grandpa, an uncle, a nursery school teacher, and so on.

Thanks to Nat Houtz,
Suggestion Circle from Lynnwood, Washington

252. My husband beats my kids, ages two and eight, and I need some help with that. I need to stay with him. He's supporting us.

- Call your local child protection agency.

- Know that you have the power to change your situation. Do it!

- Get the support you need to protect your kids.

- Call crisis hot lines, and know that you aren't alone.

- It doesn't matter if he's your husband or a stranger, child abuse is child abuse. Do whatever it takes to get him to stop it.

- Leave him and go to a shelter.
- Tell him to stop!
- Insist on counseling together.
- Get protection for you and your kids from a close male friend or relative.
- Have him arrested. Get aid while you learn to make your own living.

(See also question 253, "Keeping Two-Year-Olds Safe," and "Signs of Abuse and Neglect.")

Thanks to Melanie Weiss,
Suggestion Circle from Bellevue, Washington

253. My in-laws say my two-year-old child is going to walk all over me. They want me to use harsh discipline, slap her, or use a stick or coat hanger. Their talk scares me, and my values say not to hit her. How can I cope with them?

- When they start to tell you what to do, just let it pass through your head and don't let it in.
- Do what you think is best. This is your child.
- Hitting is abuse, period.
- Do your discipline in private so they don't get the chance to enter in.
- Say, "No, I do not let her walk all over me, and I do not need to hit her."
- Calmly explain what works for you and your child.
- If they might actively discipline your child, be sure never to leave her alone with them. Hitting with a coat hanger or stick is child abuse.

- Be a caring and loving parent. Trust yourself. Set clear limits with your child, and she will learn the rules.

- Ask them to listen to the Jason and Jennie tape, *The Terrific Twos*, by Jean Illsley Clarke. (See "Resources.")

(See also questions 241 and 252.)

Thanks to Gail Davenport,
Suggestion Circle from Alderwood Manor, Washington

254. Grandma is coming for a visit, and my two-year-old does not want to hug her. What can I do?

- Tell Grandma that her grandson will decide when to approach people.
- Get him ready for her visit; show him her picture.
- Let him hear you say that *you* love her.
- Ask him to draw pictures for Grandma to give her instead of a hug.
- Give Grandma suggestions to try, like "Play with his toys, and let him approach you."
- Let him see you hug your mom.
- Involve him in your preparation for her visit. Then leave it to him.
- Don't train him to hug when he doesn't want to.
- Call your mom and tell her about this. Ask her to help you plan how to handle it.
- Don't you or your mom make a big deal out of it.

Thanks to Nat Houtz,
Suggestion Circle from Edmonds, Washington

Chapter 32

Parents Have Needs
and Problems, Too

255. I am a working parent. I have so many things to do, I need ideas on how I can balance my needs and my child's needs when we are home together.

- Look over your routine and clear out what isn't important in order to leave more time for your child and for you.

- Decide what things you must do for yourself, and make sure to do them. Decide what things you must do for your child, and make sure to do them.

- Be sure you are not carrying the whole load yourself. Divide the work with the other adults and older children in the family.

- Clean up guilt—have fun both by yourself and with your child.

- Hire a person to help clean.

- Before you pick up your child, spend a little time on yourself. Meditate or give yourself a foot rub. Nurture yourself.

- Build some personal time into your family's routine.

- Include your child in chores like sorting laundry, tearing lettuce for the salad, and so on.

- Read *2001 Hints for Working Mothers*, by Gloria Mayer. (See "Resources.")

(See also questions 190 and 216.)

Thanks to Nat Houtz,
Suggestion Circle from Edmonds, Washington

256. When my husband comes home after work, he wants to read the paper, but our two-year-old wants his attention. My husband says he is anxious to get home to see the kids, but he wants time to wind down, too. What should I do?

- Let your husband and your child handle it themselves.

- Ask him if he could read the paper at work.

- Ask Dad to greet your two-year-old with a hug, then set the timer for twenty minutes of "alone time."

- Maybe Dad would be willing to give the child attention by letting the child help him settle down after work—helping him to change clothes and so on.

- See if they will watch "Mister Rogers" together on TV.

- Ask Dad if he could put off his wind-down time until after attention is given to the two-year-old.

- Moms need wind-down time, too. Take turns with your husband.

- Set aside some special toys the child can play with only while Dad or Mom is reading the paper.

- I roll on the floor with my kids for a while, and then read the paper.

- Invent a family greeting where everybody plays together.

- He could stop and buy a paper and read it in his car before he comes home.

(See also question 191.)

Thanks to Sandra Sittko,
Suggestion Circle from Saint Paul, Minnesota

257. I want to get over my Supermom habits and let my husband be more involved with the care of our two-year-old son. How can I get this to happen when I still don't trust my husband to watch him?

- Get out of the house to go grocery shopping in the early evening. Leave them together for a little while.

- Let Daddy do it his way even if the boy might end up dressed "funny."

- Don't pack the diaper bag when they leave on an outing together. Let Daddy do it without your coaching.

- Tell your husband when you need help. Ask him if he will do the dishes or give his son a bath.

- Be willing to begin to let go and trust your spouse and child. Take small steps, and celebrate each one.

- Watch for times when your husband takes good care of the boy and tell him.

- Get yourself a Supermom cape, and hand it over when your husband is in charge.

- Take a parenting class together.

- Decide whether you don't trust him because you want to be Supermom or because you have reason to fear for your child's safety.

(See also question 248.)

Thanks to Gail Davenport,
Suggestion Circle from Lynnwood, Washington

258. Getting dinner ready is usually a hassle. By the time I sit down, I don't want to eat. What can I do?

- Plan weekly menus at the beginning of the week. Do some of the food preparation in the morning when you feel fresh.

- Gather the family for input on who will do what for the following day's meal.

- Create one or two weeklong rotating menus.

- Meditate for ten minutes just before you start to prepare the meal.

- Use frozen casserole dishes on high-stress days.

- Let someone else cook one night a week.

- Have a snack and take a rest between 3:00 and 3:30.

- Set up a plan for the weekly menu. Delegate jobs ahead of time so you know who is responsible.

- Sing while you cook.

- Ask everyone to leave you alone while you fix dinner. Don't answer the phone or any questions.

Thanks to Gail Nordeman,
Suggestion Circle from Cincinnati, Ohio

259. My husband and I are splitting up right now. How can I make this difficult time easier for my two-year-old daughter?

- Spend more prime time with your child.

- Make sure your needs are met, and get lots of support so when you are with your child you are really there.

- Your child will probably feel angry, sad, and confused over this for a while. Accept her feelings.

- Don't go on any trips without your child for a while.

- Find someone for you to talk to so you can get support, too.

- Expect a lot of her feelings to come out indirectly. Pay as much attention as you can to her.

- Take good care of yourself so your two-year-old doesn't have to try to take care of Mommy. That is not her job.

- Explain to her as best you can exactly what is happening. Assure the child that it is not her fault. Tell her she can't do anything to change it.

- Show her lots of affection when you are with her.

- Agree with your husband to stay out of power struggles involving how you parent your child.

- Read *Divorce Is a Grown-Up Problem,* by Janet Sinberg. (See "Resources.")

(See also question 255.)

Thanks to Darlene Montz,
Suggestion Circle from Yakima, Washington

260. I still feel awful when I leave my child. What can I do?

- Call after you reach your destination.

- Leave your child for short periods of time, and increase the length of the separation as you feel comfortable.

- Don't leave him often.

- Get some help for your own guilt. Get the support of a counselor or therapist.

- Leave him with someone in whom you have a lot of trust and confidence.

- Decide that it is OK for him to start to grow up a little at a time.

- Look carefully at how each of you is learning to be away from each other. Decide how small the steps need to be.

- Remember that this is *your* separation problem. It's OK to have it, and you can deal with it. You need to deal with it so your child won't have to take care of you by clinging or using some other behavior.

Thanks to Maggie Lawrence,
Suggestion Circle from Edmonds, Washington

261. I have moved to a new neighborhood, and I need some suggestions on how to make friends with other parents.

- Go for a daily walk with your child to make yourself visible, and then approach people you see.

- If you see kids outside, go out and meet them. Eventually you will meet their parents.

- Find out if there is a baby-sitting co-op.

- Watch for people going out with their garbage, doing yard work, picking up the paper or their mail. Approach them then.

- Join a church or synagogue in the neighborhood.

- Go to the parks, playgrounds, recreation department classes, or kids' swimming lessons.

- Ask if there is a neighborhood bridge club or bowling team you could join.

- Be willing to be the "Neighborhood Mom," and invite kids over to play in the sprinkler.

- Get active in a political party.

- Have an open house, and invite the neighbors.

- Plan to get outside when the schoolchildren are leaving for school or getting home. You might even meet their bus regularly to visit and find out where families with kids the age of your child live.

- Look for toys and tricycles in driveways or yards.

(See also question 233.)

Thanks to Gail Davenport,
Suggestion Circle from Lynnwood, Washington

262. I don't get enough intellectual stimulation. I've been focusing on kids for two and a half years and I need ideas on what I can do to stimulate my mind.

- Enroll in a continuing education class at a nearby college.

- Get involved in a study group at church or at the local library.

- Do volunteer work with grown-ups in social or political groups.

- Learn a new skill—skiing, Chinese cooking, basket making, photography.

- Teach someone a skill that you already have.

- Get involved in a community action organization.

- Write letters to the editor.

- Read a difficult book.

- Have some "alone time" to talk with your partner or an interesting friend every week.

- Listen to educational tapes. You can get some at the public library.

Thanks to Nat Houtz,
Suggestion Circle from Edmonds, Washington

263. I need options for arranging child care so we can get some time alone as a couple. Please include any ideas for overnight, evening, or daytime care.

- Trade child care with a neighbor or friend.

- Set it up with relatives.

- Set up a monthly overnight or evening exchange with a family that has children close to your child's age.

- Look for recreation facilities that offer good child care, like bowling alleys and swimming pools.

- Set up a baby-sitting co-op that exchanges hours or tokens. (See "How to Set up a Child-Care Co-op.")

- Talk to scout leaders, church people, or home economics teachers for referrals of teenagers who have had some training.

- Put some energy into screening family day-care homes that accept part-time and drop-in children.

- Join a barter exchange, and trade child care for something you enjoy doing.

- Look in the yellow pages for child-care centers. Some offer evening care.

(See also question 240.)

Thanks to Gail Davenport,
Suggestion Circle from Lynnwood, Washington

Moving On to the Preschool Years

As a child grows through the twos and moves into the preschool years, your challenges and delights are bound to change. As parents, you will watch with wonder and sometimes a little dismay as your baby fades and the child emerges. You have guided your toddler through her early struggles with using a spoon and a cup and learning to climb and getting stuck. Now you will see her increase her physical competence. She will learn to race and jump and use crayons and scissors. You will listen as her language skills multiply almost explosively and she finds the ability to express pleasure and displeasure with words.

Your child has already taken her first steps toward separation and autonomy; now she will begin to learn new ways of being in her family, play group, and neighborhood. She will begin to share and to accommodate what others want. She will start to focus on her peers as people to relate to, rather than as interesting objects to explore. She will try to find out just how powerful she is. The pretend worlds she creates will provide her with many ways to develop her identity and exercise her power. However, she will still need nurturing adults who provide her with love and a safe environment within which to grow.

The next section of this book offers an abundance of ideas and suggestions for managing the challenges of parenting the preschool child. It also offers some help for you as you, too, experience and recycle the developmental steps of this stage.

These early years are the foundation of all the parenting to come, so celebrate your resourcefulness, your capability, and your own growth.

Nat Houtz

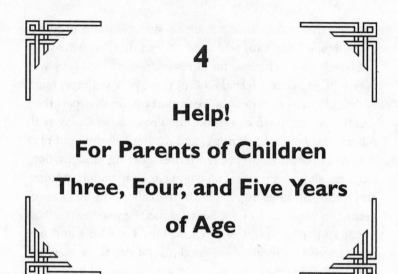

4

Help!
For Parents of Children
Three, Four, and Five Years
of Age

Ages and Stages

What is the preschool stage of development all about? You will find that the pretend play of three- to six-year-olds is charged with power themes as superheroes and monsters emerge. Feeling powerful is important to preschool children, and they can experience it in their imagination even if they often feel small and helpless in real life. Their pretend play is their way of trying on new roles and sorting out what's real from what's imaginary. Preschoolers can seem to be quite clear about what is real and what is fantasy one minute, while the next minute they can become terrified of a witch puppet or of a ghost on TV.

Words help preschoolers to feel important. The three-year-old asks, "Why?" The four-year-old says, "It's dumb and I hate it!" The five-year-old says, "How does it work?" They are learning that words have power; sassing, whining, arguing, bad language, and baby talk all surface during this period.

Friends are very important to preschoolers, and they will play with imaginary friends if they can't play with real ones. Although social experiences are important, don't expect their social interactions to run smoothly. Preschoolers' play with others is usually quite bumpy, and during a morning of play you will probably observe tenderness, caring, imagination, laughter, shouts, screams, foul language, cooperation, arguing, and hitting and kicking, as children go about the business of getting to know each other. So keep social gatherings such as birthday parties simple and short. One hour long and one guest for each year of age are good rules if you want everyone to have a good time.

There is a new awareness of the sexes during the preschool period. Hospital play is a favorite game; it is children's way of understanding their bodies. While parents will want to set limits on this play, they need not be upset about it. Around five, many boys refuse to use women's rest rooms, causing some inconvenience for their mothers. Boys have decided that there are two kinds of people in the world—male and female—and that they are male. Signs or taunts of "No boys allowed" come from groups of girls, and boys often take a "boys-only" attitude. Little boys may talk of marrying their mothers or sisters or girls they know. Girls do the same with fathers, brothers, and boys.

Two types of children may cause parents concern: the aggressive and the overly cautious. Aggressive children need large amounts of tolerance and open space. Contrary to the opinion of some, aggressive children are not necessarily hit by their parents or encouraged to hit others any more than nonaggressive children are. Still, you do not take this type of child to a china shop. These are children who grasp life rather impulsively, without a lot of forethought about the consequences. Constant setting of limits may not be effective with this type of child at this age. It is better to decide on a few important rules, such as not hurting others and not damaging property, and then to ignore temporarily some things like making noise or clutter. These children respond in the long run to a lot of gentle guidance.

Overly cautious children, on the other hand, are watchers. They don't like to make mistakes. They need adults around who say with words and actions, "You don't have to hurry. Do this when you are ready." Pressuring them to perform before they are fully able does not work.

Young children go through four stages as they learn to defend their territory. The first stage is simply hitting or grabbing to get what they need. The second stage is the use of verbal aggression—words as power. Then bribery becomes an important tool: "If you give it to me, you can come to my birthday party." Older preschoolers learn to collect allies. They learn how to gang up on each other. These acts are not good or bad in themselves; they are just steps to higher levels of socialization. When you need to, set some rules about these actions, but remember your child is handling situations the best she can with limited experience. Handling things awkwardly is better for a child than not handling them at all.

Children ages three, four, and five break rules regularly and can be quite difficult to live with at times, but their rule breaking is only the first step toward rule keeping and rule making, which will become important developmental tasks when they are ages six to twelve.

Because of frequent rule breaking, parents often wonder if they will have control of their preschoolers in an emergency. The answer is yes. Children know that their parents are smarter and stronger than they are and that parents will protect children from danger. In everyday matters, however, children will continue to balk at parental authority. It takes a preschooler a long time to teach her parents that she will no longer think the way parents say she should, that she is a separate individual person, and that she must be allowed to be herself.

Marilyn Grevstad

Affirmations for Growth—
Power and Identity

Here are some special affirming messages that will help children during this stage of growth. At this age, children are exploring their identity and ways of being powerful, acquiring lots of information, starting to learn socially appropriate behavior, developing their imagination, and trying out different ways of relating to other people.

Affirmations for Establishing Identity and Power

- You can explore who you are and find out who other people are.
- You can be powerful and ask for help at the same time.
- You can try out different roles and ways of being powerful.
- You can find out the results of your behavior.
- All of your feelings are OK with me.
- You can learn what is pretend and what is real.
- I love who you are.

You *give* these affirmations by the way you interact with the child, encourage his or her imagination, supply information to endless questions, expect cause-and-effect thinking, reward socially appropriate behavior, and enforce limits. You can also *say* these affirmations directly in a supportive, loving way.

Of course, you have to believe the affirmations yourself, or they become confusing or crazy double messages. If you don't understand or believe an affirmation, don't give that one until you do believe it. Before children can learn to respond to others in an independent, honoring way, they must establish their own identity, their sense of "this is who I am."

Since we never outgrow the need for health-giving messages, children at this age continue to need affirmations from the three earlier stages. The affirmations for Being are about our right to exist and have needs. The affirmations for Doing focus on our need to reach out and explore. The affirmations for Thinking support thinking and independence. (See the "Affirmations" sections in each of the previous parts of this book.)

Children who decided not to believe these messages at a younger age have another chance to incorporate them now. Remember, it is never too late for you to start giving these affirmations.

When you discover additional affirmations that your child needs, write them in this book and give them to your child.

Jean Illsley Clarke

Identity and Power
—Three, four, and five years of age and ever after—

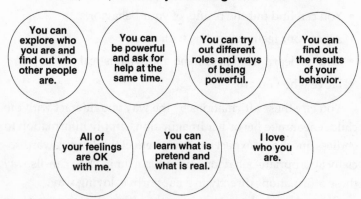

You can explore who you are and find out who other people are.

You can be powerful and ask for help at the same time.

You can try out different roles and ways of being powerful.

You can find out the results of your behavior.

All of your feelings are OK with me.

You can learn what is pretend and what is real.

I love who you are.

Copy these ovals and color them green.
Post them for daily reading.

Parents of Three-, Four-, and Five-Year-Olds Get Another Chance— Recycling

Parents often delight in young children who are trying on identity roles, learning new social skills, and developing their imagination by making up wonderful and strange things and asking a thousand questions. But sometimes those parents also feel tired. They run out of answers and patience and wonder who they are and how they got this demanding job.

One of the benefits of this period of children's growth for parents is that the parents, too, can create a new sense of autonomy. They can rework or recycle their own concept of self-identity and the ways in which they use their power, their creativity, and their imagination. (See "Parents Get Another Chance—Recycling," in the Foreword.)

Recycling the Tasks of Establishing Power and Identity

Parents of children who are busy discovering who they are and how to do things can use this period not only to support their children's growth but also to update their own identity and use of power. They can ask anew the questions "Who am I?" and "What about my relationships with all those other people?" and "Do I want to change the ways in which I relate?"

This is a good opportunity for parents to think about power. "Do I think power is good or bad in itself, or is it only the way in which people use it that makes it good or bad?" "Am I denying that I have the power to improve my life?" "Do I like the way I use my power?" "Do I whine instead of asking in a straightforward way for what I need?" "Would my family and I be better off if I bullied less? Manipulated less? Shared power more?"

The affirmations that are helpful to our children are also healthy for us. (See those listed in the previous section.) Because many of us never received or decided not to believe some of those healthy messages (or we only believed them partly), this is an ideal time to accept those messages for ourselves and to claim more of our ability to be whole, healthy, joyful adults. If you didn't get the affirmations you needed the first time around, you can take them now as you offer them to your children.

Jean Illsley Clarke

Common Pitfalls

Sometimes, as children go about their developmental tasks, they do things that are misinterpreted by parents who may be overly severe or hurtful in an attempt to stop or control those normal behaviors. Or parents who do not understand a child's needs for structure and boundaries may overindulge and encourage self-indulgence in the child.

The following behaviors of children this age are frequently misunderstood:

- Three- to six-year-old children are learning about their *identity*—including their sexual identity. This frequently leads to sexual play, including masturbation, "playing doctor," and so on. If caring adults do not realize that this is completely normal, they may overreact and physically or psychologically abuse children and give them a distorted view of their own sexuality. Parents should choose this time to explain to children that sexual organs will eventually be used to "make babies" and that sexual activity is a private activity, a source of pleasure, and a personal responsibility. It is my belief that by beginning to associate responsibility with sexuality at this stage, we as a society have the greatest hope of preventing teenage pregnancies.

- Also because these children are *learning about sexuality*, they may be practicing the flirtatious or coquettish behaviors they have seen adults model. Parents must be certain that all adults (and all baby-sitters) interacting with children know that sexually touching any child is completely wrong. It is also wrong to blame any child this age for "leading someone on." Adults are always responsible.

- Children this age are learning to *recognize the difference between fantasy and reality*. They often experiment with what is truth and what is a lie. It is important for caring adults to tell children what a lie is and to expect the truth. At the same time, they should not overreact with physical or verbal abuse if children are lying.

- Children are learning about the many *options* life offers through fantasy play. Parents should help children explore many options, not only the ones that coincide with the adult's hopes for the child.

- Because this is the *age of fantasy*, creativity should be encouraged. Many toys that "run themselves" should be replaced with blocks, with trucks and dolls without batteries, or with costumes, hats, and so on.

- Children this age are very busy learning about and *testing their own power*. If parents find themselves in a power struggle, they may inappropriately use verbal or physical abuse to "win." When parents remember that they are truly in charge, they can step out of the power struggle. They will not need to be abusive in order to "win," nor will they need to overindulge in order to placate the child. When parents know that they are in charge, both parents and children win.

- Some children this age still need to *learn toilet habits*. Caring adults may forget that children are in charge of their own bodies, and in an effort to help them learn toilet habits, they may become abusive. Both children and adults will benefit and have much happier lives if the adults acknowledge that children are in charge of their own bodies by allowing them to initiate their own toileting activities, despite the grandparents' or the neighbors' advice.

- Children this age are *using rational thinking* and show some early signs of adult behavior. Adults sometimes seize on this sign of new thinking as a signal to push children with a "hurry-and-grow-up-fast-to-take-care-of-me" message. It is important to let children be children.

Christine Ternand, M.D.

Keeping Preschoolers Safe

Children this age need careful structure for safety. Parents who do not abuse or neglect their children keep them safe by:

- Refusing to leave a child alone in the house or car
- Always using car seats or safety belts when traveling with a child in the car
- Carefully supervising a child in a shopping cart
- Continuing to cut food into small pieces
- Setting clear and firm limits for baby-sitters by discussing do's and don'ts and then leaving a list of them
- Monitoring outside play and water safety
- Making certain that other adults understand what the children need
- Teaching children what good or bad touch is and then listening carefully if children report anything that would suggest abusive behavior from other adults
- Teaching children accurate terms for all body parts, including penis, testicles, vagina, vulva, and breasts
- Teaching children ways to resolve conflict without verbal or physical attacks
- Teaching children their full name, phone number, and address
- Teaching children how and when to use 911
- Teaching children safety skills, like saying no and respecting their own and others' bodies.

If you suspect abuse of any kind, find a way to protect the child. Get help if you need it. Report the abuser to the child protection service in your area. (See "Where to Go for Additional Support," "Common Pitfalls," and "Signs of Abuse and Neglect.")

Christine Ternand, M.D.

Chapter 33

The Identity of the Preschooler

264. My four-year-old creates wonderful stories, but he creates them when I need an answer to a question. How can I encourage that creativity and yet have him give me the answer I need?

- Be clear with him when you need an answer. Avoid the words *truth* and *lying*. Say, "You make up wonderful stories, but right now I need the answer to my question."

- Use body language (a wink) or words to indicate you know when he is telling a story.

- Spend time telling stories *with* him.

- Ask, "Is that pretend or real?"

- Read him the story about the boy who cried wolf, and discuss it.

- This is typical behavior for four-year-olds. Read the chapter in Clarke's *Self-Esteem: A Family Affair* about three- to six-year-olds. (See "Resources.")

- As a family, take turns telling the same story or adding on to one that someone starts.

- When you answer his questions, make sure that you are direct with your answer. This will show him how to answer directly.

- Support his creativity by helping him record his stories on a tape recorder or having him dictate them for you to write down.

- Ask your question and allow lots of time for the story.
- At other times ask some questions in a way that he can make a choice, and honor his choice.

Thanks to Sue Hansen,
Suggestion Circle from Bellevue, Washington

265. My child was frightened when she saw a scary ghost on TV and said, "It won't come out of the TV, will it, Mommy?"

- Say, "No, it won't."
- Turn off the TV and talk about it.
- Say, "You're right, it won't come out of the TV. Some things are pretend, aren't they?"
- Say, "What you saw on TV was either made by people using machines or a person covered up by a sheet."
- Borrow or rent a VCR and camera, and let your child see herself on screen.
- Let her play ghost with a sheet if she wishes.
- Say, "When you see scary things in books or TV, you can come and ask me about them."
- Tell your child about pretend things that scared you when you were little.
- Tell her "No, it's pretend just like when you play dress-up or spacewoman."
- It's normal for kids this age to be confused about what's real and what isn't. So hang in there and be ready to answer a lot of questions like this.

Thanks to Carole Gesme,
Suggestion Circle from Wayzata, Minnesota

266. How much time is OK for a four-year-old to spend watching TV?

- Watch TV about as often as you go out to a movie. Turn it on only as a special activity to do with your family.

- Screen the content beforehand. Know why you are turning the TV on.

- Read *The New Read-Aloud Handbook,* by Jim Trelease. It tells parents how to help kids watch less TV and do more reading. (See "Resources.")

- None.

- Read *The Berenstain Bears and Too Much TV,* by the Berenstains, to your child. (See "Resources.")

- Select two quality shows that your child is allowed to watch regularly ("Sesame Street," cartoons, "Mister Rogers").

- Read Carlsson-Paige and Levin's *Who's Calling the Shots?* (See "Resources.")

- Decide how much TV you enjoy watching with your child, and let that be the determining amount.

- Dramatizations and cartoons should be monitored before age seven. Preschoolers are still working on separating fantasy from reality.

- You are in charge of the TV for your child. It is not in charge of you.

  (See also question 265.)

Thanks to Mary Paananen,
Suggestion Circle from Seattle, Washington

267. My four-and-a-half-year-old thinks our divorce is her fault. What should I say?

- Say, "No, the divorce is not your fault. Mom and Dad have different ideas about how to live, and since we cannot agree on these, we choose to live apart."

- Tell your child, "When Dad and I married, we thought we would be together all of your life. Now we don't want to be together. We both love you, and our love for you won't change."

- Say, "You might feel that our divorce was caused by you or things you have done. It was not."

- Encourage your child to talk about what she believes she did wrong to cause the divorce. Listen to her and reassure her that nobody is good all the time and that children do not cause divorces.

- Say, "Divorces are between big people. Little people do not cause them."

- Touch her often and hold her close.

- Say, "My love for your father is one thing. A mother's love for her child is different. I can stop loving your father and keep on loving you."

- Give her the affirmation "You can learn what is pretend and what is real. What is real is that adults decide about divorce. Kids do not." (See "Affirmations for Growth—Power and Identity.")

Thanks to Ellen Peterson,
Suggestion Circle from Lafayette, California

268. What do I say to my three-year-old when he asks, "Where is Daddy?" He died when my son was eight months old.

- Talk with him about his dad as often as he needs to.

- Make sure you don't give more information than your child is asking for.

- Create a special book for him about his dad with pictures and any other reminders that he may keep with him and look at whenever he wants.

- Listen for his sadness and his anger, and affirm his right to his feelings.

- Tell him the same stories about his dad over and over again, and add details as he gets older and understands more.

- Read *The Dead Bird*, by Margaret Brown, a simple and beautifully written story about some children's experience when they find a dead bird in the woods. (See "Resources.")

- Cry with him!

- *Talking About Death*, by Earl Grollman, is a book about how to discuss dying with children.

- My father died when I was three, and I wish my mother had talked about him—the little things he liked, his ideas, and what he hoped for me.

- Say, "I loved your Dad. I love you, too."

Thanks to Mary Paananen,
Suggestion Circle from Seattle, Washington

269. My daughter is shy and dreads show-and-tell at school. What do I do?

- Role-play the situation with her.

- Point out the things she does well.

- Send a note to the teacher asking for ideas on how to cope with the shyness.

- Invite classmates home to play.

- Read *The Shy Child*, by Zimbardo and Radl. (See "Resources.")

- Shy feelings are normal for kids this age. Unless it seems really extreme, accept her for doing and feeling what she needs to do and feel right now.

- Have puppet shows and plays with the family.

- Suggest she wear her most comfortable or special clothing.

- Sit down together and brainstorm. Listen to her solutions.

- Tell about times when you feel shy and what things you do, like going with a friend or watching until you feel comfortable.

- Suggest she skip it for a few weeks.

- Don't feel obligated to solve the problem for her.

- Give her the Being affirmations.

Thanks to Nat Houtz,
Suggestion Circle from Seattle, Washington

270. How can I teach my five-year-old not to be greedy? What can I say to my child who has been given a gift and thirty seconds later asks for something else new?

- Say, "OK, the toy you want costs five dollars. I'll help you figure out how you can earn the money."

- Say, "No."

- "I hear you, and I can't afford another one right now."

- "OK! Now I know what to get for your birthday."

- Ask him to think of something he wants that doesn't cost anything.

- Teach him how to say "thank-you" for the gift and that he is not to ask for more.

- Maybe he is trying to keep up with his friends. Be sure you and he take time for noncompetitive games. See the *Cooperative Sports and Games Book,* by Terry Orlick. (See "Resources.")

- Help your child appreciate his new toy. Ask him to tell you all the things he likes about it.

(See also question 313.)

Thanks to Mary Paananen,
Suggestion Circle from Seattle, Washington

271. How do you teach kids to think about feelings?

- Plan to share at dinner or family time one *feeling* about something you did during the day.

- Read books about feelings such as *Ellie's Day,* by Susan Conlin and Susan Levine Friedman. (See "Resources.")

- Give words to use: grumpy, tired, sad, joyful, lonely, or excited.

- Ask, "Where in your body do you feel that?"

- Practice saying with your children statements that tell the difference between "I think" and "I feel."

- Make a "feeling wheel" for each member of the family with a dial to point to how he or she is feeling from time to time.

- Talk with your children about their feelings and how they think others are feeling when certain things happen.

- Play this game: one person says the feeling word, and the other responds by making the face that expresses that feeling.

- Play Carole Gesme's *Ups and Downs with Feelings* games. (See "Other Learning Materials Available.")

- Let your child know that all feelings are OK to have.

- Tell stories about how you felt and what you did when you were small.

- Read the chapter about three- to six-year-olds in Clarke's *Self-Esteem: A Family Affair*. (See "Resources.")

Thanks to Elizabeth Crary,
Suggestion Circle from Seattle, Washington

272. How can I help my four-year-old daughter learn to solve problems?

- Kids this age solve lots of problems every day (what clothes to wear, what to play next, and so on). Catch your daughter doing this well, and remind her of this when she begins to solve her next problem.

- Sometimes problems need to be divided into pieces. Show her how to do this.

- Tell her that problem solving takes practice, just like skating and bike riding. Assure her that you love her and will be there if she needs to check things out.

- Read Elizabeth Crary's series of books on solving problems. (See "Resources.")

- Play the game that poses problems for kids: "What would you do if a raccoon walked into the kitchen right now?" "What are three ways to get to the park?"

- Talk out loud as you solve a problem, so she can hear you work through it.

- If she likes to draw, ask her to draw the problem and all possible solutions on paper.

- Walk through the situation yourself, using familiar objects to practice. This will let her see the choices that might be possible or not possible.

- Don't rush in and solve all her problems. Wait and say, "You can solve this problem. I will help you think of ways, if you need me."

Thanks to Mary Paananen,
Suggestion Circle from Seattle, Washington

273. What should I do about a three-year-old who has an interest in guns? I am not comfortable with it.

- Do not make an issue of it; it will pass with time.

- Talk with your child about his interest. Let him know you are not comfortable with gun play.

- It may not be an issue of violence but of budding power.

- Establish rules of gun play—such as no pointing at people, only at pretend monsters.

- Set limits such as "No gun play in the house—gun play outside only."

- Only buy squirt guns, and only let him play with them outside.

- Explain your feelings, and tell him how guns are used safely for sports.

- Children are not small adults. My son, who now demonstrates for peace, played with war toys as a child.

- It is the job of the adult to make sure all play is safe.

- I am a war veteran, and I am comfortable with pretend or homemade guns. I am against real war, and I share my values with my kids.

- Read *Who's Calling the Shots,* by Nancy Carlsson-Paige and Diane E. Levin, or read *Creating a Peace Experience,* by Mary Joan Park. (See "Resources.")

- Provide other ways for your child to express fear, concern, and anger and to feel powerful. It's OK to talk about feelings.

- It is OK not to buy him guns or allow others to buy guns for him.

Thanks to Pam McElmeel,
Suggestion Circle from Seattle, Washington

Chapter 34

Behavior Problems

274. My son talks all day. How can I get him to stop when I need to do something else? We have new twins.

- Give him a tape recorder to play with.

- Let him know he can play with a toy now, and talk about it later.

- Tell him you will have special time just for him. Set the timer so you remember, and when it rings, let him chatter on and on while you listen attentively.

- Let him sit on your lap for five minutes of attention, while you do what you are doing.

- Clearly tell him what he is going to do next. Prepare him as much as you can.

- Show him a talking place—a chair with a bear to talk to, or a box, or someplace where he can go tell his story, if he has a burning desire to do so.

- Say, "This is my time to talk. You may stay close by." Stick to it.

- Realize that this will pass. Kids this age need to ask a lot of questions. Include him in conversation whenever you can.

- Sometimes give your child total attention. Other times say, "I'm doing something else now, but I can partly listen to you."

- You are responsible for teaching him when to talk and when not to. He is responsible for his feelings. Encourage him not to feel hurt when you stop him from talking.

Thanks to Sue Hansen,
Suggestion Circle from Bellevue, Washington

275. My five-year-old colors on the walls. She does it secretly while I am caring for the baby. What can I do?

- The coloring may be her way of acting out about something else. Ask her to talk about her feelings about the new baby. Accept her feelings and suggest ways for her to deal with them.

- Set up a coloring mural on one wall in the house. Show it to people and brag about her coloring on it.

- Control the crayons. She can earn the right to use them again by using them properly.

- Expect the child to help clean the wall.

- Get a sitter for the baby, and you and your daughter have an afternoon doing what she wants to do.

- Be sure to spend fifteen to twenty minutes every day with her in one-on-one time doing what she chooses to do, not what you think would be good for her.

- Tell her stories about when she was her little sister's age and how you cared for her.

- Offer to rock her and hold her.

- Tell her she does not need to do this to get your attention; then make sure you have periods of time alone with her.

- Put the crayons out of reach. Tell her they are to be used at the table only. Enforce that rule.

- Give her lots of love and the Being affirmations. (See "Developmental Affirmations for All Ages.")

Thanks to Carol Gesme,
Suggestion Circle from Anoka, Minnesota

276. How can I handle my four-and-a-half-year-old's terrible behavior? He seems to try to get me mad. He is worse every day, and I just don't understand because the baby is so easygoing.

- Give him lots of private time with you in which you give him lots and lots of positive attention.

- Let him know he can ask for special time with you. Give it as soon as you can.

- Say, "You don't need to do that to get my attention." Then be willing to pay attention when he asks for it.

- Make sure you don't start thinking of "our good child" and "our bad child." Honor the positive as well as the negative in both.

- Double up on affirmations for Being. Read Clarke's *Self-Esteem: A Family Affair.* (See "Resources.")

- Give him lots of physical touch—carrying, rocking, and massages.

- Give more three- to six-year-old affirmations for power.

- Read him *TA for Tots,* by Alvyn Freed. Read *Discipline,* by James Windell, for yourself. (See "Resources.")

- Talk to him about the things that have happened as a result of the baby's arrival. Also say, "Gee, the baby takes a lot of time right now, doesn't he?"

- Tell him it is all right to feel angry or jealous and that he is to use words to tell you his feelings.

Thanks to Susie Montgomery,
Suggestion Circle from Walnut Creek, California

277. My child whines about everything but especially when asked to play alone. What can I do?

- Give her lots of your attention at times when she is not whining or wanting something.

- Read *Your Three-Year-Old*, by Ames and Ilg. (See "Resources.")

- Have others compliment her for using words. You do this, too. Give her no response for whining.

- Tell her to use words instead of whining. When she does, give her a hug or a sticker.

- Like a broken record, tell her each time she whines, "I don't talk to whining girls," and then don't talk to her.

- Have a family conference and ask others how they feel about the whining. Make sure no one gives her attention for it until she stops the behavior.

- Set aside special time for her.

- Explain that you will not tolerate this. Use a chart and stars to record the days when she does not whine, and then take a trip to the zoo as a reward for improved behavior.

- Explain to her that everybody spends some time alone. Use a timer, and start with fifteen minutes of play by herself.

- Tell her, "I like it when you ask for what you want in your normal voice."

- Show her what you want by using a pleasant voice, and then ask her to do the same.

Thanks to Marilyn Grevstad,
Suggestion Circle from Seattle, Washington

278. My children, ages four and three, fight in the backseat of the car while I am driving until I am terribly distracted. How can I get them to stop?

- Stop the car at the first safe place. Say, "When you are ready to follow our rules about being quiet in the car, I will go on." This works best if they are going someplace interesting.

- If what the kids are doing is not dangerous, ignore them. Sing "The Wheels on the Bus Go Round and Round" or "Old MacDonald."

- Stop the car. Tell them you feel frustrated and distracted when they behave that way and that you cannot safely drive the car until they stop.

- At the end of the drive, give stickers for good behavior. Tell them beforehand.

- Put one child in the front seat and one in the back. We make a chart by weeks for who gets to sit in the front seat.

- Play tapes they will enjoy while traveling. "Sesame Street" tapes are good for this age.

- Have a car pack of toys they can use only while in the car.

- Play a "Can you see. . . ?" game.

Thanks to Deane Gradous,
Suggestion Circle from Saint Paul, Minnesota

279. What do I do about insulting back talk from my three-year-old child?

- Ignore it. It may take a while, but eventually she won't find it interesting.

- Discipline her for it. Remove a privilege for an hour.

- Tell her people who talk back sometimes end up without anyone to play with.

- Talk to her. Help her understand your feelings.

- Use time-out. (See the section entitled "Time-Out" in this book.)

- Tell her, "Say words I like to hear like, 'Mommy, you're adorable' or 'Mommy, you're courageous.'" Then fall on your knees and say thank you. Drama is sometimes effective.

- Show her how you want her to express her feelings without using back talk.

- Have a "play" back-talk time when she sits on a stool and talks back for five minutes.

- Tell her she is a kind person and that you will be glad when she has finished trying out back talk.

- Listen to find out whether others in the family talk back and get away with it. If they do, change that and back off your three-year-old.

(See also question 280.)

Thanks to Marilyn Grevstad,
Suggestion Circle from Seattle, Washington

280. How do I solve the problem of my three-year-old calling people "stupid idiot" in the grocery store?

- Listen to yourself and other family members. If any of the other family members use "stupid idiot," have them stop. Let the three-year-old see how the older person is learning to stop.

- Say, "You're important to me. It is hard for me to hear those words. I expect you to say, 'Hello,' instead."

- Tell him he doesn't have to like everyone, but he does have to be polite.

- Make a face at him to signal him to stop.

- Ignore it. You speak pleasantly to people so he will learn how.

- Play with words: "stupid, drupid, nupid, idiot, midiot, gid-iot." Turn it into a silly game.

- Say, "I'm surprised. I don't expect you to say mean things, and I am really sorry to hear this."

- Tell him that people like to be spoken to respectfully.

- Give him lots of positive response when he does communi-cate well.

- Help him find "angry" words that are acceptable in your family.

Thanks to Roxy Chuchna,
Suggestion Circle from Albert Lea, Minnesota

281. My five-year-old has picked up some "dirty" words and hand signals from a friend who has an older brother. She has been using them around our home.

- Ignore it.

- Say, "If you'd like to use bathroom talk, please go into the bathroom and close the door. I don't want to hear it."

- Use a star chart to mark the days she goes without using the words or hand signals.

- Show her some finger-play games to use instead.

- Say, "That is inappropriate for a child your age. Please don't use it."

- Tell her to try them out in her room but not in front of other people.

- Say that it is not appropriate for her. If her friend uses it, tell the friend she is not to do that when she is with you.

- Pay attention to the times when she doesn't do it, and reward her for not doing it.

- Better to ignore it completely.

- Teach her some new words to say instead.

- Explain to her that many people regard the use of these words and motions as insulting and that you are glad to talk with her about them so she won't use them.

Thanks to Sue Hansen,
Suggestion Circle from Bellevue, Washington

282. My four-year-old lies. How do I get him to stop?

- Explain why you don't want him to lie.

- Show him that you appreciate him when he tells the truth.

- Ignore the lies. He will watch you telling the truth and learn how to do that.

- When he says something that is not true, tell him you don't believe him.

- Give him a consequence for lying. Take away a privilege.

- Tell him you will be glad when he stops lying and that you expect him to stop soon.

- State that you know it is a lie and that he makes up good stories.

- Give him a hug when he tells the truth.

- Think about why he is lying. Is it to avoid discipline? If so, is the discipline too severe?

- Spend time making up a story together. Make sure that he understands that this is different from something that really happened.

- Ask him if what he is saying is pretend or real.

- Teach him the difference between a lie and a mistake made from having inaccurate information.

(See also question 264.)

Thanks to Suzanne Morgan,
Suggestion Circle from Albert Lea, Minnesota

283. When I tell my three-year-old to do something, she either says no or just doesn't do the task. What can I do?

- Get her attention by being close to her when you give the command.

- Use a time-out. (See "Time-Out.")

- Use eye-level communication.

- Let her know that you love her whether she says yes or no.

- Ignore bad behavior and emphasize good behavior.

- Give only one direction at a time.

- Don't hurry her.

- Ask her nicely. If you get no response, pick her up firmly and put her where you want her to be.

- Look at what you are asking her to do to be sure it is suitable for a three-year-old. (See "Ages and Stages.")

- Repeat the command so that it conveys the fact that there are no choices.

- Ask her to make a choice between two things you are willing for her to do.

- Be sure you are "telling" her. Don't "ask" unless no is an OK answer.

Thanks to Margie Black,
Suggestion Circle from Eden Prairie, Minnesota

284. What do I do when my three-year-old has a temper tantrum and goes out of control when told "no"?

- Sit with him in a rocking chair, hold him tight but don't hurt him, and say, "I'm not going to let go of you until you calm down."

- Sit on the floor with your back against the wall. Wrap your arms and legs around the child and say, "I'll hold you until you calm down."

- Kneel in front of him and say, "I am not afraid of your anger. I will not let you hurt yourself or anyone else."

- Take him by the shoulders, look him straight in the eye, and say, "I'm sorry but I won't allow you to act that way. That is unacceptable behavior in this house."

- Put him in a time-out corner. (See "Time-Out.")

- Give him Being affirmations. (See "Developmental Affirmations for All Ages.") At a calm time, make statements about grown-ups being in charge of this household.

- Watch and observe if this is happening at a particular time of day. If so, find some special activities for him to do at this time. Taking a bath can be relaxing.

Thanks to Jean Clarke,
Suggestion Circle from Wayzata, Minnesota

285. How do I keep my children with me while I'm shopping?

- Use a backpack or Snugli for one, and hold onto the other's hand.
- Allow plenty of time.
- Have them stay in or push a stroller.
- Tie a balloon to each one's wrist and ask them to keep the balloons near you.
- Do not go when the children are tired, hungry, or anxious.
- Trade baby-sitting with a friend so you can go alone sometimes.
- Keep shopping trips short.
- Discuss plans and expectations in advance.
- Take a toy along for each to carry.
- For staying with you, give them a box of animal crackers. If they don't stay, put the crackers back on the shelf.
- Put a sticker on each child's hand to remind them to stay close to you.
- Role-play before the trip. Practice good "shopping manners." Give rewards afterward.

Thanks to Mary Ellen O'Keefe,
Suggestion Circle from Bellevue, Washington

286. My three-year-old hits and shoves other children.

- When it happens, pick him up and take him to his room. Don't say, "Next time," or use other idle threats.
- Use a time-out. (See "Time-Out.")
- Say, "Be gentle."

- Ask him to watch how other children play and to try ways besides hitting and shoving.

- Tell him to use words when he is angry, and reward him when he does.

- Give him a big pillow to hit and shove.

- Show him specific ways to relate to another child. Say, "Give Nicky the toy," or "Jump with Danny."

- Give him extra loving at other times.

- Look him in the eye and say, "You are capable. You can find other ways to play."

- Tell him, "That doesn't work because other children learn to do it back."

Thanks to Marilyn Grevstad,
Suggestion Circle from Seattle, Washington

287. I need help dealing with a three-year-old girl who continually bites.

- Give her time-out periods! Four minutes or less. (See "Time-Out.")

- Have her bite a piece of fruit.

- Tell her she has to stop. Mean it. Don't smile or brag about how much she bites.

- Explain that this behavior is not appropriate. Ask her what she will do to help the person she has bitten to feel better.

- Consistently explain that biting hurts people, and we do not hurt other people. Keep with it. Don't hurt her.

- Give her lots of hugging. Tell her to ask for hugs instead of biting.

- Have her choose a toy or pillow to bite.

- Ask, "Would you like to be bitten?"
- If she starts to bite you, stop her immediately. Hold her tight (don't hurt her) while you say, "No biting!"
- Give her clear "I" messages about how you feel when she bites you.
- Tell her "I love you, and I will not let you hurt me or other people."
- Teach her to kiss instead.
- Evaluate her schedule and notice when she bites. Make changes to prevent opportunities for biting, if possible.

Thanks to Carole Gesme,
Suggestion Circle from Anoka, Minnesota

288. How can we get our child to mind without hitting him? He is stubborn.

- Stop hitting him; tell him you are stopping and that he will be minding words and looks from now on.
- When you tell him to do something, look him directly in the eye and say, "I expect. . . " Have clear, definite expectations!
- Try giving your child more specific information about what you want him to do.
- Allow him to do things his own way whenever possible.
- Honor his no when it is appropriate.
- Do not give a choice when there is no choice. When there is a choice say, "Do you want to. . . ?" And honor his no if he says no.
- Explain reason and expectation and consequence.

- Define your family as a team, and tell him about his part in it.

- Teach him about times when it is important to be "stubborn" or tenacious.

- Look in his eyes at a quiet time and say, "I love you. I want to spend time having fun together. I'm not going to hit anymore."

Thanks to Mary Paananen,
Suggestion Circle from Seattle, Washington

Chapter 35

Brothers, Sisters, and Other Kids

289. I feel like a judge. I have a four-year-old and a seven-year-old. When I haven't seen the incident, how can I evaluate it when one comes to me and says she's been hurt?

- Listen to each separately.

- Tell them you will help each child file a written complaint for you to consider. Write down what they dictate. Giving attention to each usually diffuses the anger.

- Read the book *Siblings Without Rivalry*, by Adele Faber. (See "Resources.")

- You can't.

- Read Ames and Haber's *He Hit Me First*. It is about sibling rivalry and helped me learn that I didn't have to be the referee at certain ages. (See "Resources.")

- Explain that you did not see the incident so you cannot judge.

- Check to see if she is hurt and care for her. Don't talk about the other child.

- Ask, "What do you want me to do?" Be clear and definite about what you will and will not do.

- Listen to her report without evaluating. Say, "Thanks for letting me know how this incident looks to you."

- Don't try to be fair because you can't; children will expect it if you try.

(See also questions 276, 286, and 291.)

Thanks to Joanie Mack,
Suggestion Circle from Everett, Washington

290. How should I answer my child when he asks, "Do you love me or my sister the best?"

- Take your son on your lap and say, "I love you both very much. I don't think about loving one of you the best." Then look inside yourself to be sure that this is true.

- "You are my favorite four-year-old son, and no one can take your place. I love you."

- Give him all the Being affirmations. (See "Developmental Affirmations for All Ages.")

- Don't say, "I love you both the same," because each love affair is different.

- Hug him, rumple or tickle him a little, and say, "I have plenty of love for you both!"

- Say, "I don't love anyone 'the best.' Here is what I love about you. I love you because you are my son, I love the way you. . . ."

- Say, "I have a huge barrel full of love for each of you, and lots more empty barrels for when those run over."

- Say, "I love you both. You do some things better, and she does some things better, and that has nothing to do with my love."

- Say, "That question does not have an answer. Do you want me to read you a story?"

Thanks to Gail Nordeman,
Suggestion Circle from Cincinnati, Ohio

291. How can I handle teasing between my children?

- Find something that the two who are teasing can work on together as partners in a cooperative activity, like building a tent.

- Listen. If you decide the teasing is a way of having some fun or to establish position, allow it. Stop teasing that's vicious.

- Separate them.

- Read *Kids Can Cooperate*, by Elizabeth Crary. (See "Resources.")

- Establish rules about teasing for the whole family.

- Don't be a referee.

- Give your children words they may use when they are teased, such as "No one in my family is stupid."

- If their behavior is destructive, intervene.

- Read them the *Warm Fuzzy Tale*, by Claude Steiner, and ask them to give each other warm fuzzies. (See "Resources.")

- Remove yourself so they don't have an audience.

- Be sure you don't tease them.

- Young children can take time out to think. Help each of your children identify the feelings they are having.

- It's OK to stop the teasing when you've had it. Take care of yourself.

Thanks to Gail Davenport,
Suggestion Circle from Lynnwood, Washington

292. My three-and-a-half-year-old boy picks on his eighteen-month-old sister. What am I doing wrong?

- Don't waste time feeling guilty. Show him what you want him to do instead.

- Nothing, unless one of them is getting hurt. Give your son extra loving and Being messages. (See "Developmental Affirmations for All Ages.")

- Are you expecting yourself to be a "perfect mom with perfect kids"? If so, stop. It is too great a burden on the kids. Get help if you need it.

- Get time for yourself. These exploring years are demanding on the parent.

- Your daughter may be bugging her brother for attention. It takes two to tango.

- Your son is just learning how to play with others. Up until this point, most of his play has been parallel play. You can't expect them to be wonderful playmates at this age.

- Ask each of them, "What do you want from me?" and trust them to establish a relationship that is right for them.

- Make a place for your son's things where your daughter can't get into them.

(See also questions 286, 289.)

Thanks to Marilyn Grevstad,
Suggestion Circle from Seattle, Washington

293. What do I do when my children threaten or hit each other and me?

- You are responsible for a safe environment. You decide when to step in and when to keep out.

- Make sure that you and other adults are not using threats around them.

- Interrupt and offer a toy from your emergency toy box, or a snack, or a walk.

- Help your kids make a list of things to do instead of hitting.

- Tell them, "It's OK to be angry but not OK to hit."

- For threats to you, pick up the one who is threatening, give hugs and kisses, and say, "Threats don't work with me. Ask for what you want."

- Say, "Stop your threats. This is not television. Work it out."

- Don't listen to the threats. Don't respond positively or negatively.

- Close your eyes and visualize your children having fun together.

- Acknowledge their anger and help them find safe ways to express it. Hold a pillow for them to hit, provide a *big* piece of paper with bright paint for painting, or let them hit a stool with a ruler.

- Don't blame yourself. Children this age are testing their physical and verbal power.

Thanks to Samara Kemp,
Suggestion Circle from Modesto, California

294. Our four-year-old doesn't like anyone except one child in preschool. What do I say when he says to other kids, "I don't like you"?

- Explain that it is OK to feel that way and that he can keep it to himself or tell you.

- Ignore it. This may have more to do with words than feelings.

- Say, "I like you" to the kid he rejected and "I like you, too," to your son.

- Don't say, "You don't really mean that" because he may.

- I know how you feel. It sounds awful when your child says, "I don't like you." Remind yourself that he is testing out his own power and that this is a developmental stage.

- Tell him he's important and you love him. Let him have the consequences from other children, and help him see his part in them.

- Ask the teacher for suggestions. She knows the kids.

- Remember when you were this age? I loved someone one minute and hated him or her the next.

- Don't say, "Tell him you're sorry you said that," because if he isn't, it teaches him to be dishonest about his feelings.

Thanks to Maggie Lawrence,
Suggestion Circle from Edmonds, Washington

295. My five-year-old's best friend doesn't like her anymore. How can I help her?

- Give her lots of hugs.

- Listen to her.

- Don't try to make the hurt go away. It hurts to lose a friend. She will learn to handle it.

- Honor her feelings and yours. You may want your child's life always to be smooth, but it can't be.

- Make her some lemonade. Invite some kids over, if she wishes.

- Tell her you love her.

- Don't hurry her. Let her take time to get over this.

- Draw the outline of her body on butcher paper, and have the family write inside the outline the things they like about her.

- Don't make it worse than it is. The friend may be back tomorrow.

Thanks to Deane Gradous,
Suggestion Circle from Wayzata, Minnesota

Chapter 36

Not Again!
Toddlerhood Revisited

296. How can I keep my three-year-old daughter in bed at bedtime?

- Give her a choice of three things she can do in bed, such as read books, sing, or listen to tapes.

- Perhaps she is not tired enough yet. Examine your bedtime hour, and decide if you need to make it half an hour later.

- Let her know you love her and that you are in charge of bedtime, not that you are gearing up for a struggle.

- Keep a light on in the hall.

- Ask her what she needs to stay in bed.

- Keep putting her immediately back in bed over and over, firmly but gently. No talk and no fun.

- Don't spring a new bedtime plan on her at night. Tell her in the morning.

- As long as she stays in her room, don't insist that she stay in bed. You can move her into bed later.

- Get her a new sleeping bag to sleep in.

- Cut down on daytime naps.

- Try some vigorous outdoor exercise in the late afternoon and then quiet time before bed.

- Have her checked for allergies. Our daughter got up until we took out the feathers and wool.

Thanks to Darlene Montz,
Suggestion Circle from Yakima, Washington

297. My three-year-old child gets up during the night and interrupts our sleep.

- Pick him up—no words, no payoff, no anger—and put him back in bed.

- Let him sleep with you or in your room in a sleeping bag.

- During the day ask him what might help him get himself back to sleep—teddy bear, music, and so on—and make a plan with him.

- Tell him when he *can* come to your bed—in the morning, for example.

- Give him time to talk about nightmares and fears.

- Tell him what you expect: "You will stay in bed and if you wake, you will turn over and go back to sleep."

- Let the child turn on the light in his room and look at books by himself during the night, but make it clear he cannot come to your room.

- Have the less angry parent deal with it. Your anger reinforces his behavior.

- Have the more annoyed parent deal with it. He or she will be firmer and end it sooner.

- Take him back to bed and lie down with him for a few minutes.

Thanks to Ellen Peterson,
Suggestion Circle from Walnut Creek, California

298. My three-year-old is wetting her pants again. She was trained before the baby came. What can I do?

- We've been that route. Put her in diapers for now. For my child, this only lasted two weeks.

- Carry a change of clothes.

- Remind her to go to the bathroom, or take her every so often.

- Give her a treat when she goes to the bathroom or stays dry.

- Continue to use rubber sheets.

- Be sure she has alone time with you without the baby along.

- Let it be. It's a trauma for the child to have a new family member.

- Tell the child she can feel when she has to go to the bathroom, and she can ask you to go with her. There is plenty of time to go.

- Ask if she wants diapers again. If so, let her wear them.

- Give her lots of love and Being affirmations. (See "Developmental Affirmations for All Ages.")

- Put up a sign that says, "This, too, will pass."

- Listen to the tape *Is My Baby OK? Toilet Training*, by Josi Alexander et al. (See "Resources.")

Thanks to Judi Salts,
Suggestion Circle from Yakima, Washington

299. My four-year-old occasionally wets his pants and the bed. What should I do?

- Keep track of the circumstances when the accidents happen. Are the accidents happening when your child is feeling stressed? If so, do something to reduce the stress.

- Rule out any medical issues.

- Have him wear clothing he can manage easily himself.

- Remind him to go to the toilet just before bedtime.

- You know your child. Don't listen to people who say, "He should be trained by now."

- Know that when he is ready, he will stay dry. Put diapers on him at night.

- When he wets, help him calmly get into dry clothes.

- This goes away by itself with maturation.

- Talk about how he can wake up at night and go by himself. Reassure him that you will help him if he wants it.

- Don't worry about the night at all. This is not considered at all abnormal until after children are six years old. Ask your doctor about sphincter exercises. They are simple and they work.

Thanks to Judy Popp,
Suggestion Circle from Yakima, Washington

300. We were on vacation and returned to find our three-and-a-half-year-old talking baby talk again. How can I get her to speak as well as I know she can?

- Expect your child to regress a bit when you go away. It's her way of handling a difficult situation.

- Don't blame yourself.

- Tell her you are glad she is your daughter. Give her lots of Being affirmations. (See "Developmental Affirmations for All Ages.")
- Spend ten minutes with her every day doing whatever she wants.
- Give her some extra attention when she isn't talking baby talk.
- Tell her to speak clearly and that you will not respond to her baby talk. Follow through.
- Say you don't understand her. Ask her to repeat what she is saying in words you can understand.
- Don't worry about it. You know she is capable of speaking well. She will do so again when she is ready.
- It is common for three-year-olds to experiment with speech. They like to try baby talk and silly talk. Listen for ways you can join her in making a game of it.

Thanks to Deane Gradous,
Suggestion Circle from Minnetonka, Minnesota

Chapter 37

Responsibility

301. My three-and-a-half-year-old is very slow in dressing herself, and sometimes it is easier to dress her myself. I want to reward her for finishing on time, and I need some ideas.

- Reward her with special attention time. Read her a story, play with her, sing songs, go for a bird-watching walk, blow bubbles together.

- Consider what time of day it is. For instance, if it is early, you could give her a choice for breakfast.

- Don't set up dressing to be hassle time.

- Make sure her clothes are easy to put on.

- Expect your three-year-old to dawdle because she has so many things to find out about while she's dressing.

- Break her dressing into small parts with a raisin or Cheerio reward for each part completed.

- Set the timer and when it rings, you finish dressing her, gently but firmly.

- Relax and use this time as a special, unhurried time between you two to listen and talk to each other.

- Some days she just may not feel up to dressing herself. You won't ruin her if you dress her.

- Let her choose her own clothes.

- On days when it's important to you to get out of the house fast, just dress her.

- I ask my daughter each morning who she wants to dress her, and I allow her to pick out her clothes. I let her know the time limits.

> *Thanks to Melanie Weiss,*
> *Suggestion Circle from Bellevue, Washington*

302. How do I get my child to pick up his toys?

- Tell the child you will close your eyes and he can surprise you by picking up toys. Ask him to tell you when you can open your eyes for the surprise.

- Be direct, insist, and offer to help.

- Don't use "will you" or "would you" so he can say no. Say, "It's time to pick up your toys now."

- Choose a special record that you play only at pickup time.

- Read *Four Hundred One Ways to Get Your Kids to Work at Home*, by Bonnie McCullough and Susan Monson. (See "Resources.")

- Say, "I'll pick them up and keep them until tomorrow. If you pick them up, you can play with them again today if you wish."

- Divide the work, and help him. Let him know what he is to do and what you will do.

- Reward your child after he picks up by having everyone in the family clap and cheer.

- Get the toys picked up when the task is small. Don't wait until a million toys are strewn around.

- Read him the Berenstains' book entitled *The Berenstain Bears and the Messy Room*, and help him organize his toys. (See "Resources.")

- Rotate toys. Keep most of them hidden away. Bring a few out at a time. They will seem new and exciting, and there will be fewer to pick up.

Thanks to Mary Ellen O'Keefe,
Suggestion Circle from Bellevue, Washington

303. My four-and-a-half-year-old has three tasks to do after breakfast: dress, brush her teeth, and feed the cat. But she doesn't do them. Rewarding with a star doesn't work anymore. What can I do?

- Three things at one time may be too much for her. Give her one job at a time.

- Ask the child what she wants for a reward.

- Give her ample time, and praise her for each small step.

- Change to a new reward system. Try a new kind of sticker, the use of a new toy, or an art project.

- After breakfast, ring a bell for chore time.

- Give occasional rewards. Too many rewards lose their effectiveness.

- Establish six tasks and rotate three for each week. Let her pick the three.

- Don't expect her to do it perfectly.

- Tell her she is capable of doing the task, and tell her when you want it done.

- Establish a chore list for each member of the family, and let her see how different people handle their responsibilities.

Thanks to Gail Davenport,
Suggestion Circle from Lynnwood, Washington

304. My three- and six-year-olds are yelling at and hitting the dog. What should I do?

- Make sure you or other adults aren't yelling and hitting your children. Model gentleness.

- Your kids are learning about power. Give them dog-care responsibilities: feeding the dog, walking him, or letting him in and out.

- Watch with your children a TV program about a dog, and talk about how people on the show handle the dog.

- Say, "Dogs are living beings and shouldn't be hit."

- If you yell at or hit the dog, expect your kids to do the same.

- Compliment them when they are kind to the dog.

- Show and tell them exactly how you want them to interact with the dog.

- Keep them apart for now.

- Go to a dog-training class, and teach your children what you learn.

- Play dog with your kids. Take turns being dog and master, so they know how it feels to be a dog.

- Don't let the kids hurt the dog. Set limits and hold to them.

Thanks to Gail Davenport,
Suggestion Circle from Lynnwood, Washington

305. What can I do about my five-and-a-half-year-old who "forgets" her backpack regularly for school?

- Help her make a picture list of the stuff she needs for school, and post it on the door.

- The night before, have her put her backpack by the door.

- You are making her problem yours. Keep out of it.
- Ask her if she really needs to carry her backpack to school.
- Speak about the backpack when you and she are feeling great, rather than in the morning when you are in a hurry.
- Say, "Remembering your school things is your responsibility. I will not be taking them to school for you." Stick to it.
- Ask her if she wants help in remembering and what kind of help she needs.

Thanks to Ellen Peterson,
Suggestion Circle from Walnut Creek, California

306. Our four-year-old daughter will be a flower girl in a wedding. What can I do to help her?

- Have a written time schedule for you to follow, and have a place for her to play a quiet game till just before her part.
- Play wedding beforehand with veil, wedding march, and bouquet so she knows what to expect. Let her play different roles.
- Remember, she doesn't have to be perfect. People will love her anyway.
- Invent a signal system with her so she can look to you for a signal if she needs reassurance.
- Put a quarter where your little girl is to stand. When the ceremony is over, she can have the quarter.
- Put Cheerios in the basket for her to eat during the ceremony.
- Be sure she is included in the rehearsal, and walk her through it several times.

- Enjoy it with her; she'll be wonderful.

Thanks to Marilyn Grevstad,
Suggestion Circle from Seattle, Washington

307. How can I encourage my kids to be cautious of strangers without being fearful of strangers?

- Make a rule like "If you don't know the person, come and ask Mom or Dad about them."

- Start talking now about the good or bad *qualities* of people, rather than good or bad people.

- Since some children are shy and some are outgoing, make rules that fit each child.

- Role-play with them different situations and what they would do and how they would feel. Don't overdo it.

- Teach them, if lost, to find a cash register and ask the person there to help them. Walk them through it.

- Discuss out loud how you as an adult look at strangers and how you check with your feelings to decide whether you can trust them.

- Get some good books for kids on this subject: *Private Zone*, by Frances Dayee; *Safety Zone*, by Linda Meyer; *Jenny's New Game*, by Laurella Cross; and *It's My Body*, by Lory Freeman. Remember this lesson takes time to learn. They won't learn it overnight. (See "Resources.")

- Look at this as another "safety rule" that we teach our children, just as we teach them about "safety rules" in crossing the street.

(See also question 327.)

Thanks to Christine Ternand,
Suggestion Circle from Minneapolis, Minnesota

Chapter 38

Coping with Special Stresses

308. Since her father left last month, my four-year-old resists bedtime. How can I avoid threats and help her at bedtime?

- In the morning say, "Tonight I will read you two stories at bedtime and kiss you good night." Then do it and leave her room.

- Realize that this time is emotionally difficult for your child as well as for you. Give her extra hugs at night. Rock her if she likes.

- Let her know that however she feels about the absence of her father is OK.

- Rock her and sing the Being affirmations. (See "Developmental Affirmations for All Ages.")

- Encourage her to watch "Mister Rogers" on TV.

- Reassure her that you will not leave.

- See if she wants her door open, and let her have a night-light.

- Instead of sending her off to bed, you put her to bed.

- Don't threaten. Talk gently and carry her to bed.

- Go to a Parents Without Partners meeting and ask how other parents have handled this. (For information, write: Parents Without Partners, Inc., 7910 Woodmount Avenue, Bethesda, MD 20614.)

- Lie down beside her and read a story.
- Set the bedtime and tell her, "In fifteen minutes we will start your bedtime routine." Then do it in fifteen minutes.

Thanks to Margot Tobias,
Suggestion Circle from Walnut Creek, California

309. My child doesn't want to go to preschool without me. What can I do?

- Play out this school situation with him, using small figures of people, to familiarize him with the routine.
- Join a car pool so he can be friends with the other children.
- Ask him what special things he would like to do in preschool. Try to arrange it.
- Observe the preschool to find possible reasons for his not wanting to go.
- Talk to him about how he feels, and let him know you believe he can handle preschool.
- If you can, try a different preschool.
- Give him lots of recognition and encouragement.
- Have some of his school friends over to your house to play.
- Consider the possibility that he may not be ready for preschool.
- If he *has* to go because you need him cared for at that time, tell him.
- Many three-year-olds kick up a fuss but play quite happily once Mother is out of sight.

(See also "Preparing Your Child for Grade School.")

Thanks to Ellen Peterson,
Suggestion Circle from Walnut Creek, California

310. What do I do when my child comes home from preschool wiped out, has tantrums, screams, or is demanding?

- Be ready for her when she comes. Give her your attention without putting any demands on her for ten minutes.

- Your daughter may just be learning how to make transitions. Give her time.

- Pick her up at school, and make the ride home a nice transition time, with soothing music and pleasant talk.

- Rock her and sing to her, or lie down for a short rest time together.

- Let the tantrum run its course, and when it's over, offer to rock her.

- You could check out the possibility of abuse. Ask other parents if their children also have behavior problems. (See "Signs of Abuse and Neglect.")

- Don't make demands of someone in a rebellious state. It won't work.

- Hug her and say, "I'm glad to see you."

- Consider cutting down on the number of days she attends school for now.

- Maybe the experience is too demanding. Read David Elkind's book, *The Hurried Child*. (See "Resources.")

- Meet her with food.

- Shorten the length of time she is at preschool, if you can.

  (See also "Ages and Stages.")

Thanks to Nat Houtz,
Suggestion Circle from Lacey, Washington

311. My three-and-a-half-year-old throws tantrums when we come to get him after he has been playing at someone's house.

- Prearrange a departure routine. For example, put on his sweater and have him say good-bye to the dog.

- Say, "Wow, I'm glad you had a good time. Let's figure out when we can do it again." Make a date before leaving.

- Call ten minutes before to give him the "ten-minute get-ready" warning.

- Have someone else pick him up for you.

- Hug him and say, "I'm glad to see you."

- At another time, ask him what he needs in order to come home easily.

- Allow him to assert his independence in this way.

- Acknowledge his feelings about not wanting to leave.

- Set time limits for the fussing. Then pick him up and go.

- Visualize a good experience. See Clarke's *Self-Esteem: A Family Affair* for ideas about visualization. (See "Resources.")

- Allow time to play with him there.

- Remind yourself that this is a sign that he feels safe expressing his emotions with you.

- Ignore the screaming, make sure he's safe, and know that this behavior is common for kids this age.

Thanks to Ellen Peterson,
Suggestion Circle from Walnut Creek, California

312. How can I prepare my kids to go somewhere without getting hassled?

- Give them a warning, "We're leaving in ten minutes." Then when it's time, announce, "We're leaving." Honor your word to leave when you say you will.

- Say, "I'm starting to get ready," and then have a race with them to see who can be ready first.

- The night before, have them choose and take out the clothes they will wear and get their belongings ready.

- Give them a warning prior to leaving. Set consequences, and when the timer dings, follow through.

- Relax. It's OK to be late sometimes. Kids this age dawdle.

- Getting ready may have lots of parts. Help the children identify the parts; then reward them for accomplishing each one.

- Give them a reward if they are ready early.

- Allow lots of time for yourself to get ready.

- If they are not ready when it is time to go to preschool, take them in pajamas with their clothes in a sack.

- Make a rule that they are not to leave their room in the morning until they are dressed.

- Be calm.

- Visualize your children being ready on time.

Thanks to Sue Hansen,
Suggestion Circle from Bellevue, Washington

313. My son leaves a store yelling and screaming because he wanted all the items he saw. What can I do?

- Tell him no, ignore the screaming, and leave.

- Before going, tell him, "I have this much to spend on you today."

- Give him a piggy bank and pennies to save for the store.

- Before you go, tell him matter-of-factly about something specific that *you* want that you will not be getting.

- Make sure it's a good time to go to the store—that is, when neither of you is tired, hungry, or emotionally drained.

- Prepare him in the car by telling him what items you will be looking for, and tell him what behavior you expect from him.

- While at the store, make a wish list to have for special occasions and birthdays.

- Be consistent about times when he gets to choose items and when he doesn't, and decide before you go into the store.

- Say, "I choose not to buy that for you right now."

- Don't take him with you. Get someone to watch him.

- Remind yourself that the media bombard all of us with messages to buy more.

(See also question 270.)

Thanks to Pearl Noreen,
Suggestion Circle from Seattle, Washington

Chapter 39

Picky Eaters

314. I have a four-year-old who eats very slowly. What can I do about it?

- Let him time himself with a stopwatch, and try to reduce his time each day.

- Give him very small portions (one teaspoon) to begin with. If he's still hungry, he will ask for more.

- Have him serve himself. Accept his choices.

- Don't let him snack close to dinnertime.

- Honor his pace and say, "When you have had enough, you may take your plate to the sink."

- Research shows that slow eaters are much less likely to have weight problems.

- Some children are slow eaters. If he seems to enjoy his meal, even though he eats slowly, allow him the time to do so.

- Consider whether you need to be together as a family at mealtime. See if having him eat separately makes it easier for him to attend to eating.

- Give him a head start. Offer him something to nibble prior to dinner so part of his eating is done before you start.

- When *you* are done, excuse yourself and let him finish.

- Drop your membership in the "Clean-Your-Plate Club," and when others are through, take his plate whether he's finished or not.

Thanks to Betty Beach,
Suggestion Circle from Minnetonka, Minnesota

315. My child does not eat at the evening meal. I am worried about her nutrition. What can I do?

- Have fun things to eat with, like a huge spoon or tongs.

- Remember that many children eat in cycles at this age—a month of eating well and a month of eating like a bird.

- Put an array of healthy food on a buffet; then let her serve herself and eat what she wants.

- Don't worry. She can get what she needs from breakfast and lunch.

- Invite the child to help you cook, and offer her tastes as you go.

- Routinely prepare a vegetable or fruit snack one and a half hours before dinner, and then don't allow her to eat after that until dinner.

- No snacks between lunch and dinner. Hunger is your best ally.

- Have dinnertime when she needs it (at her own time, not necessarily the rest of the family's).

- Do not allow toys at the table.

- Don't fix special food just for her.

- Let her help plan some menus. Teach her to include a protein, vegetable, and starch.

- Examine the atmosphere at the dinner table. Is it enjoyable for her?

Thanks to Marilyn Grevstad,
Suggestion Circle from Seattle, Washington

316. How can I get my children to stay at the dinner table?

- Use a special plate that means "You're the Special Person of the Day."

- Let the children choose what they want to eat (within reasonable limits).

- Evaluate your mealtime. Is it when the children aren't hungry or are so tired they can't concentrate?

- Have "special" dinners (perhaps foods from other countries), and include the children in preparing table decorations—specially folded napkins, place cards, and so on.

- Tell them when they leave the table that they are finished eating. No more food till breakfast.

- Make sure they have comfortable chairs where they can see what's going on.

- Play "restaurant" in which you use your best table manners, dress up, and set out good dishes.

- It's impossible for most kids to sit still for very long.

- Serve food in muffin tins or on doll dishes.

- Why is it important to you? Tell your child why.

Thanks to Marilyn Grevstad,
Suggestion Circle from Seattle, Washington

317. My child is always asking for candy, and I don't want her to have very much of it. What can I do?

- On Saturday, let her choose three pieces from a jar of candy, and make it clear that Saturday is the only day you will give her candy.

- Don't buy it. Say no. It's OK for her to be angry if she wants to.

- Buy individually wrapped snacks like cheese cubes. Part of the fun of candy is opening little packages.

- Ask your dentist to talk with her and use visual aids.

- At the store, let her choose her favorite nonsugar snacks for the week.

- Tell her what you know about sugar. List the effects.

- Don't let her watch TV! It is loaded with candy advertisements.

- Together, make nutritious snacks like whole-grain cookies with raisins, granola bars, or yogurt Popsicles.

- Tell her, "We don't have or eat candy in our house." Be sure you follow that rule, too.

- Say, "I'd be glad to buy you stickers instead of candy."

- Give her hugs instead.

Thanks to Melanie Weiss,
Suggestion Circle from Bellevue, Washington

318. My five-and-a-half-year-old declares himself a vegetarian for a week every once in a while. What should I do?

- This is a personal preference issue. Meat is not the only source of protein. Check out other high-protein foods.

- If it makes you feel better, make sure he takes vitamins.

- Read John Robbins's *Diet for a New America,* and offer him lots of fresh fruits and vegetables. (See "Resources.")

- If he continues to be a vegetarian for longer than one or two weeks, check out his diet with your doctor or a dietitian. Growing children may need supplements not normally noted in vegetarian cookbooks.

- Listen to him. He's a smart kid! That's a healthy way to eat.

- Don't make an issue of it.

- Respect his ideas, and involve him in exploring different options or meal preparations.

- Use cashew butter, almond butter, and peanut butter.

- Think of him as trying out a new role—"Vegetarian."

Thanks to Becky Monson,
Suggestion Circle from Minnetonka, Minnesota

Chapter 40

Things to Do

319. What can I do with my preschooler on a rainy day?

- Get the book *Rainy Day Activities for Preschoolers,* by the Mercer Island Preschool Association. (See "Resources.")

- Don't resort to TV. Instead, develop a rainy-day routine. For example: "On rainy days we can wear pajamas till 11:00, then we have a picnic in the laundry room, then we go for an umbrella walk."

- Cook together; make fancy hors d'oeuvres.

- Keep a box of toys and art materials hidden away just for rainy days.

- Invite another preschooler over to play and get out a box of dress-up clothes. Anything will do, even cut-off pant legs or sleeves. Kids love being silly.

- For some part of the day say, "You know where your toys are. You decide what you will do while I read my book."

- Allow your child to play with water at the sink. Add food coloring or bubbles.

- Scrub the kitchen floor together.

- Take a trip to the library for books, records, and tapes. Then snuggle down together for listening time.

- Build spaceships with whatever—blocks, furniture, pillows, boxes, or blankets.
- Use real sewing things. You can sew together.

  (See also question 320.)

  Thanks to Carole Gesme,
  Suggestion Circle from Minneapolis, Minnesota

320. How can you keep three- and four-year-olds entertained and help them enjoy the ride when carpooling to preschool and back home?

- Plan the seating arrangement for peace! You decide.
- Play song and story tapes. (*Wee Sing and Play Book and Cassette*, by Beall and Nipp, is good.) Bring granola bars or grapes.
- Give stickers for good behavior.
- Play games: "I spy with my little eye," the alphabet game, rhyming words, "I'm thinking of . . . ," and so on.
- Sing or tell stories.
- Ask about jobs people do, the weather, seasons, holidays, or preschool events, and enjoy the children's answers. If there is a favorite seat, rotate who sits in it.
- Look for things: motorcycles, stop signs, water towers, fire hydrants, VW Bugs.
- Play Faires's *Sing Yes!* audiotapes, which offer affirmations set to music. (See "Resources.")

  Thanks to Gail Davenport,
  Suggestion Circle from Lynnwood, Washington

321. I will be driving across the country with my daughters, ages twenty-four months and four and a half years. I would like traveling tips.

- Attach a shoe bag to the backseat or some other part of the car. This is a handy place to store toys, snacks, and toddler training cups full of juice.

- Contact AAA to map a route with the rest stops marked.

- Take turns in different seats in the car. Rearrange the children and parents a couple of times each day.

- Take along a cassette recorder with story tapes for the children and a blank tape for recording your own sing-along.

- Give fruit for a snack. It's juicy and won't make the children thirsty like most other snacks.

- Gift wrap an assortment of small toys and activities. Open one periodically. They don't have to be new toys.

- Don't try to cover too many miles at once. Break the trip into short sections of travel each day, making frequent stops to get out and exercise.

- Try to arrange your seating so one adult can focus on one child.

- Cover an old record jacket with felt, and cut out felt pieces for the kids to stick on it.

(See also question 320.)

Thanks to Gail Davenport,
Suggestion Circle from Alderwood, Washington

322. How can I prepare my child for a move?

- Ask him to choose some favorite things to carry with him in his suitcase. Let him help pack the rest.

- Pack his things last.

- Help him say good-bye to his room, the kitchen, the yard, and so on.

- Read him the Berenstains' *The Berenstain Bears' Moving Day*. (See "Resources.")

- Tell him you love him, and give him lots of hugs. Attending to your child is more important than having things packed perfectly.

- Tell him why you are moving. Mark moving day on a big calendar.

- Get *Help for Kids! Understanding Your Feelings About Moving*, by Gesme and Peterson, and help your child do the activities described in it.

- Make time for fun. Have a going-away party with his friends, and give each one your new address.

- If he cries about leaving, let him cry and comfort him.

- Use a baby-sitter while you are packing.

- Show on a map where you will be moving, and let him follow the route. If driving or flying, have a little celebration as you cross each state line.

- Don't use this time to throw away his old toys. Preschoolers are very attached to "things."

- Give him pictures of the new house and a picture of the old house to take.

Thanks to Pearl Noreen,
Suggestion Circle from Seattle, Washington

323. How can I help my child wait for a big event that is a month away?

- Don't tell him about it too far in advance, if possible.

- Make a paper chain with a link for each day until the event, and remove a link each day.

- Don't talk about it all the time.

- Change the focus from what's in it for him to what he can do for others—making gifts, wrapping them, decorating the house.

- Say, "It really is hard to wait. Let's make a list of three things you can do to get ready."

- Draw pictures of what he imagines is going to happen. You could draw, too. Decorate the room with the pictures.

- Plan tiny weekly events to prepare for the big event.

- Try to de-emphasize it. Keep routines normal.

- Have your child mark off or put a sticker on the calendar as each day passes so he can keep track.

Thanks to Ellen Peterson,
Suggestion Circle from Alamo, California

Chapter 41

Bodies and Sex

324. My five-year-old was playing with a friend in the bedroom. My husband opened the door and found them masturbating. Our rule is that this behavior is OK for our son *alone* in his bedroom. We need suggestions for appropriate consequences for breaking that rule.

- Be honest with your son about your feelings.

- After the friend has left, tell your son not to forget the rule again.

- Do not allow the kids to play in the bedroom with the door closed.

- Review your rules about private parts to him. Don't impose special consequences now, unless he knew them ahead of time.

- Don't blame yourself or think your son is bad. He is just trying to learn about bodies. Treat it seriously, but don't *take* it seriously.

- You could decide on some consequences to occur if it happens again. Say, "You can't play in your bedroom with a friend for two days."

- Matter-of-factly tell them both they have broken the family rule and not to break it again.

- Send his friend home.

- Don't send the friend home. It will make it seem like they've committed a crime.

(See also "Time-Out.")

Thanks to Sue Hansen,
Suggestion Circle from Bellevue, Washington

325. My five-year-old daughter touches the private parts of mannequins in department stores. She lifts clothing and looks. What can I do?

- Say, "You may not do this."
- Get her a set of dolls with genitals, and set the rule that it is OK to explore at home but not in public.
- Go with her to check out some mannequins. She's just curious.
- Be honest that this is embarrassing to you and that you expect her not to play with mannequins in stores.
- Check museums or children's museums for displays of body parts. Take her to see them.
- Together read *Where Did I Come From?*, by Peter Mayle, and giggle over the pictures. (See "Resources.")
- Ask your doctor if she has any models of body parts.
- Bathe together and use this as an opportunity to talk about bodies.
- Remember, it's OK to be curious.

Thanks to Sue Hansen,
Suggestion Circle from Bellevue, Washington

326. My five-year-old son stayed overnight at the home of some five- and eight-year-old friends. His friends were inserting their penises into each other's anuses and trying to urinate. My son was resistant but finally was coerced and really enjoyed it. He came home excited and wanted to teach his three-year-old brother. I don't want to teach him his body is dirty. How can I stop this behavior?

- Approach it from a hygiene angle. Say, "It is not a clean place to put your penis. It is the body's wastes that are unclean, not your body." Don't overreact. Kids are very interested in bodies at this age. Read Joe Kaufman's *How We Are Born, How We Grow, How Our Bodies Work, and How We Learn*. (See "Resources.")

- Say, "Your brother has private parts of his body that you may not touch."

- Compliment your son on resisting. Then read Lory Freeman's *It's My Body* with him. (See "Resources.")

- Say, "That probably did feel good, but don't do this with other boys. Sex is between adults. It is something special you will enjoy when you are older."

- Talk with the other parents. Let them know what their kids are doing.

- You're doing well to keep the communication open.

Thanks to Melanie Weiss,
Suggestion Circle from Bellevue, Washington

327. How do you handle a four-year-old girl who was sexually molested by her grandfather and others? She tries to play with the genitals of her three-year-old friend and of men we know, and she lies on the floor and spreads her legs.

- Take care of your own feelings about this. Get counseling support for yourself and for her.

- Make sure she has lots of active kids to play with.

- Watch her and compliment her for appropriate play with the friend.

- Read her *It's My Body*, by Lory Freeman. (See "Resources.")

- When she lies on the floor, get her up and get her started in a new activity.

- Enroll her in tumbling or swimming classes to help her appreciate her body.

- Give her a lot of love.

- Say, "I will not allow people to touch you in your private places, and I won't allow you to do that to others."

- Children who have been sexually molested frequently confuse sexual touch for love or think that sexual behavior is the only way to get love. Be sure she gets lots of holding, rocking, wrestling, and other appropriate touching.

- Keep her away from her grandfather.

(See also "Where to Go for Additional Support.")

Thanks to Sara Monser,
Suggestion Circle from Lafayette, California

Chapter 42

Hassles with Other Adults

328. My parents favor my sons over my daughters. What can I do?

- Tell your parents quite frankly that this bothers you and why.

- Did they do this when *you* were little? Get in touch with your feelings about this.

- Let the girls know you are glad they are girls, and let the boys know you are glad they are boys.

- Tell your parents how confusing these messages are to children who are just learning to identify their own sex.

- Ask your parents to favor your daughters also.

- Tell your children you love them.

- Every generation has its hang-ups and its gifts.

- If this bothers your children, talk to them and listen to them.

- If you think this situation is too bad, don't let them see their grandparents.

- Don't try to make your parents into something they are not.

Thanks to Carole Gesme,
Suggestion Circle from Anoka, Minnesota

329. My children sometimes go to Grandma's for a weekend. Grandma won't follow the children's schedules, and she lets them run her.

- Tell Grandma how you want things done and how you feel about what she is doing.

- You may not be able to change your in-laws. Tell them straight what you want, and then decide if the price of going to Grandma's is worth it.

- Grandparents are for loving kids. Let her do it her way.

- Make sure your children are safe. If not, find someone else to keep the children.

- Listen to Jay O'Callahan's tape *The Little Dragon and Other Stories*, which is about relationships between grandmas and grandkids. (See "Resources.")

- Write a list for Grandma. Include nap schedule, food likes, and so on.

- Decide on a few things that are really important to you; insist on these and let the rest go.

- Grandmas are meant to be different from parents and are important people to your kids.

- Kids can learn that there are different rules at different houses. Make sure the rules are safe, and encourage them to talk about "alikes" and differences.

- Tell Grandma that you know she will be in charge and to make sure the weekend is enjoyable for her, too.

Thanks to Marilyn Grevstad,
Suggestion Circle from Seattle, Washington

330. How can I cope during a weekend stay with my in-laws, who are not very tolerant of my five-year-old son's behavior? This causes my spouse to react strongly toward our son also.

- Plan activities away from their home each day of your stay.

- Ask your husband to treat your son the same way he usually does.

- Take good care of yourself for two days before you go.

- Tell your husband why you would prefer to stay home.

- Let your son know you love him.

- Stay out of your husband's or in-law's anxiety. Make a list of "Good Parent Rules" for yourself.

- Be specific with your husband before the trip about the discipline you and he will use.

- Ask your in-laws to state the two most important rules for your son to follow at their house.

- Start them reminiscing about your husband's childhood, especially when he was five.

- If it's too intolerable, have them come to your house next time.

- Ask your son to figure out how to get along with his grandparents and father.

- Take a look at the boy's behavior. Is it normal five-year-old stuff, or does he need some training in manners?

Thanks to Deane Gradous,
Suggestion Circle from Wayzata, Minnesota

331. My boyfriend is too strict with my child. What should I do?

- Explain to him that you will handle the situation.
- If he's physically or emotionally abusive, dump him.
- Listen to his side of it. Maybe you are too lenient. Think about it, and decide if this fits.
- Tell him what you want him to do.
- Don't hassle this issue in front of your child. Talk, listen, and share child-care expectations when you are away from your child. This is an issue between adults.
- Ask him how he was treated when he was her age. Tell him how you were treated and what you want for your daughter. Talk about personalities, expectations, and discipline.
- Take a parenting class together.
- Get an unbiased opinion.
- Put up a poster of normal child behaviors at this age as a reminder to you and your boyfriend.

(See also "Ages and Stages," "Common Pitfalls," and "Keeping Preschoolers Safe.")

Thanks to Ellen Peterson,
Suggestion Circle from Lafayette, California

332. How can I handle the parent of a three-year-old who spanks or slaps her child in my presence in my home? I disapprove.

- You can call a child protection service.
- Tell her the rule at your house is that no one gets hit.
- Put up a sign: "People are not for hitting. Children are people."

- Share with her the section on what to do instead of hitting from Clarke's *Self-Esteem: A Family Affair*. (See "Resources.")

- Talk to the parent about spanking at a time when the three-year-old is not present.

- My friend and I tell each other about times we feel like hitting and don't; this helps us both.

- Don't walk away. Tell her how you feel.

- Talk about how you feel like hitting sometimes but you don't do it; let your friend see and hear how you handle this with your child.

- Tell your friend all the reasons you like her. Then share your beliefs about discipline without spanking.

Thanks to Harold Nordeman,
Suggestion Circle from Cincinnati, Ohio

333. Our three-year-old son prefers me, and this disturbs his mother. How can we respond to him when she wants to give him something and he will only take it from Daddy?

- Mom can say, "Your dad's busy right now. I'm here now to give you this. If you want it, it's yours!"

- Arrange for him to have time alone with you.

- Remember, Dad, that his attachment to you is a stage and won't last forever. Have fun with him.

- Tell yourself it's not anyone's fault.

- Point out to your wife all the ways in which she is a good mom.

- Agree between you not to get your feelings hurt by this. Don't be manipulated.

- Say, "Hey, I really love it that you want it from me, but I'm busy right now."
- Read about triangles and family maps in *New Peoplemaking*, by Virginia Satir. (See "Resources.")
- Know that this has happened in many households and that kids have still grown up to love both parents.

Thanks to Craig Halversen,
Suggestion Circle from Coon Rapids, Minnesota

334. My husband, from whom I am separated, gives our three- and six-year-olds a dollar allowance for chores they do while visiting him. The children expect it from me, too, but I can't afford it. What can I do?

- Say, "We don't use the same set of rules here."
- Have some chores that your children do because they are part of the family.
- Can't blame them for giving it a try! Give each a hug and simply say you don't have the money.
- Don't give them money just because he does. Decide what you want to do, and do it your way.
- Give your children the allowance *you* can afford in order to give them experience in handling money, not as a reward for chores.
- Tell them that isn't how you choose to spend your money. Your children are learning that people do things differently. That's valuable.
- Your kids love you because you're you—not because of how much allowance you give.
- Teach them about other types of rewards.

- Say, "Your dad and I do this differently. It's OK for you to love us both."

- Read *My Mother's House, My Father's House,* by C. B. Christiansen, to your children. (See "Resources.")

Thanks to Linda Witt,
Suggestion Circle from Cincinnati, Ohio

335. How do I get my husband to help with the house and the kids?

- Be specific. Don't say, "I want help." Say exactly what you want, and write it down.

- Use *fair* delegation. Let him be responsible for things he enjoys. Split jobs you both hate.

- Point out how you will both benefit when he helps. You will have a better disposition, and he and the kids will know each other better.

- Get mad.

- Discuss the roles of both parents. Ask him what he expects a dad to do. Your ideas may not be the same. Negotiate a compromise.

- Be flexible. Sometimes I don't feel like doing much, and sometimes he doesn't. Trade off.

- When I feel desperate, I say, "It's your turn, and I mean it."

- Don't talk about it when you're heated up. Go away someplace and talk about it.

- Go off by yourself.

- List all the things to be done. Together decide which ones he will do.

- Read Harriet Lerner's *The Dance of Intimacy*. (See "Resources.")

Thanks to Sara Monser,
Suggestion Circle from Lafayette, California

336. My day-care person won't let my three-year-old son wear the women's clothes from the dress-up closet. I think it's OK.

- Talk to the day-care person directly, and tell her that it's OK with you.

- Ask her why, and listen to her reasons.

- Explain to your son that some people don't understand that kids like to dress up in all kinds of ways. Make sure he has dress-up clothes at home.

- Check out another day care.

- Let him wear something special from home so he can feel "dressed up."

- Tell the provider, "He has a great imagination. Kids can pretend to be anything they want. Pretending doesn't make things come true. Some days he pretends he is a dinosaur. Please let him wear all of the dress-ups."

- I used to feel funny about my son dressing up, too, until I read *Growing Up Free*, by Letty Pogrebin. Give it to your day-care provider. (See "Resources.")

- Tell your provider please to let him have free access to the dress-up closet but please to let you know if he does it to the exclusion of other play.

Thanks to Sara Monser,
Suggestion Circle from Lafayette, California

337. My child has several friends who have their own Nintendo games. When he goes to their houses, that is all they play. I feel this is not what preschoolers should be doing. How can I handle this?

- Talk to the parents of these children before your child goes to visit. Share your feelings with them.

- See "Ages and Stages" and "Resources" for age-appropriate activities.

- Read *Who's Calling the Shots,* by Carlsson-Paige and Levin, for more information on the effects of watching the tube. (See "Resources.")

- Have the other children play at your house.

- Maintain your limits at home.

- See if you can find other children for your child to play with.

- Talk with your child about other people's values and your values.

- Trust your feelings. If you think it's not OK, keep him home.

- In this computer age, a little Nintendo is better than none, but more Nintendo is not better than some.

Thanks to Melanie Weiss,
Suggestion Circle from Bellevue, Washington

338. I don't want my father to be alone with my daughters, because he molested me as a child. How should I handle this?

- Don't leave your daughters alone with your father ever, even if you get criticized for it!

- Tell your father you remember what he did and that he is never to touch your children.

- You, as the parent, are responsible for your daughters' safety. Don't expose them. (See "Keeping Preschoolers Safe" and "Signs of Abuse and Neglect.")

- Remember, grandchildren don't have to stay overnight for sexual abuse to happen.

- Be aware that molestation can take place in the afternoon when Grandpa takes the kids to the zoo or for an ice cream cone or even when they are coming home from church, at a movie, or on the way to the circus.

- Don't leave your sons alone with your father, either!

- Protect your children from any known offender by *never* leaving them alone with that person.

- People do better at protecting their own kids from abuse if they get help for their own, so be sure to do that if you haven't. You deserve to have help in recovering from this abuse. (See "Resources—Protecting Your Children from Abuse.")

- Expect other family members to support you, and if they don't, stand firm alone.

Thanks to Survivors Support Group,
Minneapolis, Minnesota

Chapter 43

Parents Have Needs, Too

339. When is *my* time? How do I get my child to respect my right to be with friends and on the phone?

- Make it clear when you will spend time just with him and when you will spend time talking to adults. Give him his time first.

- Stop and talk to him. Explain your need to talk to adults.

- Keep some special quiet toys by the phone, to be played with only while you're talking.

- You are important. Arrange with your neighbor to watch your child while you are with friends or when you want a long phone conversation.

- Don't be too long on the phone. Save long talks for nap time.

- Don't always answer the phone. Tell the child you are choosing to be with him instead.

- Reward the child with hugs for a few minutes of quiet while you are on the phone.

- Help your child arrange a special time with a friend, and tell him when you have special arrangements with your friends.

- Congratulate yourself on having a healthy child who is pushing you and others to find out what the limits are and how he can be part of the action.

- Meet a friend at the park and talk while the kids play. They are happy, and you are happy!

Thanks to Sandy Keiser,
Suggestion Circle from Cincinnati, Ohio

340. Our three-year-old daughter and seventeen-month-old son climb onto the pool table where I keep my Avon samples. How can I keep them off?

- Keep taking the children off the table. State the rule of staying off.
- Establish private places for each member of the family to keep their stuff. Remind the children.
- You deserve your own space. Claim it!
- Set up an alternative climbing apparatus or trampoline nearby for them to climb on.
- Remember that you establish rules differently for different ages. Change the environment for the toddler, and make consequences for the three-year-old.
- Could you build a cover of plywood to set over the pool table and Avon samples?
- Get them their own Avon samples or little jars and lids, and remind them to play with their own samples, not yours.
- Find a new space, like a cupboard, that you can lock. It isn't safe for little ones to eat your products. Protect your children.

Thanks to Marilyn Grevstad,
Suggestion Circle from Seattle, Washington

341. I am too busy. I feel guilty about my busy scheduled days and worry that my child is not getting enough of my attention. What can I do?

- Make a list of tasks, prioritize them, and include some time for yourself and for your child each day.

- Find a good preschool where your child can have fun and get lots of attention from other people. Work fast while she is gone, and give her attention while she is at home.

- Pay attention to your own feelings and needs as well as other people's.

- My mom worked, and I learned lots from watching her figure out how to get things done and from listening to her stories about her work.

- It's OK to say no. You don't have to do everything now.

- Don't stay "in worry." Look at your choices and decide what is best for you and your child in your situation at this time.

- Instead of thinking "only two hours," think, "I've got two hours, and that's lots of time."

- Look at your old "good mom rules." Rewrite them to work for you now. Read more about this in Clarke's *Self-Esteem: A Family Affair*. (See "Resources.")

- Invite the child to help you at meetings by helping you get the room ready, serve refreshments, and so on.

- Foster a spirit of cooperation.

Thanks to Susie Montgomery,
Suggestion Circle from Lafayette, California

342. My in-laws criticize me a lot. How can I not feel condemned? They will be spending ten days with me.

- Don't forget, this is their point of view, and you can say, "Thank you, I'll think about that."

- Say, "I don't do things the way you do. There are lots of different ways of doing things. This is the way I'm doing it now."

- Say to yourself, "I am a duck, and this criticism is so much water off my back."

- Tell them to stop it.

- Remove yourself and think of a response you can give next time. Rehearse.

- Whenever you feel threatened, use centering and leveling techniques. Stand or sit straight, and breathe deeply. Read *The Centering Book,* by Gay Hendricks and Russel Wills. (See "Resources.")

- Say, "I feel hurt when you say that. Please tell me about something I do well."

- Write an affirmation for yourself, give it to a friend, and ask her to read it to you when you call. Call once every day and listen. (See "Developmental Affirmations for All Ages.")

- Remember, children deserve to hear their parents honored, not abused. If the criticism is too much for you or your children to tolerate, ask your in-laws to leave.

- Read *Peace Is Every Step,* by Thich Naht Hahn. (See "Resources.")

Thanks to Cindy Vernatter,
Suggestion Circle from Cincinnati, Ohio

343. What about me? As my child practices the independence I am fostering, I no longer feel needed.

- Say to yourself, "Isn't this neat? This is what I'm working for."

- Ask a friend for a hug, and celebrate your success with your child.

- You will always be needed, but the ways in which you are needed will change.

- Think of how your own needs change over time.

- Take care of the child in you! Start a new hobby, buy yourself a present, or take a friend to lunch.

- It's OK to mourn the loss of your child's babyhood.

- Write a letter to yourself about this new experience and what you feel, and read it whenever you need to.

- Think about your child at ages nine, fifteen, and twenty-three and how you would feel if he were not independent.

- Read the adult affirmations to yourself morning and night for three weeks, and then see how you feel. (See the Interdependence section in "Developmental Affirmations for All Ages.")

Thanks to Mary Paananen,
Suggestion Circle from Seattle, Washington

344. The clod and I are getting a divorce. How can I prepare my child?

- Prepare your child by giving the facts as they occur rather than letting it out all at once.

- Get some help for yourself so you can say something other than "the clod." Find ways to let out your feelings that do not involve your daughter.

- Provide opportunities for her to associate with other loving adults and with children who have survived divorce.

- Tell the child's teacher.

- Continue as much of your regular routine as possible, and structure some high-quality times with your child.

- Tell her, "When we got married, we loved each other very much. Now our love for each other has changed, but love for children doesn't change. We will continue to love you."

- Say, "Though things are changing, you are important, and we will always be your mom and dad."

- Say, "This is not your fault. Big people get divorces for their own reasons. Little people do not cause them."

- Tell her about the future—where she will be living, with whom, about visitations, and so on.

- Take care of yourself, and do the best you can. Remember you don't have to be perfect.

Thanks to Mary Paananen,
Suggestion Circle from Seattle, Washington

345. I have just moved here. How do I find new friends?

- Find a church to attend, and volunteer to help.

- Take a fun class. Pick one that might attract people who like to do things you enjoy.

- Go on outings—fairs, hikes, community holiday celebrations and festivals—and talk to people at these events.

- Be active in groups involving kids: La Leche League, school, preschool, Sunday school, parenting class.

- See if there is a baby-sitting co-op. Ask parents in grocery stores, parks, and so on. If you can't find one, start one. (See "How to Set up a Child-Care Co-op.")

- Pursue a hobby—bowling, flower arranging, playing an instrument—and find a group to do it with.

- Join a preschool, baby-sitting, or food co-op.

- Stay around after meetings or classes. This is when people get to know each other.

- Offer to teach a skill you have.

- After a meeting or class, invite the group to your house for coffee.

- I remember that lonely feeling. Taking care of *you* is more important than unpacking all the boxes.

Thanks to Sandra Sittko,
Suggestion Circle from Saint Louis, Missouri

346. What should I look for in choosing a preschool?

- Take your child's personality and needs into consideration.

- If you want to be involved, look for a cooperative preschool. You can take your time and find one that's just right for you and your child, or you can start one yourself.

- Look for a preschool in which social skills will be learned. These are important tasks for preschool children.

- Look for a preschool in which the child will have fun. Don't worry about academics yet.

- Look for invitations to the children to participate but no forced activities.

- Check on these things: the teachers' credentials, reputation, the schedule (time outdoors and so on), the adult-to-child ratio, who watches the kids, whether parents are welcome, meals, field trips, outside specialists, amount of indoor climbing equipment, the cleanliness of the school, and how they handle sick children.

- Listen to the opinions of friends who share your values.

- Is the discipline positive or negative?

- Observe the children at the preschool. Are they happy? Are they listless? Are they out of control?

  (See also "Preparing Your Child for Grade School.")

  Thanks to Marilyn Grevstad,
  Suggestion Circle from Seattle, Washington

Preparing Your Child for Grade School

All the parents I know would like their children to be at the top of their class. We all want our kids to bring home the gold stars. However, most of our kids, like us, will be somewhere in between the top and the bottom. That's OK, because there are lots of gifted children in the world, and some have gifts that comply with school ideals and some have gifts that shine elsewhere.

The preschool years are a time when children get to know themselves in relation to other people in the world. It is a time of preparation for "school age." Parents who are thinking ahead ask, "How can I help my children succeed in elementary school? Is there some way I can give them a head start?"

As a preschool teacher, I notice that very bright children often have advanced verbal skills. They may learn to count at an early age; they may learn their colors at an early age; they may memorize the alphabet at an early age. Parents sometimes mistake these verbal indicators as *causes* of intelligence. "If only I can get someone to teach my child the ABCs, colors, and counting, he will be bright, too." Then preschool panic sets in, and parents want to push.

Pushing doesn't help. Don't push your children into learning about symbols before they are ready. If you do, they will develop a distaste for numbers and letters. Let *them* lead *you* down the academic road. Respond to their questions about letters and numbers just as you do to other questions about what life is about. That's all the teaching you need to do.

Don't send them to a pushy preschool. They'll learn to hate learning and think of school as a place where grown-ups make them do things they don't want to do. Preschool should be fun.

See your children as the very capable persons they already are. All things happen in their own good time. You can help your children more if you rejoice in what they have already learned about the world, their neighborhood, their family and friends, and above all themselves, rather than focusing on what they don't know yet. They have already accomplished quite a lot in a very short time.

Love them and believe in them. Children do better in school when they see themselves as lovable and capable. When parents believe their children are lovable and capable, their sons and daughters believe it, too.

Give your children lots of hands-on learning experiences, things in which they use their bodies as well as their minds. Help them engage fully with life. To do this, provide as many of those activities traditionally loved by preschoolers as you can. In this way, your children will have had a rich array of experiences before they begin formal schooling. These experiences will help them develop the skills they need in order to learn the "basic skills" at school. To support this process, you can provide the following:

sand	clay and mud
pretend-play props	books and stories
water	things to climb on
glue and stuff to glue	swings
paper	musical instruments
scissors	outdoor time
paints	records, songs
markers, pencils, pens	field trips to stores
Play-Doh	wheel toys
friends	banks, doctors, parks

Good preschools can be a great benefit. The best kind are those in which children have long periods of time to play with each other and the materials just listed. Parents who can share their preschoolers' enthusiasm for life will be able to provide many experiences, materials, and field trips for their children without benefit of preschool, but preschool does offer experiences that are hard to duplicate at home because it also offers groups of children to play with.

Preschool does not have to be expensive. Cooperative preschools are usually low in cost because parents provide staff help. Many parents form play groups where several children rotate from house to house and parents take turns being the host-teacher. This is an excellent way to provide preschool at almost no cost. In addition, most day-care centers include a preschool program.

If you choose to send your children to preschool or kindergarten, find a school that fits your children, rather than expecting your children to mold to the expectations of the school. This kind of compliance is difficult for a child and may result in lowered self-esteem.

If your children are quite active and love to climb, find a school that includes running and climbing as part of the curriculum. They will feel good about themselves and will be willing to learn new things once they have had their fill of active play. If one of your children is quite shy, find a school with a minimum of pressure to perform in front of a group. When allowed to do his own thing unobtrusively, your shy child will in time feel safe and will warm up to the supportive adults and friendly children who are around. In other words, find a school that will allow your children to be who they are and that will offer them new experiences as well.

Two helpful things you can do for children at home are to read to them and to talk to them. Books to own and regular trips to the library for interesting books will help them develop a love of reading. (When they are ready, sometime between ages six and nine, they will learn *how* to read.) When you talk to children, you build their vocabulary, teach concepts, and offer them your own enthusiasm for life. It is this enthusiasm for what you see, hear, and feel and for the everyday challenges and joys of life that will help them love learning for the rest of their lives.

Marilyn Grevstad

How It Feels to Be a Parent of a Preschooler

Raising a child of this age is a highly emotional experience. For example, one parent wrote:

I am a parent of a four-and-a-half-year-old, and I experience a buffet of emotions toward him every day.

My child's changeable nature is very challenging to deal with. You never know when you might say or do the wrong thing! His resulting explosiveness can be very exasperating. He tests my patience with demands, rigidity, noisy teasing, and nonstop activity that easily gets "out of bounds." Sometimes I feel so weary.

On the other hand, I *love* the *fun* we have. I delight in his silliness in play and language and in the places his imagination has taken us. I feel tenderness and warmth for my boy during moments when he is eager to please and to be sweet and affectionate. I have learned that I can encourage this behavior by giving him the opportunity to think and cooperate in his own time. It's exciting to watch him grow at his own rate.

Sue Hansen

Moving On to the School-Age Years

While learning about their own sense of power and identity is the focus of three- to six-year-olds, the main job of six- to twelve-year-olds is to build on that sense of identity and to experiment with, learn about, and develop their own structures and ways of keeping themselves safe.

Before elementary school age, parents provide almost all of the structure for their child. But as children grow older, they gradually become more responsible for and participate in establishing some of their own boundaries, structures, safety, and standards for behavior.

Six- to twelve-year-olds are often delightful and fun to be with. They take pride in their own activity, in figuring out what to do, and in learning how to be themselves and how to be active participants in a group.

You can expect continued change in the way your children manage themselves with you. You will notice children becoming more involved in problem solving and in anticipating and making choices. You will also see more verbal negotiating, reasoning, and comparing with others as your children examine and challenge your rules and develop internal rules of their own.

As children move into adolescence, their task is to develop a sense of personal identity, to explore their sexuality, and to continue separating from you. They will need your love and guidance as they become more independent.

"Will they be able to cope?" "What is my role in their lives?" "How well are we preparing for the teenage years?" These are questions parents ask. *Help! For Parents of School-Age Children and Teenagers* is ready to aid you in that process.

Mary Paananen

Appendixes

Developmental Affirmations for All Ages

Being
(Stage I—Birth to Six Months)

- I'm glad you are alive.
- You belong here.
- What you need is important to me.
- I'm glad you are you.
- You can grow at your own pace.
- You can feel all of your feelings.
- I love you and I care for you willingly.

Exploring and Doing
(Stage II—Six to Eighteen Months)

- You can explore and experiment, and I will support and protect you.
- You can use all of your senses when you explore.
- You can do things as many times as you need to.
- You can know what you know.
- You can be interested in everything.
- I like to watch you initiate and grow and learn.
- I love you when you are active and when you are quiet.

The reader is encouraged to photocopy and post pages 380–383.

Thinking
(Stage III—Eighteen Months to Two Years)

- I'm glad you are starting to think for yourself.

- It's OK for you to be angry, and I won't let you hurt yourself or others.

- You can say no and push and test limits as much as you need to.

- You can learn to think for yourself, and I will think for myself.

- You can think and feel at the same time.

- You can know what you need and ask for help.

- You can become separate from me, and I will continue to love you.

Identity and Power
(Stage IV—Three to Five Years)

- You can explore who you are and find out who other people are.

- You can be powerful and ask for help at the same time.

- You can try out different roles and ways of being powerful.

- You can find out the results of your behavior.

- All of your feelings are OK with me.

- You can learn what is pretend and what is real.

- I love who you are.

Structure
(Stage V—School Age)

- You can think before you say yes or no and learn from your mistakes.

- You can trust your intuition to help you decide what to do.

- You can find a way of doing things that works for you.

- You can learn the rules that help you live with others.

- You can learn when and how to disagree.

- You can think for yourself and get help instead of staying in distress.

- I love you even when we differ; I love growing with you.

Identity, Sexuality, and Separation
(Stage VI—Teenagers)

- You can know who you are and learn and practice skills for independence.

- You can learn the difference between sex and nurturing and be responsible for your needs and behavior.

- You can develop your own interests, relationships, and causes.

- You can learn to use old skills in new ways.

- You can grow in your maleness or femaleness and still be dependent at times.

- I look forward to knowing you as an adult.

- My love is always with you. I trust you to ask for my support.

Interdependence
(Stage VII—Adults)

- Your needs are important.

- You can be uniquely yourself and honor the uniqueness of others.

- You can be independent and interdependent.

- Through the years, you can expand your commitments to your own growth, to your family, your friends, your community, and to all humankind.

- You can build and examine your commitments to your values and causes, your roles and your tasks.

- You can be responsible for your contributions to each of your commitments.

- You can be creative, competent, productive, and joyful.

- You can trust your inner wisdom.

- You can say your hellos and good-byes to people, roles, dreams, and decisions.

- You can finish each part of your journey and look forward to the next.

- Your love matures and expands.

- You are lovable at every age.

Signs of Abuse and Neglect

Child abuse and neglect are prevalent—perhaps epidemic—in our society today. We editors feel strongly that all children are to be valued and cherished. We believe that children will be better protected when parents know the signs of child abuse.

Signs of abuse can vary with the age of the child. Listed here are signs that should arouse a parent's suspicions. If you find yourself worried or concerned about an abusive relationship between your child and another adult or older child, check it out.

Physical and behavioral signs that may indicate neglect or abuse include:

- A child who is not growing appropriately (not gaining weight or length)
- Diaper rash that's getting worse or is not clearing up when the child is in the care of others
- Pin-size marks around the eyes or blood in the white part of the eye, which may indicate that the child has been shaken
- Circular bite marks, either adult- or child-size
- Hand-slap marks on the face or elsewhere
- Bruised or tender fingertips from little hands being slapped
- Bruises on the thighs or upper arms
- Straight-line marks on the skin from abuse with a belt or a ruler

- Inappropriate sexual or violent play with dolls
- Unwillingness or overwillingness to display the genitalia
- Any bruises around the genitalia.

If you suspect abuse of any kind, find a way to protect the child. Get help if you need it. Report the abuser to the child protection service in your area. (See all the "Common Pitfalls" sections and "Where to Go for Additional Support.")

Christine Ternand, M.D.

How to Start a Backyard Center

A "Backyard Center" is a program that provides parent education and support for families with newborns to five-year-olds. There are two types of Backyard Centers: Parent-Infant Support Groups (birth to two-year-olds) and Home-style Preschool Play Groups (two- to five-year-olds).

Parent-Infant Support Groups of six to eight families meet in each other's homes on a rotating basis. Parents bring their infants (birth to twenty-four months), and the host or hostess leads discussions on a selected parenting topic, leads Suggestion Circles, and leads baby songs and infant stimulation exercises for the infants.

In the Home-style Preschool Play Groups, the parents rotate being play-group hosts for the two- to five-year-old children from all the families. One helper parent assists the host, and the rest of the parents have the time off. After the children have played in each home, the parents and children meet for a "cycle" meeting, using the same meeting format as the Parent-Infant Support Groups.

Any interested parents can begin their own Backyard Center group. The key to the success of the group will be the commitment of the members. The goals of the group are decided by the members. The meetings should be fun, flexible, and something to look forward to.

*How to Start Your Own Backyard Center
Parent-Infant Support Group*

Recruiting Members

Make use of hospital birth records, YWCA and YMCA preschool programs, physicians, Lamaze classes, co-op baby-sitting groups, community bulletin boards, and local newspaper ads in order to find possible members.

Organizing

When four or more families have expressed interest, meet with them and do the following:

1) Decide on the day of the week, time of day, length of the meeting, and how frequently to meet (the most popular times are weekly or biweekly for one or two hours).

2) Discuss a rotation system in which each family takes a turn as the host/discussion leader of the group.

3) Exchange addresses and phone numbers and any other pertinent information.

4) Plan your calendar for the month.

Designing the Format

Each meeting can be divided into four parts: (1) a parenting topic, (2) Suggestion Circles, (3) baby songs and exercises, and (4) a snack.

1) *Parenting Topic.* The host parent selects from the following:

• Present a topic or article from a magazine, book, or newspaper to the group (for example, "Sleep Disturbance," "When to Wean Your Baby," and so on).

- Share information on community activities, workshops, and programs offered that are appropriate for parents of infants so that other members of the group are aware of what's going on in your community.

- Organize a craft project (making a mobile or homemade toy).

- Arrange to attend a class or workshop together.

- Arrange for a speaker to present information on such topics as nutrition (how to make your own baby food, for example), appropriate and safe toys, stimulating language, self-esteem (your own and your child's), reading to infants, and how and when to discipline.

2) *Suggestion Circle.* The lead parent asks who wants a Suggestion Circle. Follow the guidelines in this book under "How to Lead a Suggestion Circle."

3) *Baby Songs and Exercises.* Babies love to be sung to, and singing can calm down a whole troop of crying babies. Adapt any song you know to a baby exercise. It's fun, and babies don't mind if you sing off-key! Parents can practice doing infant stimulation using infant exercises or massage books. (See "Resources.")

4) *Snack Time.* This is optional, but it provides an excellent time for conversation and sharing of concerns.

You can organize a Backyard Center Home-style Preschool Play Group in the same way, except that the parents' meetings are held only after the children have played in each home. You can organize your Backyard Center program on your own, or you can persuade a school district, YMCA, YWCA, or other community agency to sponsor it.

The Backyard Center program originated in 1975 in the Yakima School District in Washington State, and it is designed to provide cost-effective parent education and support to families of newborns to five-year-olds. In Yakima, the school district offers help in recruiting and organizing the groups and provides facilitation skills training for group members.

Judith L. Popp

How to Set up a Child-Care Co-op

1) Start small. Four to ten families allow several possible exchanges without many complications.

2) In order to begin with trust, start out with people you know, whose child-rearing ideas are similar to yours. Then have current members sponsor new members.

3) Visit each other's homes with your children before you leave your child for care. The environment should feel familiar and safe to both parents and child.

4) Decide whether your co-op will be limited to babies and preschoolers or will also include school-age children. Remember that homes are best equipped for the ages of the children who live there.

5) Set some geographic boundaries for your co-op.

6) Discuss whether your co-op will be used for daytime, evening, weekends, or overnight care.

7) Establish a health policy. Include guidelines for dealing with sick children, and provide a medical release form to be signed by the parents and left for each child being cared for.

8) Recommend that members carry liability insurance.

9) Select a secretary, and rotate the job.

10) Develop a system for recording hours of care provided and received. The secretary can keep an index card listing the care given (+ hours) and care received (– hours) for each family. Total the hours on the cards each month, and pass them on to the next secretary.

11) Decide if you want to arrange care through the secretary only or between members. If you arrange time among yourselves, report hours only to the secretary.

12) When more than one child from a family is left for care, decide how to credit each member. Two children could total either two times or one and a half times the total hours.

13) The member arranging for care should leave emergency information with the caregiver (including destination, car license, and phone number).

14) Members must agree on whether the caregiver will be allowed to run errands with the children in the car.

15) Insist on using car safety seats, and leave your child's seat with the caregiver.

16) If a meal will be served to your child, decide whether the caregiver will receive an extra half-hour credit.

17) Provide each member with a membership list, rules, guidelines, and emergency forms. If you can't get someone to donate duplicating costs, spread the cost among the members.

Gail Davenport

Time-Out

What Is Time-Out?

Time-out is a technique used to interrupt unacceptable behavior for one or two minutes by removing the child from the "scene of the action." Time-out is a calming device, not a punishment.

When and Where to Use It

Use a time-out for stopping inappropriate behavior before it reaches oppressive or assaultive proportions or for serious violations of your family's rules. Put the child in a safe, boring place within your view.

The time-out should be short enough (a minute or less for young children) so that the child has a chance to go back to the original situation after the time-out is over and learn acceptable behavior.

Procedure

If your child is under two and a half, pick him up, remove him from the scene, and tell him some ways to change his behavior. As he learns this procedure, his brief time-out can take place in your lap.

Before using a time-out, see if your child understands the concepts of "wait" and "quiet." (Children usually do between two and a half and three and a half years.)

The first few times, do this:

1) Explain a time-out to the child.

2) Explain when it will be used.

3) Walk the child through the steps.

4) Time the quiet time only (not the whining or crying).

5) Tell the child the time-out is over when the time is up.

6) Return the child to the situation, and reinforce appropriate behavior.

This summary of the time-out strategy is from Elizabeth Crary's *Without Spanking or Spoiling*. (See "Resources.") See her book for a more complete description of the uses and pitfalls of using time-outs.

The Editors

How to Lead a Suggestion Circle

A Suggestion Circle is an efficient tool for collecting high-quality options for solving a specific problem. It takes three to five minutes to collect suggestions from a dozen people. Unlike brainstorming, participants offer only their best suggestions. Here is how to run one:

1) The leader invites people to sit in a circle and asks a person in the group (called the "focus person") to share a problem. (Deal with only one problem in each circle.)

2) Have the person state the problem specifically and briefly. For example, a parent might say "Jason, my two-year-old, refuses to go to bed at night. When we put him in his crib, he climbs out as soon as we leave the room. How can I get him to stay in bed?" Questions of clarification should be answered briefly so that the group understands the problem.

3) Ask someone to be ready to record the suggestions made so that the person with the problem has a written list to take home.

4) Ask each person in the group to think of his or her best idea.

5) Invite whoever wishes to start to offer a concise, one- or two-sentence suggestion like this: "Keep putting him back to bed, gently but firmly." Then the next person in the circle should offer a suggestion or say, "I pass."

6) In response to each suggestion, the person with the

problem says, "Thank you." No one should comment on or add to another's suggestion.

7) When everyone has had a turn, the leader may choose to ask those who passed if they want to offer a suggestion.

8) When the circle is complete, the leader invites the person to take the suggestions home, consider them, and use them in a way that makes sense for him or her.

Nat Houtz

Telephone Circle

1) When you have a problem that you need help with, phone six friends.

2) Clearly and quickly explain the problem to each friend, and ask for his or her best suggestion. Writing the problem out before you call may help you state it more clearly.

3) Listen to the suggestion and write it down.

4) Do not comment on the suggestion, other than to say, "Thank you."

5) After you have phoned each friend, look over your list of suggestions and decide which to use. Acknowledge the support that you have received from your friends.

Sandra Sittko

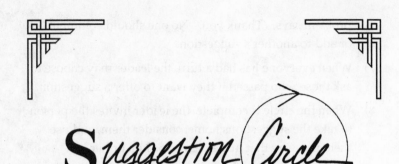

Suggestion Circle

- One problem, one sentence

> Think
> One best suggestion,
> one sentence
> Write

- Thank you
- Think, choose and use

Leader's Checklist for Clean, Clear Leadership of a Suggestion Circle

___ I explained clearly to the people in the group how a Suggestion Circle works. (I may have decided to run one for myself first with a new group.)

___ I posted the Suggestion Circle poster.

___ I helped the focus person to clarify his or her situation so that the focus person, the group, and I all held a common understanding of the problem.

___ I made a contract with the focus person to listen to all the suggestions offered and to say only "Thank you," and I supported the focus person in keeping that contract.

___ I made clear that the "thank you" was for the person's willingness to give a suggestion and was not a comment on the quality of the suggestion.

___ I reminded the group to offer their best (high-quality) ideas, one at a time, in a concise sentence or two, and I praised them for doing that.

___ I reminded myself and the group of the ground rules, particularly the right to pass, and enforced them as needed.

___ I offered the opportunity to have someone in the group write down the suggestions for the focus person.

___ I returned to group members who passed the first time around in case they wished to offer a suggestion later.

___ I invited the focus person to consider the suggestions and to use them in a way that fit for him or her; I also invited the focus person to report back to the group but emphasized that there was no pressure to do so.

___ I ran the Suggestion Circle in three to ten minutes, depending on the size of the group.

___ If there were more than twenty people, I divided them into groups of ten to fifteen and got others to help lead so we could run simultaneous circles.

Deane Gradous

Where to Go for Additional Support

If you have tried the ideas offered by the Suggestion Circles in this book, talked with your family and friends, read some child-rearing books, and still feel stuck with a problem, here are some places where you can call for additional help or where you can find out about parenting classes. If you have difficulty finding a telephone number after looking in both the white and the yellow pages, call any of these sources and ask them to help you find the number you need.

Community Services

Parent-education organizations

Crisis or hot-line numbers

YMCA, YWCA, or a local church or synagogue

Parents Without Partners International

Chemical abuse treatment centers

Chemical abuse prevention programs

Community civic centers

Women's or men's support groups

Battered women's and children's shelters

Childbirth education groups

La Leche League or other breast-feeding support groups

Planned Parenthood and other family-planning centers

Alcoholics Anonymous

Parents Anonymous

Sexual assault centers

Local hospitals

Private Services

Psychologists, social workers, psychiatrists, therapists, family counselors

Schools

Community education (run by the local school district)

Colleges or universities

Community or junior colleges

Vocational and technical schools

Government

Community mental health services

Public health nurse or department

Child protection services

Family service agencies

County and state social service agencies

Head Start programs

Interview the persons who will help you to see if they know about the area in which you need support. If you don't get the help you need, go somewhere else until you do.

The Editors

Resources

Ages and Stages

Ames, Louise B., and Ilg, Frances L. *Your Five-Year-Old: Sunny and Serene.* New York: Dell, 1981.

———. *Your Four-Year-Old: Wild and Wonderful.* New York: Dell, 1989.

———. *Your Three-Year-Old: Friend or Enemy.* New York: Dell, 1980.

———. *Your Two-Year-Old: Terrible or Tender.* New York: Delacorte Press, 1980.

Badger, Earladeen. *Infant Toddler: Introducing Your Child to the Joy of Learning.* Englewood Cliffs, NJ: McGraw-Hill, 1981.

Calladine, Carole. *One Terrific Year.* New York: Harper & Row, 1985.

Caplan, Frank. *The First Twelve Months of Life.* New York: Bantam Books, 1984.

Clarke, Jean Illsley. *The Terrific Twos.* Plymouth, MN: Daisy Tapes, 1983.

———. *The Wonderful Busy Ones.* Plymouth, MN: Daisy Tapes, 1983.

Coles, Robert. *The Spiritual Life of Children.* Boston: Houghton Mifflin, 1990.

Fraiberg, Selma. *The Magic Years: Understanding and Handling the Problems of Early Childhood.* New York: Doubleday, 1984.

Galinsky, Ellen, and David, Judy. *The Preschool Years.* New York: Times Books, 1988.

Greenspan, Nancy Thorndike, and Greenspan, Stanley I. *First Feelings: Milestones in the Emotional Development of Your Baby and Child*. New York: Penguin Books, 1989.

Jessel, Camilla. *From Birth to Three*. New York: Dell, 1990.

Johnson & Johnson. *First Wondrous Year*. New York: Macmillan, 1984.

———. *Your Toddler*. New York: Macmillan, 1980.

Kersey, Katherine. *Helping Your Child Handle Stress*. Washington, DC: Acropolis Books, 1989.

Klaus, M. H., and Klaus, P. *The Amazing Newborn*. Reading, MA: Addison-Wesley, 1985.

Leach, Penelope. *Babyhood*. New York: Knopf, 1983.

———. *The First Six Months*. New York: Knopf, 1987.

———. *Your Baby and Child: From Birth to Age Five*. New York: Knopf, 1987.

———. *Your Growing Child*. New York: Knopf, 1989.

Levin, Pamela. *Becoming the Way We Are*. Deerfield Beach, FL: Health Communications, 1988.

Nilsson, Lennart. *A Child Is Born*. New York: Delacorte Press/Seymour Lawrence, 1990.

Pushaw, David. *Teach Your Child to Talk*. New York: Dantree Press, 1977.

Segal, Marilyn, and Adcock, Don. *Your Child at Play: One to Two Years*. New York: New Market Press, 1989.

White, Burton L. *The First Three Years of Life: The Revised Edition*. Englewood Cliffs, NJ: Prentice Hall, 1991.

Self-Esteem

Clarke, Jean Illsley. *Self-Esteem: A Family Affair*. San Francisco: Harper & Row, 1985.

Steiner, Claude. *Warm Fuzzy Tale*. Rolling Hills Estate, CA: Jalmar Press, 1977.

Values

Riley, Sue S. *How to Generate Values in Young Children*. Washington, DC: National Association for the Education of Young Children, 1984.

Robinson, Jo, and Staeheli, Jean. *Unplug the Christmas Machine*. New York: Quill-William Morrow, 1982.

Loving and Bonding

Brazelton, T. Berry, M.D. *Infants and Mothers*. New York: Dell, 1983.

Buscaglia, Leo. *Living, Loving, and Learning*. Greenwich, CT: Fawcett, 1985.

Kaplan, Louise J. *Oneness and Separateness*. Franklin Park, IL: La Leche League International, 1983.

Karnes, Merle B. *You and Your Small Wonder*. Circle Pines, MN: American Guidance Service, 1982.

Klaus, Marshall H., and Kennell, John H. *Bonding: The Beginnings of Parent-Infant Attachment*. Mosby, NY: Johnson & Johnson, 1982.

Leboyer, Frederick. *Loving Hands*. New York: Knopf, 1985.

McClure, Vimala Schneider. *Infant Massage: A Handbook for Loving Parents*. New York: Bantam Books, 1989.

Montagu, Ashley. *Touching: The Human Significance of the Skin*. New York: Harper & Row, 1986.

Health

Food

Lansky, Vicki. *Feed Me! I'm Yours*. Minneapolis, MN: Meadowbrook Press, 1982.

Robbins, John. *Diet for a New America*. Walpole, NH: Stillpoint Publishing, 1987.

Sanger, Sirgay. *Baby Talk Parent Talk: Understanding Your Baby's Body Language.* New York: Doubleday, 1991.

Satter, Ellyn. *How To Get Your Kid to Eat—But Not Too Much.* Palo Alto, CA: Bull Publishing, 1987.

Toilet Training and Bodies

Alexander, Josi, et al. *Is My Baby OK? Toilet Training.* (Audio-tape.) Los Angeles: PIPS Parent House, 1983.

Brooks, Joae G. *No More Diapers!* New York: Dell, 1983.

Gordon, Sol. *Girls Are Girls and Boys Are Boys.* Buffalo, NY: Prometheus Books, 1991.

Mack, Alison. *Toilet Learning: The Picture-Book Technique for Children and Parents.* Boston: Little, Brown, 1983.

Quackenbush, Marcia, and Villarreal, Sylvia. *Does AIDS Hurt?* Santa Cruz, CA: Network Publications of ETR Associates, 1988.

Protecting Your Children from Abuse

Cross, Laurella Brough. *Jenny's New Game: How to Protect Children Against Kidnapping and Assault.* Englewood, CO: L. B. Cross (P.O. Box 4025, Englewood, CO 80155), 1984.

Dayee, Frances S. *Private Zone: A Read-Together Book to Help Parents Help Children Deal with and Prevent Sexual Assault.* New York: Warner Books, 1982.

Freeman, Lory. *It's My Body.* Seattle, WA: Parenting Press, 1983.

Hart-Rossi, Janie. *Protect Your Child from Sexual Abuse.* Seattle: Parenting Press, 1984.

He Told Me Not to Tell. Renton, WA: King County Rape Relief, 1979.

Meyer, Linda D. *Safety Zone: A Book Teaching Children Abduction-Prevention Skills.* Edmonds, WA: Franklin, 1984.

Sleep

Brown, Saul L., M.D., and Reid, Helen. *Infant and Toddler Sleep Disruptions.* (Audiotape.) Los Angeles: Preschool and Infant Parenting Service, 1983. (Write to: Preschool and Infant Parenting Service, 8730 Alden Drive, Los Angeles, CA 90048)

Ferber, Richard, M.D. *Solve Your Child's Sleep Problems.* New York: Simon & Schuster, 1986.

Jones, Sandy. *Crying Baby, Sleepless Nights.* New York: Warner Books, 1983.

Thevenin, Tine. *The Family Bed: An Age-Old Concept in Child-rearing.* Garden City Park, NY: Avery Publishing Group, 1987.

Crying/Tantrums

Ayllon, Ted, and Freed, Mori. *Stopping Baby's Colic.* New York: Putnam Publishing Group, 1989.

Taubman, Bruce, M.D. *Curing Infant Colic.* New York: Bantam Books, 1990.

Relationships

With Others

Ames, Louise B., and Haber, Carol Chase. *He Hit Me First: When Brothers and Sisters Fight.* New York: Dembner Books, 1982.

Clarke, Jean Illsley. *Ouch, That Hurts! A Handbook for People Who Hate Criticism.* Plymouth, MN: Daisy Press, 1983. (Write to: Daisy Press, 16535 9th Ave N., Plymouth, MN 55447)

Crary, Elizabeth. *Kids Can Cooperate.* Seattle: Parenting Press, 1984.

Faber, Adele. *Siblings Without Rivalry*. New York: Avon, 1988.

Grollman, Earl A. *Talking About Death: A Dialogue Between Parent and Child*. Boston: Beacon Press, 1991.

Lerner, Harriet Goldhor. *The Dance of Anger*. New York: Harper & Row, 1989.

———. *The Dance of Intimacy*. New York: HarperCollins, 1990.

Zimbardo, Phillip G., and Radl, Shirley L. *The Shy Child: A Parent's Guide to Preventing and Overcoming Shyness from Infancy to Adulthood*. New York: McGraw-Hill, 1981.

With the Environment/World

Lavie, Arlette. *Half a World Away*. New York: Child's Play International, 1988.

Thich Nhat Hahn. *Peace Is Every Step*. New York: Bantam Books, 1991.

Behavior

Temperament

Budd, Linda S., Ph.D. *Living with the Active Alert Child*. Seattle, WA: Parenting Press, 1993.

Ilg, Frances L., and Ames, Louise B. *Child Behavior*. New York: Harper & Row, 1982.

Turecki, Stanley. *The Difficult Child*. New York: Bantam Books, 1989.

Discipline

Cherry, Clare. *Parents, Please Don't Sit on Your Kids*. Belmont, CA: Pitman Books, 1985.

Crary, Elizabeth. *Without Spanking or Spoiling: A Practical Ap-*

proach to Toddler and Preschool Guidance. Seattle, WA: Parenting Press, 1979.

Carlsson-Paige, Nancy, and Levin, Diane E. *Who's Calling the Shots?* Santa Cruz, CA: New Society Publishers, 1990.

Windell, James. *Discipline: A Sourcebook of Fifty Fail-Safe Techniques for Parents.* New York: Macmillan, 1991.

Responsibility

Crary, Elizabeth. *Pick Up Your Socks.* Seattle: Parenting Press, 1990.

McCullough, Bonnie, and Monson, Susan. *Four Hundred One Ways to Get Your Kids to Work at Home.* New York: St. Martin's Press, 1982.

Parenting

Berends, Polly Berrien. *Whole Child/Whole Parent.* New York: Harper & Row, 1987.

Biddulph, Steve. *The Secret of Happy Children: A New Guide For Parents.* Sydney, Australia: Scarborough House, 1984.

Biddulph, Steve, and Biddulph, Shaaron. *The Secret of a Happy Family: How to Find Freedom, Fulfillment, and Love Together.* New York: Doubleday, 1989.

Brazelton, T. Berry, M.D. *On Becoming a Family.* New York: Dell, 1982.

———. *Toddlers and Parents.* New York: Doubleday, 1989.

Bumgarner, Norma J. *Mothering Your Nursing Toddler.* Franklin Park, IL: La Leche League International, 1982.

Elkind, David. *The Hurried Child: Growing Up Too Fast Too Soon.* Reading, MA: Addison-Wesley, 1988.

Greene, Bob. *Good Morning, Merry Sunshine.* New York: Atheneum, 1985.

Kersey, Katherine C. *The Art of Sensitive Parenting.* Washington DC: Acropolis Books, 1983.

Kurcinka, Mary Sheedy. *Raising Your Spirited Child.* New York: HarperCollins, 1991.

Meeks, Carolyn Ann. *Prescriptions for Parenting.* New York: Warner Books, 1990.

Pogrebin, Letty C. *Family Politics: Love and Power on an Intimate Frontier.* New York: McGraw-Hill, 1983.

———. *Growing Up Free.* New York: Bantam Books, 1981.

Rogers, Fred, and O'Brien, Clare. *Mr. R. Talks with Families About Divorce.* New York: Berkley Books, 1987.

Sullivan, S. Adams. *The Father's Almanac.* New York: Doubleday, 1980.

Trelease, Jim. *The New Read-Aloud Handbook.* New York: Penguin Books, 1989.

Grandparents

Aldrich, Robert, and Austin, Glen. *Grandparenting for the '90s: Parenting Is Forever.* Escondido, CA: Robert Erdman, 1991.

Bloomfield, Harold H. *Making Peace with Your Parents.* New York: Ballantine Books, 1983.

The Boston Women's Health Collective. *Ourselves and Our Children.* New York: Random House, 1978.

Elkind, David. *Grandparenting: Understanding Today's Children.* Glenview, IL: Scott, Foresman, 1990.

Faber, Adele, and Mazlish, Elaine. *Your Guide to a Happier Family.* New York: Avon, 1990.

Working Parents

Greenleaf, Barbara Kaye. *Help: A Handbook for Working Mothers.* New York: Berkley Books, 1979.

Lowman, Kaye. *Of Cradles and Careers: A Guide to Reshaping Your Job to Include a Baby in Your Life.* Franklin Park, IL: La Leche League International, 1984.

Mayer, Gloria Gilbert. *2001 Hints for Working Mothers.* New York: Quill, 1983.

Olds, Sally Wendkos. *The Working Parents' Survival Guide.* New York: Bantam Books, 1989.

Babies

Brazelton, T. Berry, M.D. *Infants and Mothers.* New York: Dell, 1983.

———. *What Every Baby Knows.* New York: Ballantine Books, 1988.

Carson, Mary B. *The Womanly Art of Breast-Feeding.* Franklin Park, IL: La Leche League International, 1983.

Clarke, Jean Illsley. *The Important Infants.* (Audiotape.) Plymouth, MN: Daisy Tapes, 1983. (Write to: Daisy Tapes, 16535 9th Ave N., Plymouth, MN 55447)

Eagan, Andrea. *The Newborn Mother: Stages of Her Growth.* Boston: Henry Holt, 1987.

Eiger, Marvin, and Olds, Sally. *Complete Book of Breast-Feeding.* New York: Bantam Books, 1987.

Fonda, Jane. *Workout for Pregnancy, Birth, and Recovery.* New York: Simon & Schuster, 1982.

Gonzalez-Mena, Janet, and Eyer, Dianne Widmeyer. *Infancy and Caregiving.* Palo Alto, CA: Mayfield, 1980.

Greenberg, Martin. *The Birth of a Father.* New York: Avon, 1986.

Laskin, David. *Parents' Book for New Fathers.* New York: Ballantine Books, 1988.

Pryor, Karen. *Nursing Your Baby.* New York: Pocket Books, 1991.

Spock, Benjamin, M.D., and Rothenberg, Michael, M.D. *Baby and Child Care*. New York: Pocket Books, 1985.

Stein, Sara. *That New Baby*. New York: Walker, 1983.

Parents

Clarke, Jean Illsley, and Dawson, Connie. *Growing Up Again: Parenting Ourselves, Parenting Our Children*. New York: HarperCollins, 1989.

Galinsky, Ellen. *Between Generations: The Six Stages of Parenthood*. New York: New York Times Books, 1981.

Hendricks, Gay, and Wills, Russel. *The Centering Book*. Englewood Cliffs, NJ: Prentice Hall, 1989.

Lakein, Alan. *How to Get Control of Your Time and Your Life*. New York: NAL, 1989.

Lansky, Vicki. *101 Ways to Tell Your Child "I Love You."* Chicago: Contemporary Books, 1991.

Satir, Virginia. *New Peoplemaking*. Mountain View, CA: Science & Behavior Books, 1988.

Marriage and Divorce

Fisher, Bruce. *Rebuilding: When Your Relationship Ends*. San Luis Obispo, CA: Impact Publishers, 1981.

Parents Without Partners, Inc., 7910 Woodmount Avenue, Bethesda, MD 20614.

Sinberg, Janet. *Divorce Is a Grown-Up Problem*. New York: Avon, 1978.

Wallerstein, Judith, and Blakeslee, Sandra. *Second Chances*. New York: Ticknor and Fields, 1989.

Activities/Games

Beall, Pamela, and Nipp, Susan. *Wee Sing and Play Book and Cassette.* Los Angeles: Price Stern, 1983.

Broad, Laura Peabody, and Butterworth, Nancy Towner. *The Play-Group Handbook.* New York: St. Martin's Press, 1991.

Burtt, Kent, and Kalkstein, Karen. *Smart Toys for Babies from Birth to Two.* New York: Harper & Row, 1981.

Faires, Darrell. *Sing Yes!* (Developmental affirmation song tapes). Hazelwood, MO: Shalom Publications, 1988.

Gesme, Carole. *Ups and Downs with Feelings: Twelve Starter Games, Three to Six Years.* 1985. (Write to: 4036 Kerry Court, Minnetonka, MN 55345)

Gordon, Ira J. *Baby Learning Through Baby Play.* New York: St. Martin's Press, 1970.

Hagstrom, Julie, and Morrill, Joan. *Games Babies Play: A Handbook of Games to Play with Infants.* New York: A & W Visual Library, 1981.

Hendrickson, Karen. *Baby and I Can Play.* Seattle: Parenting Press, 1990.

———. *Fun with Toddlers.* Seattle: Parenting Press, 1990.

Levy, Dr. Janine. *The Baby Exercise Book.* New York: Pantheon, 1975.

Mercer Island Preschool Association. *Rainy-Day Activities for Preschoolers.* Mercer Island, WA: Mercer Island Preschool Association, 1983.

Orlick, Terry. *Cooperative Sports and Games Book.* New York: Pantheon Books, 1978.

Segal, Marilyn. *Your Child at Play: Birth to One Year.* New York: Newmarket Press, 1986.

Segal, Marilyn, and Adcock, Don. *Just Pretending: Ways to Help Children Grow Through Their Own Imaginative Play.* New York: Penguin Books, 1982.

Shea, Jan Fisher. *No Bored Babies*. Seattle: Bear Creek Publications, 1986. (Write to: Bear Creek Publications, 2507 Minor Avenue E., Seattle, WA 98102)

Warren, Jean. *More Piggyback Songs*. Everett, WA: Warren Publishing House, 1984.

Books for Children

Aliki. *Feelings*. New York: Greenwillow Books, 1984.

Ancona, George. *I Feel: A Picture Book of Emotions*. New York: Dutton, 1977.

Berenstain, Stan, and Berenstain, Jan. *The Berenstain Bears and the Messy Room*. New York: Random House, 1983.

———. *The Berenstain Bears' Moving Day*. New York: Random House, 1981.

———. *The Berenstain Bears and Too Much TV*. New York: Random House, 1984.

Brown, Margaret W. *The Dead Bird*. New York: Harper & Row, 1989.

———. *Goodnight Moon*. New York: Harper & Row, 1984.

Cain, Barbara. *Double-Dip Feelings*. New York: Magination Press, 1990.

Christiansen, C. B. *My Mother's House, My Father's House*. New York: Puffin Books, 1990.

Conlin, Susan, and Friedman, Susan Levine. *Ellie's Day*. Seattle, WA: Parenting Press, 1989.

Crary, Elizabeth. *I Can't Wait*. *Children's Problem-Solving Series*. Seattle: Parenting Press, 1982.

———. *I Want It*. *Children's Problem-Solving Series*. Seattle: Parenting Press, 1982.

———. *I Want to Play*. *Children's Problem-Solving Series*. Seattle: Parenting Press, 1982.

———. *My Name Is Not Dummy*. *Children's Problem-Solving Series*. Seattle: Parenting Press, 1983.

———. *I'm Lost*. *Children's Problem-Solving Series*. Seattle: Parenting Press, 1985.

———. *Mommy Don't Go*. *Children's Problem-Solving Series*. Seattle: Parenting Press, 1986.

DePaola, Tomie. *Nana Upstairs and Nana Downstairs*. New York: Penguin Books, 1978.

———. *The Knight and Dragon*. New York: Putnam, 1980.

Freed, Alvyn. *TA for Tots*. Rolling Hills Estate, CA: Jalmar Press, 1977.

Gesme, Carole, and Peterson, Larry. *Help for Kids! Understanding Your Feelings About Moving*. Minneapolis, MN: Pinetree Press, 1991.

Kaufman, Joe. *How We Are Born, How We Grow, How Our Bodies Work, and How We Learn*. New York: Golden Press, 1975.

Kunhardt, Dorothy. *Pat the Bunny*. New York: Golden Press, 1942.

Marzollo, Jean. *Close Your Eyes*. Los Angeles: Pied Piper Books, 1981.

Mayle, Peter. *Where Did I Come From?* Secaucus, NJ: Lyle Stuart, 1973.

McKinnon, Elizabeth. *Great Big Holiday Celebrations*. Everett, WA: Warren Publishing House, 1991.

O'Callahan, Jay. *The Little Dragon and Other Stories*. (Storytelling audiotape.) Write to: 90 Old Mount Skirgo Road, Marshfield, MA 02050.

Pappas, Michael G. *Sweet Dreams for Little Ones*. New York: Atheneum, 1989.

Scott, Ann H. *On Mother's Lap*. New York: McGraw-Hill, 1972.

Spier, Peter. *People*. New York: Doubleday, 1988.

Stein, Sara. *That New Baby*. New York: Walker, 1984.

Williams, Joy. *Red Flag Green Flag People*. Write to: Rape and Abuse Crisis Center of Fargo-Moorhead, P.O. Box 1655, Fargo, ND 58107, 1980.

Williams, Sarah. *Round and Round the Garden*. New York: Oxford University Press, 1983.

Magazines, Newsletters

Creating a Peace Experience. Little Friends for Peace, 4405 29th Street, Mount Rainier, MD 20712.

Dads Only. P.O. Box 270616, San Diego, CA 92128. Monthly newsletter filled with suggestions to help dads interact with kids and wives.

Growing Child. 22 N. Second Street, Lafayette, IN 47902. Monthly guide to growth and development coordinated to your baby's birthdate.

Mothering. P.O. Box 1690, Santa Fe, NM 87504. Quarterly. Alternative birthing and parenting ideas.

Parents Magazine. 685 Third Avenue, New York, NY 10017. Monthly. Covers topics from infancy through adolescence.

Working Mother. 230 Park Avenue, New York, NY 10169. Monthly. Covers issues about careers and families.

Your Big Backyard. National Wildlife Federation, 1400 16th Street NW, Washington DC 20036-2266. Close-up photos that spark three- to five-year-old children's curiosity.

Index

Abduction, 155

Abuse, preventing,12, 20–21, 107, 143–44, 155–56, 207, 251–52, 267–68, 288, 290–91, 335, 352, 361–62, 384–85

Activities, 165, 182, 240

Affirmations, xix, 4–5, 6–7, 38, 44, 60, 62, 63, 91, 94, 100–101, 102–3, 145, 178, 192–93, 195, 283–84, 286, 295, 297, 304, 311, 317, 324, 326, 333, 366, 380–83

Aggression, 280–81

Allergies, 220, 323

Anger, 189, 192, 196, 204–5, 208, 217, 226, 273, 304, 311, 316, 320

Appetites, 22, 190, 237, 340–41

Asking for help. *See* Help for parents; Self-care; Responsibilities,

Attention, 60–61, 132, 210–11, 216, 233, 240, 271, 273, 303, 304, 305, 310. *See also* Bonding; Competition

Attention span, 111–112

Baby talk, 280, 325–26

Babyproofing. *See* Childproofing

Baby-sitters. *See* Child-care providers

Baby-sitting co-op, 169

Backyard Center Play Group, 171, 386–89

Bathing, 33, 34, 151, 208–9, 223, 350

Bath time, 151

Bed, 2, 33, 121, 136, 144, 220–24, 322–23. See *also* Sleeping

Bedroom, 136

Bedtime, 116–21, 220–24, 322–23, 333–34

Birthdays, 338

Biting, 9, 124–25, 140–41, 145–46, 211–12, 217–18, 313–14

Bonding, 20, 36–45, 75, 224

Books. *See* Reading

Bored, 204

Bottle, 29, 230

Bottle-feeding. *See* Nursing

Breast pump, 27–28, 29, 74, 79, 80, 123

Breast-feeding, 22–29, 74–75, 79–80, 122–30, 168, 230–37

Bribery, 235, 281

Bundling, 17, 83

Burping. *See* Gas

Candy, 160–61, 342

Car, 85, 98, 106, 141, 249, 254, 306

Car seats, 11, 84, 85, 86, 107, 141, 149–50, 219, 290

Car pool, 334, 345

Caution, 280–81

Child-care co-op, 148, 169, 171, 250, 257, 275, 277, 368, 390–91

Child-care providers, 11, 16, 34, 39, 47, 48, 53, 54, 59, 75, 77–83, 84, 86, 87, 115, 143, 145, 147–48, 152, 155, 168, 170, 180, 181, 183, 185, 186, 235, 243, 247, 250, 257–58, 262, 277, 360

Child development, 1–3, 41, 65–66, 75, 97–99, 104–5, 107, 161–62, 189–91, 196–97, 200, 203, 214, 225–26, 258, 279–82, 287–89, 310, 361, 371–72

Childproofing house, 104, 106, 153–54, 163, 252, 253

Choices, 124, 187, 201, 214, 234–35, 310–11, 314, 322, 328

Chores, 52, 62, 87–88, 182–83, 328–29, 330, 358–61

Chores, sharing. *See* Responsibilities; Partners

Christmas, 154

Classes, 276, 368

Climbing, 190–91, 253, 364, 373

Clothing, 12, 244, 324-25, 337

Colic, 2, 14–15

Coloring. *See* Drawing

Comforting, 16, 231

Competition, 91, 94, 110–11, 132

Consistency. *See* Discipline; Routines

Control, 288

Cooperative preschool, 369, 373

Cooperation, 214–19

Coping, 243–50

Counseling, 21, 31, 50–51, 143, 177, 267, 268

Couple. *See* Marriage relationship; Partners

Crawling, 98, 107–8,

Creativity, 288, 292–93

Crib, *See* Bed

Criticism, 261–62, 264–65, 366

Crying, 2, 9, 12, 13–21, 31, 53, 78, 118–19, 159–60, 181–82, 247

Cuddling. *See* Loving

Cup, baby, 123, 124, 230, 231

Dawdling, 327–28

Day care. *See* Child-care providers

Death, 296

Development. *See* Child development

Developmental stages. *See* Child development

Diapering, 82, 107, 138

Diapers, 12, 18, 25, 137, 162, 226, 324–25

Diet, 128–30, 233–34, 343

Discipline, 19–20, 104, 107, 196, 258–59, 268, 306

Dishwasher, 151–52, 252

Divorce, 295, 367–68

Doctor, 14, 18, 20–21, 23, 26, 81, 118–19, 122, 123, 124, 142, 177, 238, 249, 350

Drawing, 300, 303–4

Dress-up, 344, 360

Dressing and undressing, 209–10, 244, 327–28, 329, 337

Drugs, 51, 83, 178

Earaches, 249

Eating, 1, 11, 106, 122–30, 230–37, 272–73, 339–43

Electrical outlets, 106, 254–55

Emotions. *See* Feelings

Entertaining toddler. *See* Play

Exercise, 146, 249–50, 322

Exhaustion. *See* Fatigue

Ex-husband, 165, 266–67

Expectations, 203, 214, 264

Exploring, 104, 114–15, 124, 131, 138–48, 157–62, 163, 172

Fairness, 316–17

Fantasy, 279, 288, 292–93, 360

Fathers. *See* Partners

Fatigue, 57, 66, 104, 143–44, 150, 168–69, 170–71

Favorites, Favoritism, 157–58, 317, 353, 357–58

Feeding, 15, 22–29, 31, 79–80, 89–90, 122–30, 232

Feelings, 31, 93, 111, 182, 192, 273–74, 298–99, 303, 320–21

Fighting, 216–17, 306

Finger foods. *See* Solid food

Fingernails. *See* Nails

Food. *See* Eating; Nutrition

Forgetting, 56–57, 330–31
Friends, 55, 56, 60, 77, 145–46, 215, 275, 280, 320–21, 368
Fussing, 15, 16–17, 20–21, 84, 86–87
Games, 141
Gas, 14, 25, 26
Glasses, 159
Going home, 243–44, 336
Grandparents, 67–72, 153–54, 157–62, 252, 260–61, 268–69, 352, 353–55, 366
Grief, 10, 296
Grocery shopping. *See* Shopping
Guilt, 64–65, 172–73, 185–86, 270, 274–75, 318–19
Handicaps, 176–77
Hate, 208
Helping, 92–93
Hitting, 145–46, 211–12, 281, 312–13, 314–15, 319–20, 330, 356–57
Holidays and special events, 134, 154, 255–56, 348
Household management. *See* Time management
Housework. *See* Time management
Hugging, 113, 230, 241–42, 247, 269, 313, 321, 335

Hurting, 241–242, 313
Husbands. *See* Partners
Identity, 285–86, 287, 292–301
Ignoring negative behavior, 186, 204, 208, 210, 260–62, 306, 307, 309
Illness, 26–27, 177–78
Imagination, 279–80
Imitation, 190
Infant stimulation. *See* Stimulation
In-laws. *See* Grandparents
Intercourse. *See* Sexual intercourse
Isolation. *See* Loneliness
Jealousy, 47–48, 135, 239, 304
Junk food, 160–61, 235
Kissing, 162–63, 314
La Leche League International, 23, 27, 231, 368. *See also* Nursing
Language, 2, 3, 190, 199–200, 279–80, 281
Learning, 3, 190
Leaving child, 181–82, 247, 274–75
Limits, 93, 166, 189, 192, 212–13, 244, 245, 258, 269, 281
Loneliness, 58–59, 267
Love, 4–5, 9, 44, 91, 317
Loving, 42, 62, 113, 158

Lying, 309–10
Management. *See* Time management
Making love. *See* Sexual intercourse
Marriage, 46–53
Marriage relationship, 46–53
Massage, 13, 27, 40, 49, 59, 60, 62, 81, 120
Memory, 56–57
Messes, 236
"Mind." *See* Discipline
Mothers, 16, 17. *See* Partners
Moving, 275–76, 347, 368–69
Music. *See* Singing.
Nails, 139–40
Naps, 31, 33–34, 54, 98, 117, 119–20, 170–71, 223, 227
Needs: adult, 47–48, 67, 83; baby, 11–12, 18; child, 76, 192, 270–71; parents, 7, 20–21, 31, 34–35, 54–66, 73–74, 94, 167–86, 270–77, 363–70. *See also* Asking for help
Negative behavior. *See* No (saying)
New baby, 133, 238–39, 304, 324
Night. *See* Feeding; Sleeping
Nintendo, 361

Nipples, 29, 79, 90, 123, 230
No (saying), 151, 189, 192, 194–95, 196, 201, 253, 310
Nursery rhymes, 149
Nursing, 14, 22–29, 47, 79–81, 89–90, 118, 122–30, 168, 230–37
Nutrition, 340–41, 343
Older children, 93, 131–36, 144–45
Outings, 337–38
Outside help. *See* Help for parents
Pacifiers, 22, 45, 71, 81, 83, 117, 118, 201–2
Pain, 65
Pandemonium hour, 144–45
Parenting, 4, 7, 53, 55, 63–65, 69, 179. *See also* Bonding
Parents Anonymous, 20
Parents Without Partners, 171, 333. *See also* Self-care
Partners, 17, 43, 46–53, 59–60, 68–69, 82, 87–88, 88–90, 164, 166, 176, 179, 224, 271, 272, 355, 359–60. *See also* Responsibilities, sharing
Patience, 54
Pediatrician. *See* Doctor
Pets, 330
Physician. *See* Doctor
Pinching, 11

Play, 200, 240, 253, 344–48
Play-Doh, 246
Play group, 132, 177, 203
Playmates, 238–42, 316–21,
    336
Playpen, 144, 147, 150, 170
Poisons, 252
Poking, 110. *See also* Hitting
Potty chair, 225, 227, 228
Pouring, 232–33, 236
Power, 200–13, 214, 225, 226,
    228, 285–86, 288
Pregnancy, 60–61, 91–92
Preschool, 334, 335, 369–70,
    371–74. *See also*
    Cooperative preschool
Pretend. *See* Fantasy
Problem solving, 299–300
Public embarrassment,
    245–46, 350
Puppets, 214, 256, 297
Pushing, 241, 371–72
Readiness. *See* Child devel-
    opment
Reading, 111–12, 120, 224,
    373–74
Recovery from childbirth,
    49–50
Recycling theory, xx, 6–8,
    102–3, 194–95, 285–86
Refrigerator, 248
Regression, 322–26

Relatives, 62, 88, 134. *See also*
    Grandparents
Relief. *See* Help for parents
Resistance, 194, 196, 219
Resources, 401–14
Responsibilities, sharing, 17,
    24–25, 52, 64–65, 73–74,
    82, 87–88, 92–93, 176, 180,
    182–83, 224, 264, 272
Responsibility, 327–33
Rest. *See* Fatigue
Returning to work. *See* Work
Rhymes, 112, 141, 199
Rituals, 115, 116, 118, 191
Rocking, 13, 14, 120–21
Role-play, 297, 332
Routines,116, 169, 223
Rules, 202–3, 253, 258,
    281–82, 349–50
Running away, 208, 254
"Running wild," 163
Safety, 11–12, 149–56, 198,
    251–56, 290–91, 332,
    361–62
Schedule. *See* Time manage-
    ment
Scratching, 211–12, 241
Screaming, 206, 208–9,
    212–13, 247, 335, 338
Self-care, 13, 20–21, 31, 35,
    54–66, 69–70, 83, 94, 122,
    143–44, 167–79, 270–77

Self-esteem, 160, 179, 226, 261
Separation, 115, 192, 194–95, 196–97, 221, 262, 263, 273–75, 333–34
Sex: of child, 10
Sex-role stereotyping, 112–13
Sexual abuse. *See* Abuse
Sexual intercourse, 48–50, 136, 167, 168–69. *See also* Loving, Massage
Sexual play, 49, 287, 349–50, 351
Sexuality, 46, 48, 107, 280, 287–88, 349–52
Shampooing, 99, 139
Sharing, 109, 110–11, 131, 182–83, 215
Shoes, 113–14
Shopping, 84, 152–53, 254, 312
Shyness, 297, 373
Sibling rivalry, 239, 316–17, 318–19
Siblings, 106, 131–37, 238–42, 316–21
Sick baby, 26–27
Singing, 85, 100, 116, 120, 125, 209, 273
Single parents, 171–72, 179, 221–22, 260–61
Sitters. *See* Child-care providers

Sleep, 34–35, 98, 116–21
Sleep problems. *See* Bedtime
Sleeping: baby, 1, 9, 30–35, 116–21; parents, 31, 34, 136, 323. *See also* Fatigue
Smoking, 230
Snacks, 341
Solid food, 28, 106, 116, 117, 124, 128–29, 233–34, 235
Soothing. *See also* Rocking
Spacing children, 137
Spanking, 207, 356–57
Spills, 232–33
Spoiling, 17–18, 44
Spouses. *See* Partners
Stereotyping, 112–13
Stimulation: infant, 33, 40, 83; intellectual, 276
Store, 307–8, 312
Stories, 139, 223, 224, 292–93, 333
Storytelling, 224. *See also* Reading
Strangers, 251–52, 332
Streets, 254, 264
Stress, 204, 222, 227, 325, 333–38
Stubborn, 314–15
Sucking, 2, 45, 71, 81, 230. *See also* Pacifiers
Suggestion Circle, xv–xvi, 394–97

Support groups, 398–99

Swaddling. *See* Bundling

Talking, 190, 302–3, 305, 307–9, 373–74

Tantrums, 142–43, 189, 196, 204–13, 311, 335, 336

Teasing, 318

Teething, 15, 117, 125, 141

Telephone, 147, 173, 246–47, 363–64

Thinking, 192, 194–95, 199, 202–3, 289, 298–99

Threats, 319–20, 333–34

Time concept development, 190, 247

Time management, 52, 169, 365

Time-out, 202, 211, 212, 241, 305, 310, 312, 392–93

Time for self, 59–60, 169

Toilet training, 99, 161–62, 190, 196, 225–29

Toileting, 2, 118–19, 225–29, 288, 329

Touch, 11, 40, 42

Touching, 40, 113, 126. *See also* Loving, Massage

Toys, 85, 114, 131, 133, 138, 209, 215, 217, 245, 300–301, 328–29

Travel, 39, 84–90, 141, 248–49, 262–63, 346

TV, 142, 218, 260–61, 265–66, 293–94

Twins, 218

Undressing. *See* Dressing

Values, disagreement about, 160, 164, 183–84, 260, 361

Visualize, 114, 210, 213, 336, 337

Waking at night. *See* Sleep

Walking, 97, 98, 113–14, 190, 240

Washing hair, 99, 139

Water play, 229, 236, 344

Weaning, 122–30, 230–37

Wedding, 331–32

Wet pants. *See* Toileting

Whining, 199–200, 234–35, 280, 305

Wives. *See* Partners

Work, 51–52, 61–62, 68–69, 73–76, 92–93

Working parent, 73–76, 180–86, 270–71

Yelling, 205, 207, 212, 217, 330, 338

Other Learning Materials Available

All of the following materials can be ordered from Daisy Press, 16535 9th Avenue N, Minneapolis, MN 55447.

Affirmation Ovals are laminated colored ovals that come in different sizes as bookmarks, punch-outs, or stickers. Each set contains all fifty-four affirmations.

Developmental Tapes, by Jean Illsley Clarke, are audiocassette tapes that present important information about children and the nurturing they need. Told in both male and female voices, they are useful tools for adults and for helping older children understand their little brothers' and sisters' needs and behavior. Each is twelve to eighteen minutes long.

The twelve *Ups and Downs with Feelings* starter games for ages three to six and the seven *Explorer* games for ages six to adult, by Carole Gesme, help children and adults recognize, name, and be responsible for their feelings.

The *Love Game,* by Carole Gesme, is an everybody-wins board game that lets people absorb unconditional love messages while they follow the directions indicated by the roll of the dice.

Feeling Faces Paper People, by Carole Gesme, includes over one hundred pieces to color and cut. Match the feeling faces to the vests and sweatshirts with messages for growth and health.

The *Sing Yes!* audiocassette, by Darrell Faires, contains sixty-three singable, easy-to-remember songs based on the affirmations. A sampler tape of fourteen songs is also available. Sung by both male and female vocalists.

WE: A Newsletter for People Who Care About Self-Esteem includes theories and activities, edited by Jean Illsley Clarke.

About the Editors

Jean Illsley Clarke, M.A., is the author of the book, *Self-Esteem: A Family Affair*, coauthor of *Growing Up Again*, and the creator of parenting programs based on both of these books. The Suggestion Circle technique comes from those programs. She teaches people how to facilitate groups and has written *Who, Me Lead a Group?* She is a transactional analyst, a nationally certified parent educator, and a mother of three. She and her husband, Richard, live in Minnesota.

Gail Davenport, B.A., is the coordinator of parent education at Edmonds Community College in Washington. She is a facilitator of "Self-Esteem: A Family Affair" classes, works with parents of toddlers and preschoolers, developed a baby-sitting cooperative, and participated in an elementary school parent cooperative. Each spring and summer, while her husband Aaron is running his commercial fishing boat, Gail and their daughters, Daysha and Lena, tend to the family's horses.

Marilyn Grevstad is most often found surrounded by children. She is a parent educator for Shoreline Community College in Seattle. She directs the North City Cooperative Preschool, where parents and their infants, toddlers, and preschoolers learn together. She and her husband, Ben, are the parents of four young men, Kris, Kurt, Hans, and Nels, and one young woman, Fritzi. Marilyn facilitates "Self-Esteem: A Family Affair" classes.

Sue Hansen, B.A., lives with her husband, Don, and two young children, Jacob and Betsy, in Washington. Parenting is her present full-time vocation. She is a trained facilitator of Self-Esteem: A Family Affair parenting classes. She feels a great deal of gratitude for the many resources available to parents today.

Nat Houtz, B.A., is a parent educator at Edmonds Community College, a research analyst at the Parenting Clinic at the University of Washington, and a facilitator of Self-Esteem: A Family Affair parenting classes. She has been a preschool, infant, and toddler teacher in parent cooperatives. Nat is director of Parent Education Associates. She is raising two daughters, Robin and Rachel.

Samara Kemp, R.N., B.S.N., a single parent since 1974 to Bradford, Brett, Darren, and Shawni, cares for pregnant moms and dads and newborn infants as a labor and delivery room nurse and public health nurse. Samara also teaches holistic techniques for optimum health and facilitates Self-Esteem: A Family Affair classes and childbirth education. She lives in California.

Maggie Lawrence, M.A., has been a parent educator for eight years and is a psychotherapist in Edmonds, Washington. She is married, has two sons, and lectures in the United States and Australia on parenting and healing from abuse.

Darlene Montz, M.Ed., teaches college-level parent involvement classes. She also writes a weekly newspaper column and tapes "parenting commercials" for Yakima radio stations. She and her husband, Fred, feel lucky frequently to find their three grown children, their spouses, and three grandchildren at the Sunday dinner table, which is more likely to offer take-out pizza than Norman Rockwell turkey.

Gail A. Nordeman, B.A., leads workshops on parenting in the United States and Europe. She cofounded and directs A Growing Place, an educational and counseling center in Cincinnati, Ohio. She is a registered nurse with a clinical provisional teaching membership in the International Transactional Analysis Association. She also is the mother of five children.

Mary Sleeth Paananen, R.N., B.S.N., is a Washington facilitator of Self-Esteem: A Family Affair classes. While Mary worked on this book, she, husband Terry, and son William, five years, were joined through adoption by Jon, six years, Jeff, four years, and Erin, three years. The children provided Mary with a constant source of "Whys," "Try this," and "Ahas!" Mary has worked with multiply handicapped children and their families, tending to their medical as well as their supportive and nurturing needs.

Ellen Reese Peterson, B.A., is the mother of two children and has been leading parents' groups since 1978 in California. She is a cofounder of the Nurture Company, a nonprofit parent education organization, and of Newborn Connections, a one-to-one support program for new mothers. She also directs a high school peer counseling program. She is completing a master's degree in transpersonal counseling psychology. She believes parenting is our most important work.

Judy Popp, M.Ed., and husband, Harry, have three adult children who went through their explorer stage while Judy was completing both bachelor's and master's degrees in education. Previously the director of early childhood programs for the Yakima School District in Washington State, Judy created its Home-School Partnership program and now is an infant and toddler teacher. Judy has been active in parent education efforts for over twenty-five years and has spearheaded many school and community networks. Judy gets multigenerational learning about exploring from her mother, Marjorie, and grandchildren, Casie Elizabeth, Travis, and Chandler.

Judith-Anne Salts, B.A., was coordinator of the Yakima School District's Backyard Center program and designer of its Parent-Infant Support Groups. Formerly a first-grade teacher, she derives practical expertise from her life with her husband, Dennis, daughter Robin, and son Christopher.

Melanie Weiss, M.Ed., has been an art teacher, has worked with residents in a psychiatric hospital, and has done volunteer work with child protective services. She is a trained facilitator of Self-Esteem: A Family Affair parenting classes. She is the parent of Eli, Adam, and Evan. After experiencing the continuous changes and needs of a growing family, she has come to appreciate the opportunity for personal growth that children offer us all.